W. ZAGORSKI
('Lech')

Seventy Days

Translated by
John Welsh

GEORGE MANN . MAIDSTONE

W. Zagorski
SEVENTY DAYS

Copyright © W. Zagorski, 1957

First published in the United Kingdom by
Frederick Muller

This edition first published by George Mann, 1974

ISBN 0 7041 0049 5

Printed by R. Kingshott & Co. Ltd.,
Deadbrook Lane, Aldershot, Hampshire
for George Mann Limited, 40 Bower Mount Road
Maidstone, in the County of Kent

INTRODUCTION

By General T. Bor Komorowski

On 25 April 1943 Soviet Russia made use of various trifling pretexts in order to break off diplomatic relations with the Polish Government in London. From this time on, hostile Soviet propaganda directed against Poland increased in intensity. Moscow, for instance, accused the Polish Government of 'favouring the Germans' and the Underground Home Army of 'inactivity and collaboration with the German occupying forces in Poland'. This was at a time when the Home Army of over 300,000 men was carrying out intense and uninterrupted sabotage and diversion behind the German front. The Russians were well aware of this. Yet the Soviet partisan units which were ravaging the eastern territories of Poland adopted an unmistakably hostile attitude towards any Home Army units they met. Many cases are known of Soviet partisans trying to ambush and destroy Polish units.

When the German front line began to move back in the face of the Red Army, near the end of 1943, it was clear that the Russians would penetrate into Polish territory as they followed the withdrawing German forces. Thus Poland now found herself fighting in the same camp as the Russians against the Germans. The Western Allies at this time regarded Soviet Russia as a loyal and trustworthy ally. Nevertheless, Soviet Russia had broken off diplomatic relations with Poland, and her attitude was becoming increasingly hostile and aggressive towards Poland. Consequently we began to wonder what attitude our Home Army should adopt towards the Red Army, when the latter entered Poland in pursuit of the Germans who, although in retreat, were not yet defeated. This was the question which the Commander-in-Chief of the Home Army had to ask the Polish Commander-in-Chief in London to clarify. The Polish Government at once answered by issuing 'Instructions' ordering the Home Army to continue its fight against the Germans despite the political and military attitude of the Soviet Union. This involved the risk of undertaking military action without obtaining any co-operation from the Red Army, and it also meant that we had no means of telling how the Red Army would behave towards our men of the Home Army when the fighting started. At the time, this policy seemed by far the best, since any respite in fighting the Germans would have meant that Poland's contribution to the common war effort would at once have been cancelled out, not only in the eyes of Soviet Russia but also of the Western Allies.

Repeated attempts by the Polish Government to re-establish diplomatic relations with Soviet Russia and thus to create conditions favourable for co-operation between the Home Army and the Red Army were fruitless, due to the negative attitude of the Soviet Union. Even attempts by Mr. Eden, the then British Foreign Secretary, to reach agreement in this respect during his visit to Moscow in October 1943 came to nothing. Soviet Russia put forward increasingly impossible demands, requiring, for instance, the Poles to yield half their territory to her, and also making the reopening of talks dependent on certain changes in the constitution of the Polish Government, which would have secured her a more submissive attitude. Soviet Russia also made it quite clear that she had every intention of enforcing her own will on Poland by the use of strength.

The Commander-in-Chief of the Home Army carried out the 'Instructions' issued by the Polish Government by giving the necessary orders, which included the concentration of individual Home Army units into larger fighting units along what was seen as the German line of retreat. These units were then to start fighting as the Germans withdrew.

Protracted battles between the Russians and the Germans had begun by the spring of 1944 in eastern Poland—the Kowel-Wlodzimierz region. Units of the Home Army which had been temporarily formed into the 27th Infantry Division took part in these battles. The local Soviet commanders were only too pleased to use the support which these Polish units provided. They repeatedly asked Polish units to undertake specific action and to provide them with support in their own battles. It began to look as though relations between the Home Army and the Red Army might work out in the field of battle. Yet, when the Russians were forced to withdraw in the face of a German counter-attack, they abandoned Home Army units in the field without informing them of their intention to retreat. As a result, Polish units were surrounded by the Germans, and the Poles had to fight their way out single-handed, with many casualties.

It was not until the end of June 1944 that the Russians started a big offensive in the Witebsk–Orsza–Mohylew region, where they broke through the German lines and shattered the 'Heeres Gruppe Mitte', which consisted of four armies. Two of these (the 4th and 9th Armies) were destroyed, while the 3rd Panzer Army withdrew, after heavy losses, along the Dzwina River towards Riga. Only the 2nd Army, which had been out of range of the main attack, avoided massacre by hasty retreat in the direction of Brest on the Bug River.

In the space of three weeks the Red Army was able to seize an area of some 250 square miles, and by mid-July they had reached the Kowno–Grodno–Pinsk line, and were ready to go into action again.

Then strong Russian forces moved forward from the southern front. Hitherto these forces had remained inactive. The attack of the 1st Bielorussian Army Group, under Rokossowski, emerged from the Kowel region and moved towards Warsaw. They took Lublin, and by the end of July had reached the outskirts of Warsaw, which the Germans were defending by means of an extended bridge-head. Then the 1st Ukrainian Army Group, under Marshal Koniev, moved into the attack in the direction of the central Vistula River. Farther to the south, the 4th Ukrainian Army Group had also attacked, and by the end of the month the central Vistula had been seized as well as the line of the San River, and the German forces which had been cut off there were driven back into the Carpathians.

The German defeat on the Eastern Front was now complete, and was the more disastrous for them in that it was linked with an Allied offensive in the West, so that the Germans were unable to bring up reinforcements to replace their enormous losses here in the East. The Russians' superiority was overwhelming. In the report of the 'Heeres Mitte Gruppe', dated 21 July 1944, the Russian forces thrown into the attack were estimated as 160 divisions and independent brigades, while the Germans had only sixteen divisions at their disposal. General Guderian, Chief of Staff of the German forces in the East, was to state at the Nürnberg Trials, that twenty-five German divisions were completely destroyed, and that the entire front at this stage consisted only of scattered remains trying to withdraw beyond the Vistula.

As the front line moved across Polish territory, units of the Home Army went into battle in accordance with the orders they had been given. Polish Home Army units hurriedly formed into infantry divisions, and also large partisan groups took part in the fighting throughout the country, from the Eastern Frontier up to the line of the Vistula, and they inflicted heavy losses on the Germans. The heaviest fighting, in which units of the Home Army took part, occurred during the capture of Wilno and Lwow and in the Lublin area.

The Soviet commanders in the field were very well disposed towards the Polish units. They were generous in their praise, and promised awards and distinctions as they continued to urge the Poles to co-operate closely with them. But as soon as fighting ceased in a given area, the attitude of the Russians at once changed. They demanded immediate subordination to the Soviet command, and in cases where this was not forthcoming, they did not hesitate to arrest the Polish commanders who, on the pretext of 'agreeing to further co-operation', the Russians would invite to their headquarters. Polish units, deprived in this way of their commanders, would then be surrounded, disarmed and deported into the interior of the Soviet Union. News of these treacherous devices on the part of the Russians reached Home Army headquarters only after a good deal of delay and often in a roundabout manner, since the Russians used first of all to arrest the Polish radio-operators, thus ensuring that their trickery was not made known.

Nevertheless, these episodes did not go unnoticed when the time came for the Polish Underground to decide what was to be done.

By this time we knew full well, from what had happened along the Eastern Front, that most towns were only captured by the Russians at the cost of fierce fighting and destruction to the towns themselves. The Germans continued to defend the more important centres of communication, particularly when these were larger towns situated on rivers. Thus the feverish preparations by the Germans to defend Warsaw meant that the city was not likely to escape this fate and was threatened with widespread destruction. The only way of preserving Warsaw from total destruction was for the Underground to start fighting inside Warsaw at once, and thus to hasten the end of the coming battle. It looked to us as though the enormous superiority of the Russians in man-power over the Germans, if supported by organised fighting within Warsaw itself, meant that we would have every chance of victory and would also mean the end of the battle in a short time.

Yet even the very great sacrifices which units of the Home Army had already made in the fighting in Poland had passed unnoticed and had aroused no response in the outside world. Thus we felt that the battle for Warsaw would have both to call forth a response from the world and also to proclaim our will for independence. The liberation of Warsaw by her own soldiers was to be the most eloquent witness we could produce, and was at the same time to give the lie to Soviet accusations of Home Army 'inactivity and collaboration with the Germans'.

Our plans for the liberation of Warsaw had already been worked out well in advance, and were known to all commanding officers and units. These plans formed part of a general over-all plan which was to be put into effect in the event of a general uprising should the Germans at any time suffer complete col-

lapse. But under the circumstances this general uprising throughout the country could no longer be considered. However, that
section of our plans concerned with Warsaw presented no great
difficulties in execution, and the Commander-in-Chief in Warsaw was ordered to prepare to carry it out.

At the end of July the civilian authorities of the Polish Underground decided, in view of the situation in the front line, that
Warsaw as the capital of Poland must be liberated by Poles.
These civilian authorities and the Home Army military commanders would thus emerge as hosts in control of their own
territory in relation to the Red Army as the latter moved in.

Once this had been decided, only the choice of the proper time
to start fighting remained to be taken. This was no easy matter,
since a premature outbreak would have had serious consequences.
Supplies of food and ammunition in the capital were sufficient for
from seven to ten days. On the other hand, delay might well can-
cel out the advantages to be gained by surprise. But there was
also the danger of 'provocation' by Communists or irresponsible
persons. Any minor incident might well have brought about an
outburst which none of us could have controlled or used. This
was particularly so in view of the tense atmosphere among the
civilians in Warsaw and their fierce desire to be revenged on the
Germans for their cruelty during the Occupation. But the greatest
difficulty of all was that we found it impossible to reach any
agreement whatsoever with the Soviet Headquarters as to action.

From 28 July we could hear the noise of battle on the outskirts
of Warsaw. Soviet aircraft held the skies over the city and its
surroundings. Soviet tanks were making deep inroads into the
defences of the German bridge-head. Places only ten miles outside Warsaw were already held by the Russians.

It was on 29 July that Moscow radio began to appeal to the
people of Warsaw to start fighting at once and to promise us
quick support.

On 31 July a Soviet communiqué announced the capture of
the Commander of the 73rd German Infantry Division which
had been defending the bridge-head. In the afternoon of this

same day, Soviet tanks were reported to be within the bridge-head and its defenders in confusion. We expected the Russians to strike at Warsaw at any moment. Faced with this situation, the Home Army command considered that the time had come to start the battle for Warsaw. As Commander-in-Chief of the Home Army, in agreement with the Warsaw representative of the Polish Government, I ordered fighting to start on 1 August at 5 p.m. Forty-thousand men of the Home Army were to go into battle inside Warsaw.

It is this battle and the events connected with it which Captain Zagorski describes in this book.

I feel that a few words should be added here, in an attempt to clarify the attitude of Soviet Russia to the Warsaw Insurrection.

Once we had started to fight in Warsaw, the Russians not only broke off all fighting on the outskirts of Warsaw but also at once adopted a very hostile attitude, even though it was their radio which had appealed to the people of Warsaw to take up arms. Throughout the first two weeks of the Insurrection, when broadcasting stations in the West were giving detailed news of the fighting in the city, Moscow never mentioned us. Then, from the middle of August, Moscow started to put out a violent campaign of accusation against the Polish Government and the commanders of the Home Army, whom Moscow held responsible for starting the Insurrection.

Despite repeated requests to Stalin personally by Prime Minister Churchill and President Roosevelt, Soviet Russia gave us no help in the fighting capital. By denying the use of her bases to aircraft, Soviet Russia made it impossible for the Western Allies to come to the help of Warsaw at a time when their support might have meant victory.

When the Russians attacked again in the direction of Warsaw in mid-September, they had no difficulty in reaching the banks of the Vistula. Here only the river itself separated them from positions held by the Insurgent units. Yet once again—and this time against their own interests—the Russians gave us no assistance. They stood with their rifles stacked on the opposite bank of the river, and the only help they gave us was to drop small supplies of food and ammunition—not so much in order to help but as concessions to the demands which were being made at this time by the Western Allies.

Telegrams sent by me as Commander-in-Chief of the Home Army to Rokossowski, the Soviet Commander, remained unanswered. When it became clear to us that it would soon become impossible to continue the battle in Warsaw, I informed Rokossowski, by radio, that if Warsaw did not obtain help within three days, fighting would have to cease, owing to the shortage of ammunition and food. This message, too, remained unanswered.

By abandoning Warsaw thus to the Germans, Soviet Russia revealed her attitude to Poland in its true colours to the rest of the world. Soviet Russia never intended Poland to be free; instead, Poland was to become her satellite, subservient to her will and obedient to her commands.

SEVENTY DAYS

30 July to 7 October 1944

Sunday, 30 July

Today as every day I called at Stas-the-Sailor's little café for news, as it's always safest to know what is happening in Grzybowska Street and in the rest of Warsaw. Stas-the-Tailor and Czes, both unshaven and a little tight, were sitting at one of the tables. They were arguing about how many people had responded to the Germans' appeal for help in building barricades on the eastern outskirts of Warsaw. The German authorities asked for a hundred thousand men for this purpose. But Stas held that not a single Pole had replied to the appeal, while Czes was insisting that there had been one—but one only.

Stas drew me to one side, behind some crates. Then he handed me a scrap of paper, tightly folded.

'What are you waiting for, Lech?' he then asked.

'What do you think I'm waiting for? For my orders, of course.'

'That's all very well for you—but what are the big-shots waiting for? The Red Army may be here tonight or tomorrow at the latest.'

But Warsaw seems calm. There are strong German patrols in the streets, though they are not arresting people or even checking papers or searching them, except here and there in the deserted side-streets. Someone from Praga, on the far side of the Vistula, says he distinctly heard artillery fire during the night, in the east and south.

I went back to my workshop to hide the scrap of paper Stas had given me. Opening it, I read: 'Poles! To arms! The time has come when we are about to destroy the Germans. Night and day the Red Army is fighting the Germans on Polish soil, and is driving them to the west. Your fellowcountrymen are fighting with the Red Army as a Polish Army under Generals Rola-Zymierski and Berling. . . . Italy, Rumania, Bulgaria and Finland—until recently the allies of Germany—are now fighting against Hitler. Yugoslavs, Greeks, Czechs and other freedom-loving nations have taken up arms against their German oppressors and are driving them from their countries. . . . Poles! Arise and fight for the freedom of your fatherland and for the happiness of your children. Destroy your age-old enemies, the Germans! Take up arms and give battle to the Germans wherever you find them. Every bullet fired at a German brings the joyful hour of liberation nearer. The mighty Red Army is hastening to your relief. It is bringing you freedom! Arise against the Germans. Attack them and prevent them from carrying off what they have looted, destroy the bridges and roads, seize or burn their stores, give them no peace either by day or night! Revenge and death to the German invaders!'

There was no signature, but now it's clear to me why Stas has taken to using phrases like 'What are *you* waiting for?' instead of 'What are *we* waiting for?' This is what his recent meetings with the 'Sindicalist' political group has done for him.

I went to keep an appointment with the man we know as Mecenas. He told me that no final decision as to action has been reached yet, but that the decision may be made at any time. I wanted to know what is to happen to my secret printing press. My own opinion is that we shouldn't reveal its existence too readily. Even if we don't need to use it for a time, we must keep it ready for use as long as the war continues and until the political situation becomes clearer. Still, I'd like someone else to take over the press, as this would give me more freedom for fighting when the Insurrection begins.

Mecenas agreed to this in principle, but he has to talk it over with someone higher up. Today he urged me to get as much paper as possible ready for the printing of leaflets. He is to let me have the text of the leaflet tomorrow.

On my way home, I saw heavy machine-guns in position in the newly erected cement block-houses on Warsaw street-corners.

Monday, 31 July

Again this morning I went to see Mecenas. On the way, I saw that there are already fewer carts and rickshaws crammed with Germans and 'Volksdeutsch' and their loot than there were yesterday. I expect the more cowardly ones have already fled, leaving only those who are actually on duty—and, of course, those who are sure of some kind of motor transport, so that they can get out of the city at the last minute. However, I gather that orders have been issued by the German authorities, forbidding individuals to quit Warsaw so that the roads are left clear for military transport. In fact, traffic in the streets leading to the bridges out of Warsaw is well under control, and there were military columns moving freely in both directions.

I found several people in Mecenas' office, and the atmosphere was that of an ordinary business office, with no signs of the caution and secrecy to which, after so many years of conspiracy, we've become accustomed. People were talking loudly and vigorously. Kazimierz, as usual, spent the week-end with his wife at Kobylka, about ten miles outside Warsaw, and he'd had to walk back into town. He claimed that he'd seen the first Soviet tanks near Kobylka early this morning. On the way back to Warsaw, however, he'd seen no full-scale German defences at all. Now he wanted to go back to Kobylka at once, to avoid being cut off from his family, and he believes he could still get back on foot in the confusion which reigns on the other side of the Vistula, providing the area isn't already held by the Soviet infantry.

Everyone was excited by this. What are we waiting for now? The 'Lublin Committee' in their Soviet limousines? Colonel Orzech reminded us of the Underground plan for an uprising known as 'The Storm', which still holds good.

'Damn the plan,' someone exclaimed bitterly. 'The Reds will

pick us up, singly or in groups, and we'll be deported to Russia just as they deported the Home Army men who captured Wilno. There must be an insurrection throughout Poland. What does it matter if we haven't enough arms and the Germans are still too strong? Once we've seized a big enough area, they'll send in our own parachute brigade.'

Someone else tried to calm him.

'That's as may be. But Warsaw isn't Wilno. Here in Warsaw the Reds would have to disarm tens of thousands of us, and arrest as many again, including all the members of our Council of National Unity, whose names are known throughout the whole world. Even the Reds wouldn't dare.'

This argument was convincing. Yet we all decided that further delay was out of the question. The Communists might seize the lead at any moment, and give the order for fighting to start. True, they're numerically very weak, and only have a few units, but this would suffice to give them the opportunity to make chaos out of a situation like ours and to wreck our own plans. Indeed, the atmosphere in Warsaw is already so tense that even without orders being given serious fighting may start in Warsaw at any time. The truth is that people here have been reduced to a state of almost unendurable nervous tension following five years of German occupation and it's something of a miracle that Warsaw has been so highly disciplined up to now. But can we count on what amounts to a miracle?

I was given the text of the leaflet for printing. I'd expected some sort of political manifesto, but it turned out to be instructions to the people of Warsaw how to behave towards the Soviet Army when it enters the city. It says that the Soviet Union is no ally of Poland, 'we all know the hostile acts committed by the Soviet Union towards Poland both in the past and now that the Reds have crossed into Polish territory. On the other hand, we must not forget that Russia is an ally of our Western friends in the common fight against Hitler Germany. So it is right to help the Soviet Army in their fight. The sooner the front line and with it the main forces of the opposing armies cross Poland, the better it will be for us Poles. Therefore, no hostile acts towards the Soviet forces can be tolerated, nor must we let ourselves be provoked into any activities which might then be used as pretexts for repressions and brutality.' Orders issued by the Soviet Army are to be obeyed, but at the same time the leaflet makes it clear that certain matters can only be dealt with by the legal authorities of the Polish state. The leaflet also appeals to everyone to behave in a way befitting hosts in their own territory.

Although the leaflet isn't official, it seems to me that it will be a useful and necessary guide for the first encounter between the people of Warsaw and the Red Army. Mecenas says that the text has been agreed upon by all interested parties in the Polish Underground.

I am to print as many as possible. And for the first time I am going to print something on our secret printing press which is intended for open distribution as soon as Warsaw has been liberated from the Germans.

Back home I learned that someone from Praga has brought news that all the workmen who were sacked last Saturday from the big instrument factory there have been recalled to work. The two German directors of the factory were caught outside Warsaw, trying to flee, and have been brought back: now, in front of the factory workers, they have both been shot for sabotage and desertion.

Stas-the-Sailor has managed to get hold of a whole lorry-load of vodka—'on the cheap'. The lorry driver, a German soldier, wanted the lorry unloaded at once, as he had the opportunity to get away from Warsaw with something more profitable. So Stas asked me to let him store the vodka in my cellar. This is useful, for now that the cellar is empty you can hear the sound of the printing press through the wall. Czes and I helped carry the cases of bottles downstairs, and we stacked them where, last December, the death sentence was carried out on Wlodek, and where the floor is still a little uneven, despite the earth we put into his grave. Stas said he didn't know how to thank us; Czes winked at me comically.

Stas-the-Tailor's son turned up at his home last night. Last March I managed to have him transferred to an Underground diversionary unit. He hasn't been home for three nights. He changed his underclothes and took an extra pair of socks. Nobody asked him any questions: only his mother, despite his protests, provided him with some sandwiches to take when he left again.

When I got home, I went into the workshop, gave the signal, opened the trap-door leading into the underground passage and climbed down the iron ladder. Proofs of the leaflet were ready for correction.

The air is hot and close, as though there's rain or a storm coming. Barbara, my wife, is on guard upstairs.

Tuesday, 1 August

This is it. Fighting has started in Warsaw.

We heard the first shots at about half-past four this afternoon. I was helping Staszek count the leaflets we've printed when Tadeusz called me upstairs. He and Czes were worried, as Barbara had not yet got back from seeing Mecenas.

We went out of the gateway of the house cautiously, for there was firing going on in the streets. A car full of Germans in uniform drove fast along our street. Immediately behind them came another car, full of young men in black raincoats, firing at them with revolvers.

Then everything became quiet again. Our street was empty, and someone was belatedly closing up his shop. The shutters squeaked as he fastened them. At last Barbara ran across. Breathlessly, she started telling us that she'd only just left Mecenas when shooting began. They were also shooting in the main streets.

Now we could hear intermittent firing near by and machine-gun fire farther away. Opposite, on the other side of the street, is the Dering factory used by the Germans for the manufacture of fuses, in a big building which formerly belonged to the Jewish Council in Warsaw. We knew that some twenty well-armed

German guards were behind the closed gates of the factory. A hundred yards farther on, in the police barracks in Ciepla Street, a reserve force of the civil police was stationed.

I went into the workshop and asked for two of our home-made bombs, two revolvers and all the pre-war hand-grenades, which someone had once given me and which I'd put by. I shared these with Czes. Tadeusz produced a P·38 revolver from a secret box. When Stefan came home from his shop in Zelazna Street, it turned out that he, too, had a gun—a fine Steyer. Czes wanted to disarm the factory guards at once, but I wouldn't let him. We kept our weapons hidden under our jackets.

Suddenly a detachment of men appeared in the empty street. Some wore belts and civilian clothes, others had red-and-white arm-bands, but only a few were armed. It was difficult to make out who was in charge and even who belonged to the detachment. Czes went over to them and pointed to the factory gates.

'Lads—there's some Germans in there,' he shouted.

Shooting flared up. The gates gave way before a mighty heave. The Germans were all standing in the yard with their hands up, but no one paid them any attention. The first men in grabbed the Germans' rifles. Workmen and girls came out of the building into the yard.

Then someone shouted that the German directors of the factory were in an office on the first floor. What was to be done with them? Nobody in the crowd was able to control the confusion that followed. Someone ordered the Germans to strip 'so they can't make a bolt for it', and some workmen seized the Germans' clothes. Evidently they had been ready for hasty departure, for there were in their suit-cases clean pyjamas, which they then took out in order to have something to wear.

Gradually the yard emptied. By now the guards—disarmed— had been locked in the guard-room. Someone called from the street. A middle-aged man in a car was listening to a report by a tall youth.

'Thanks. Now, collect your men together and take them to Dabrowski Square. I'll see you there.'

The first wounded man was lying in our bedroom, near my
workshop. His wounds had been dressed and he was conscious.
He kept saying he didn't want to endanger us, and that he'd clear
off; but we couldn't let him go. Barbara and Wanda, a tall dark
woman who lives near by, cleaned his blood-soaked bandages
and brought some water. I gave orders for the wounded man to
be taken down into the hidden cellar, to the printing press,
should any Germans appear in the street.

It was dark by this time, and the street was empty again.
Officers of the Home Guard stood at the gateway. Someone said
that the police, dressed as civilians, were leaving their barracks in
Ciepla Street. Some of us hurried there to take their arms from
them. I stood in the street, with a revolver and hand-grenade, and
listened. I could hear machine-gun fire from various directions
and heavy explosions farther away.

We do not know what is happening in Warsaw—not even in
the nearest streets. We don't know whether anyone has given the
order for fighting to start. But we all realise that now, after five
years of occupation, the storm of freedom is sweeping through
the streets of Warsaw.

The rule of the Germans in our street has come to an end. The
dark sky is illuminated by a glow in the west, but we were looking east. Hundreds of Russian tanks are approaching from that
direction; perhaps even now they have already reached our side
of the Vistula. But before they enter our street, we will take
control in the name of the Republic of Poland.

Heavy rain started to fall. Someone came up to me and threw
a German officer's coat over my shoulders.

'Lech, for goodness' sake! You'll be soaked and catch cold.'

Wednesday, 2 August
                                        No one can have slept in Warsaw
tonight.

At midnight I drew up a list of volunteers. One of the first was
Alexander, who had a detachment of men in Mokotow but

didn't know precisely when the Insurrection would start and was caught by the Insurrection in a house in our street. Now he cannot get back to his men. Alexander is an old friend of mine, a fair-haired man of thirty-eight who used to work for the Łódz City Council. Several others are in his position, with their units in other districts of the city; a few lads who have been living for the past months in the woods round Warsaw have joined us, too. Some are armed, while others managed yesterday and during the night to get hold of revolvers or single grenades.

At dawn we made a reconnaissance of the situation in our neighbourhood. We are almost surrounded. To the east Grzybowski Square is under heavy fire from several directions. Apparently a fair number of the enemy's forces are surrounded in the area of Pilsudski Square and they also hold the Saxon Park. Our patrol encountered another little group of Polish rebels in Zelazna Brama Square, which is under fire from the Saxon Park. The block-house on the corner of Walicowa and Chlodna Streets is held by German gendarmes and is difficult to attack, as there's a company of gendarmes at the corner of Chlodna and Zelazna Streets, keeping the whole length of both streets under fire from their machine-guns.

All the same, people take the risk of crossing these streets and, in their search for relatives or their families, they manage to reach nearly all the districts of Warsaw, except those on the right bank of the Vistula, and these people are the bearers of the most contradictory accounts of the way the fight is going. Our little enclave, which includes our own Grzybowska Street and Ciepla and Krochmalna Streets, also includes a small detachment of the Home Guard, who are, however, practically unarmed. A secret group of the Underground 'Security Forces' came into the open during the night in the police barracks in Ciepla Street: they seized the barracks and, as they had no contact with any other authority, they reported this to us. We handed over seven German directors and technicians of the Dering factory, who were still dressed in nothing but their pyjamas, as well as seventeen prisoners of the 'Werkschutz', and got a receipt for them. We set one of them free: he came from a family of Germans long settled in Warsaw, and who had sometimes been able to warn his Polish acquaintances when they were in danger and who had provided us with a good deal of valuable information.

Volunteers continued to turn up in increasing numbers. There were so many that I had to form several smaller groups. I put Alexander, Tadeusz and Stefan in command of a group each.

The wife of Stas-the-Tailor brought us some thirty red-and-white armbands, but there weren't enough to go round. At nine o'clock, the group commanders reported to me that we now have three groups of eighteen men each, including a high proportion of trained N.C.O.s. We hung out a red-and-white flag on the Dering factory, which our detachment now occupies. Then, as though this were a signal, Polish flags appeared on all the houses in the streets around.

Standing to attention, everyone sang the hymn, 'Not yet is Poland lost. . . .'

I suppose it wasn't, after all, to be wondered at that people were in tears. Everyone wanted to do something, to help somehow. And today, in our street, everything was shared, everything was free. . . .

A plump little man with bushy whiskers, wearing a revolver in his belt, reported to me as 'Cavalry Sergeant Strzelczyk', Quartermaster of an Underground unit of the 'Nationalist' movement. He also claimed to be a part-owner of the chemist's shop in our street. He handed over six grenades, and said that he had a private car which we could make use of (he got hold of it yesterday), as well as a warehouse full of food. The owner of the chemist's shop has handed over to us all the medicine and bandages in his shop, as well as 500 empty bottles and a good store of petrol.

I appointed Mr. Strzelczyk Quartermaster of our unit with the baking of bread as his most urgent task. I gave him two men to help guard the food store. Then I arranged for the petrol to be put into bottles and gave instructions for the collection and storage of as much sulphuric acid and chloride of potassium as possible, as these are essential for making incendiary anti-tank missiles.

The women and girls from our street, who have voluntarily undertaken to provide meals for the soldiers, asked me how many dinners to get ready. The answer was as many as possible—at least two hundred: for our unit is growing all the time, and everyone working in the unit, including civilians, must get their dinner. They have taken over the kitchen in the Dering factory.

A small lorry drove up, and its driver asked to be taken on. His name is Sikora, he was wounded at Narvik and was in a German hospital until they discharged him as unfit for any military duties. But he insisted that he's ready for anything.

And I had a job for him. We'd already three wounded who had to be taken to hospital. But the streets were under fire, we couldn't carry them—so could Sikora try to reach the hospital through these streets by driving very fast? Even though the Germans certainly won't take any notice of it, we thought it would look better if he had a Red Cross flag on the lorry. And Sikora's face lit up.

'I'll do it, sir—see if I don't!'

With him went Wanda, Marta and Halina, who are already on duty as our first ambulance squad. We have a doctor, too, Dr. Leopold, although, unfortunately, he is not a surgeon. This ambulance unit has been strengthened by two other girls who have managed to reach our street. One, Ola, has a degree in classics, while Kasia has a degree in philosophy. Both, like Wanda, took courses in nursing in 1939, as did many other young Poles faced with the threat of German aggression.

Mecenas joined us at noon, bringing with him today's issue of the 'News Bulletin'. Now at last we have it officially that the order for the fighting to start in Warsaw was issued by the Commander-in-Chief of the Home Army, General Bor. The Commanding Officer of the Insurrection is the officer in charge of the Home Army, Warsaw area, Colonel Monter, whose headquarters are in the 'Victoria' Hotel in Jasna Street, not far from us. The Germans have been cleared from almost the whole of the area in

the City Centre, though they are still holding out in the main Post
Office building in Napoleon Square. Although the far side of
Marszalkowska Street is fairly near, it is still difficult to get across,
and Mecenas advised me to make contact for the time being with
the nearest Group Headquarters in Twarda Street. He then gave
me a note to the officer in command of the 'Chrobry II' group,
Major Lig.

Mecenas was interested to get a short account of what has happened so far in our street—how we captured the street, formed a
unit, and also that we are keeping dark the existence of our
printing press and the two printers, Henio and Staszek. He went
off cheerfully.

I took Alexander and his group of men with me to report to
Major Lig, leaving Tadeusz in command till we got back. We got
through fairly easily to the Group Headquarters, where we found
a big block of flats which they had taken over. The inner courtyard
and ground-floor flats were crowded with young men and women
wearing arm-bands but unarmed. Major Lig read Mecenas' letter,
and asked me how many men I had and how we were armed.

'I have twenty men—with revolvers, grenades and petrol-
bottles.'

'You're just in time, then! I've just heard that German tanks
are entering Towarowa Street and we have no men on this side
of Towarowa. I want you to go to Kazimierz Square and—if the
Germans are there—to throw them back at any price. Then
occupy the Borman factory, and arrange to defend it. Report
back to me when this is done. If I can, I'll have you relieved then,
and we can talk.'

'Very good, sir.'

We crossed the deserted streets without meeting any other
rebels until we reached Kazimierz Square. Our boots slipped on
the pavements, which were covered with broken glass and, here
and there, splashes of blood. Small groups of civilians emerged as
soon as they caught sight of our red-and-white arm-bands, and
shouted and waved to us, to show the direction in which the
tanks were moving. We could hear the tanks already.

Someone pointed out to us the easiest way through the shattered windows of the Borman factory. Then someone else placed a ladder against one wall and led the way over the roofs until, looking down, we could see six tanks moving in our direction. S.S. men, wearing black shirts, were leaning out of the open conning-towers. A pistol fired two bursts of shots from just behind me—it was a lad from my group who had not been able to wait for the order to open fire. Instantly all the tank conning-towers slammed to and the barrels of their guns moved in our direction.

Again someone showed us a gap in the roof, through which we jumped, and made our way into the first-floor rooms of the factory, immediately above the tanks. I hadn't counted them, but all at once it seemed to me that my group of men had doubled in size. Big glass vessels containing petrol stood along the walls, and someone took out a battered tin which he impatiently filled. One lad threw a bomb, others hurled bottles of petrol. The first tank snarled to a halt like a horse-fly pierced with a pin and stopped there, damaged. The crew of the second tank, which had gone up in flames, jumped out of it.

When, a few minutes later, we were barricading the western end of the streets leading off Kazimierz Square, there must have been about a hundred of us. Paving-stones were soon heaved up to make entrenchments, backed with sandbags, furniture and anything we could lay hands on.

When, at dusk, we were returning to our own street, a powerful explosion shook the surrounding buildings. The German gendarmes, surrounded by a group of Poles on the corner of Chlodna and Walicowa Streets, had blown up their own cement blockhouse and the near-by school buildings as well.

Thursday, 3 August

Two pictures stand out clearest of all from yesterday's 'baptism of fire'. The first is the sight of the battlefield that was Towarowa Street, with an overturned

tramcar, street-lamps and trees shattered. Here and there in the
street were dead Germans—and our own people. One man, with
a red-and-white arm-band, was still alive. He managed to raise
himself to his knees, but at that moment he was mown down by
a burst of shots fired by an S.S. man from the open cockpit of a
tank.

The second picture is that of a civilian. Seeing that the fuses of
the bottles full of petrol which we were throwing went out as
we threw them, he raked shavings into the window of the factory,
soaked them in petrol, set them on fire and, from where he stood
in the flames, he hurled in the blazing bottles. It was he who set
the tank on fire, not we.

It was as bright as day all night long in our street. The Germans
still hold the Saxon Park and have dug themselves in. They set
fire to the booths that stood in a market-place near by, and these
booths flared up like dry straw. We didn't even try to put them
out. Instead, we erected barricades by the light of the conflagra-
tion, and closed off the entry into our street. We have extended
the area we hold on the other side as far as Zelazna Street, as the
German stronghold on the corner of Chlodna Street has now
been wiped out. We have also taken over the entire square and
the Mirowski covered market.

Our unit was so large by reveille that it needed reorganising,
and I have put each officer formerly in command of a squad
in command of a platoon, each consisting of two squads. The
fighting strength of our three platoons amounts to 100 people,
but over half are armed with nothing but bottles of petrol. Anyone who has a rifle or revolver doesn't get any grenades. Each
group is further divided according to its weapons into riflemen,
grenade-throwers and 'bottlemen'.

I didn't see Stas-the-Sailor at roll-call. Then, a little later, I
caught sight of him on the first-floor balcony over the printing-
works.

'How about it, Stas?' I called up. 'Three days ago you asked me
what we were waiting for!'

'I'm surprised at you, Lech. Why should I stick my neck out, just because some general or other decides he wants to go down in history books?'

'It's up to you. You're grown up now. . . .'

The messenger I left yesterday at Headquarters in Twarda Street ran up at about ten o'clock with an order from Major Lig telling me to send the strongest possible detachment to the railway post office where they're withstanding a heavy attack. I can only send one platoon under Stefan, but I armed them as best I could. They took Sten-guns and three rifles, as well as revolvers and half our grenades. Stefan's wife went with him as a messenger for maintaining direct contact with us.

There were more wounded on the corner of our street and Rynkowa Street. First a man, an hour later a girl. This has brought the total of 'incidents' on this corner to four. Each casualty was hit by a single bullet from a rifle. It was impossible to make out where these shots were coming from, but the wounds—with big torn holes—made it clear that the sniper is using 'dum-dum' bullets. When the lads heard this, they began to cut notches in their ammo, and it was only the threat of taking away his arms from any man found with a notched bullet which made them desist.

I stationed a sentry to prevent people from using this dangerous crossing, and gave instructions for a way to be made by breaking through the cellars of the houses in Rynkowa Street. People say that underground passage-ways like this have been made everywhere in Warsaw, so that one can get anywhere and avoid streets which are under fire.

I stationed Corporal Adam, our best marksman, to track down the dangerous sniper. This was a stroke of luck, for when I went up to the barricade again a little later, Adam was just about to take aim. There, on the roof of the six-storey block of flats on the corner of Graniczna Street, just visible behind a chimney-pot, was a German, also taking aim. Adam fired first; a moment later, the German let his rifle fall and toppled off the roof like a doll. Adam was the hero of the day in Grzybowska Street.

Yesterday I heard that twenty 'Kalmucks', who'd been taken prisoner from the Soviet Army, were hiding in the Dering factory. The Germans had been using them for the heaviest and dirtiest work in the factory. As nationals of races whom the Germans were trying to win over, they were picked out of various general prisoner-of-war camps, but they had refused to enter any of the German auxiliary forces. I said they were to be told that they're free now, and can go where they like and do as they choose. But it turned out that they have all stayed behind and wished to speak to me.

So I went to see them. They weren't 'Kalmucks' at all, but Georgians, Armenians, Daghestanis and Tartars, with a few Ukrainians. One claimed to be a Moslem 'Mullah', and it was he who told me that they are well aware of what is going on. They thanked me for liberating them and for the food we'd been giving them, but they didn't want to leave nor to be fed for nothing. So they all very anxiously asked to join the Polish 'Home Army'. I couldn't decide this myself, nor had I arms for them. If they wanted to, I said, they could stay with the unit, and work would certainly be found for them. They agreed to this willingly, but also asked for their application to be passed on to higher authority, for they would like to be soldiers and have the right to wear our red-and-white arm-bands.

When I came away from them, I found the wife of Edward Iwanski waiting for me. Edward is a Communist and member of the 'Polish Workers' Party'. We know them both well enough, for they live in the left wing of the house where I have my printing press, and in fact their presence has meant continuous and redoubled vigilance on our part. Edward used to work from time to time making Christmas-tree decorations, but this was only for show, for we found out that he used to get a regular and fairly good wage from the Party. Now his wife wanted us to let him join our unit.

'Why doesn't he come to see me himself?' I asked, with feigned indifference.

'He doesn't like to. He thinks you'll refuse. In the Party, they told him to wait and not get involved. But how long are we to wait? Don't leave him out.'

'Ask him to come here.'

So he appeared, and I sent him to join Alexander's group. But there are still some people who are uncertain of the political background of the Insurrection, and talk as if they want to rid themselves of their own doubts.

'People say that Bor's a Fascist,' said a little man with a reddish growth of beard on his chin.

I gave him a copy of the 'Worker' newspaper, issued by the Socialists.

'See for yourself,' I replied. 'In any case, don't you know that the chairman of our Council of National Unity is Kazimierz Puzak, who's a Socialist?'

'So what?' someone else put in. 'You're only opening up the way for them, and they'll seize power over your heads.'

Aircraft have begun to appear over Warsaw. But they are German Stukas, not Soviet planes. They fly low to drop their bombs. Witek, who used to be a bos'n in the navy until he injured his leg in 1939 fighting near Gdynia, has reported as a volunteer, and I put him in charge of our Home Guard detachment. Everyone in our street knows and trusts him.

We still have no clear picture of the advance of the Red Army on the far side of the Vistula, but it seems likely that the Germans may undertake a desperate attempt to break out of Warsaw towards the west—which means they will have to get through the streets we hold. The bombing of our sector and the grouping of tanks in the Saxon Park seem to support this idea. So our main task is not to let a single German break out of Warsaw.

I gave the order for the digging of anti-tank ditches while Alexander's platoon man the barricades. All the houses must be left open and accessible, through the cellars as well as on the first floor. I insisted that a strict watch must be kept on the roof-tops, and also required that all weapons held by civilians should be handed in to us. Anyone in possession of arms is either to report for duty with us or hand in his arms to the officer commanding

Home Guard. Then I ordered sentry-posts to be set up in the streets to check identities and, if necessary, to search anyone trying to pass through.

Within a couple of hours a good many revolvers and rounds of ammunition had been handed in by men not belonging to any groups. At dusk, the sentry-post in our street arrested a civilian who refused to give any explanation of what he was doing and would not let them search him. When he was brought in to me he was cursing and blinding, but at last gave his name as 'Filip'.

I showed him one of our home-made bombs and suddenly he grinned. It turned out that he had made it himself.

'Where did you get it from?' he asked. 'This was one of the first I ever made. One just like it was used last April, in the assassination of the S.S. General Krueger, in Cracow.'

'Filip' has a well-hidden workshop in Krochmalna Street, which is parallel to our street. A few moments later and we'd become friends. I have guaranteed him protection for his workshop and any help he needs. Then, before midnight, he brought me a fine gift—four new home-made bombs. These are to strengthen the defence of his workshop, of our printing-press and of the whole sector.

Friday, 4 August

Now at last, after twenty-two hours, we have had news of Stefan, who has been taking part in the fighting at the railway post-office building. This building has been going from hand to hand. However, this is only to be expected, for the building stands astride the lines of the main railway tracks. As long as we hold it, the Germans cannot use the railway; while the Germans holding the main railway station about a quarter of a mile away are cut off. When our men had finally taken it, they were able to cross the Jerusalem Way and reach the Tourist Hotel. Stefan's men have occupied a part of this building, but it still contains a number of Germans in other rooms.

Stefan's platoon was lucky too. Only a few of his men were wounded, and in addition they managed to get hold of some arms and ammunition. But it doesn't look as though they'll be able to go back here today. Stefan's wife, Zosia, who brought me this report, collected some clean clothes and socks for the lads, as well as bandages and some food, for they are very short of food. Communication is difficult, for there are German tank columns in the Jerusalem Way.

But unexpected support appeared in our streets to replace Stefan. Another group of about twenty lads has joined Alexander and his men on the barricade at the corner of Rynkowa Street. Their leader, a young cadet who was probably trained in a secret Underground course during the Occupation, has taken charge and has no time for any of us. But we learned from his men that they are a platoon of Kilinski's battalion, and that yesterday they took part in the capture of the main Post Office in Napoleon Square. They are to stay with us for twenty-four hours, and will then be relieved. My lads envy them their brand-new bank-notes, stamped 'First Insurgent Pay'.

I sent out more patrols to the west and north. Because the presence of the gendarme company in the block-house on the corner of Chlodna and Zelazna Streets is worrying me—we can hear heavy firing from that area—I myself led the patrol to the north. On the way we came across a temporary field hospital. A rebel group was attacking the Germans in the area, and in Bank Square there was complete confusion. Handfuls of men and women were ransacking the deserted shops. People said that there had been fighting in Theatre Square, and we could still hear intermittent firing. We returned through empty streets.

Tadeusz's patrol brought the news that the Goods Station and the western part of Towarowa Street are strongly held by the Wehrmacht. Meanwhile, German tanks have been emerging from the Saxon Park and coming up to within fifty yards of our positions, firing a few shots and then withdrawing. This is happening in several places, and it looks as if they are trying to test our resistance. But we can do nothing, for we have no anti-tank weapons or even anti-tank ammo for rifles. We must wait for them to come still closer.

We are also totally defenceless against aircraft, which come over in increasing numbers. The first bombs have fallen in our sector, some blocks of flats in near-by Krochmalna Street have been demolished, but without any dead. Small incendiary bombs have also been dropped, several dozen at a time falling on roofs, in the courtyards and streets, whistling in an alarming way as they come down.

But our Home Guard group has put up a good show and put the fires out before they could spread. Fire broke out in the Dering factory, but here, too, it was soon localised by the use of plenty of sand. When the German aircraft came over again they dropped both explosives and incendiaries; then turned and flew in again, very low, to spray the roof-tops with machine-gun fire and prevent us putting the fires out.

But over half the incendiaries failed to explode, and Tadeusz has carefully collected these, for he claims that they can be used to make hand-grenades. He has tested some by dropping them from the balcony into the asphalt paving of the empty court-yard.

Even though we had no serious losses, the aircraft overhead and the bombing have caused some anxiety among the civilians. Some people believe that the flags we've put out incite the bomber attacks and make their targets clear to the pilots. It seems to me, though, that the bombing is neither accidental nor confused, and that the German pilots have their targets determined in advance, probably on the basis of accurate information. This should be easily obtainable, since, in fact, anyone can cross from our sector into that held by the Germans. But for the sake of peace and quiet, I ordered the flags to be taken down.

But people's impatience is directed mainly against the Red Army.

'It was they who told us to start fighting—but what now?'

A rumour is going round to the effect that a British officer and escaped prisoner-of-war has managed to reach General Rokos-sowsky's Headquarters, where he described the situation in Warsaw and urged the Russians to speed up their attack. But the Reds told him that they must wait for more infantry, since their tank columns are too scattered and have by-passed Warsaw, and that Warsaw cannot be taken without infantry. The rumour goes on that the Englishman then pointed out that the 40,000 men of the Home Army who are now fighting in Warsaw con-stitute sufficient infantry, and that it is only the Russian tanks which are needed to turn the fight into a victory. But he couldn't convince the Russians.

At two o'clock another air-raid started—the fourth today. But they dropped leaflets this time instead of bombs. Civilians and soldiers alike were amazed to read an order calling for immediate cessation of fighting by all units of the Home Army, and for them all to withdraw to their original positions. These leaflets claim that we have had to start parleys with the Germans as a result of the difficult attitude adopted by the Russians towards our Prime Minister Mikolajczyk, who is now visiting Moscow officially, and also as a result of the way the Soviet Army is behaving. The leaflet was signed by 'Bor, Commander of the Home Army'. But the alarm caused by this was short-lived, for everyone realised that it was nothing more than an attempt on the Germans' part to trick us. People warned each other not to touch the leaflets, while others burned them, and in the end our spirits went up and our will to fight redoubled. Evidently the Germans are lacking man-power if they are reduced to this sort of cheap trickery.

Then some old girls came rushing up from the direction of Ciepla Street, waving white rags tied to long bits of stick, screaming breathlessly that 'it's all over', that 'the Germans are everywhere', that they'd 'only just escaped with their lives'. But people snatched their sticks and white flags away from them.

'It's the same trick again, like the leaflets. The Germans must have sent them, the stupid old cows.'

Saturday, 5 August

I'm beginning to think that
Filip is off his head altogether. Yesterday his workshop collapsed
during the bombing, with a large number of hand, home-made
bombs in it. It beats me why the whole place didn't blow up and
greatly increase the general destruction. As the fuse-caps on his
home-made bombs have no delaying action, you have to treat
them as though they were eggs. Already one of our lads has been
killed when a bomb exploded in his coat pocket. And yet tons of
stone and steel collapsed on Filip's workshop—and nothing
happened.

Of course I have forbidden anyone to go near the workshop.
Even moving a few bricks might set off the bombs.

When Filip arrived and saw what had happened, he dived
straight into the wreckage, and he's been rooting about there
ever since, indifferent to the darkness and the bombing by day.
Now and again he emerges with battered and shapeless bombs
to say that he doesn't think it right to take such battered objects
to Area Headquarters, but that, after all, the shape of the bomb
isn't what matters and it's a pity to waste them. He says he can
guarantee each one which he brings us.

Jadzia, who brought us news last night of the death of Mecenas,
and who spent the night with us, has decided to stay here. But first
she has had to go to Area Headquarters, which is about a quarter
of a mile away, and ask to be transferred, as strictly speaking
she is on their strength and they might suspect her of desertion.

'But they won't make any difficulties, for I'm not of any use
there,' she said. 'Besides, they'll find plenty of other girls to take
my place. You've no idea, Lech, of the crowds of people hanging
about there, of the heaps of paper the amateur clerks surround
themselves with—and it's all useless and serves no purpose except
to make things difficult for the people who really want to do
something. It's quite different here. Everyone's got something
definite to do; you're like one big family. Probably you don't
realise what a splendid atmosphere there is here, but it's given me
new strength.'

Perhaps she was right. None of us had thought of it, but in fact the atmosphere is good and everyone's hard at work.

Since 2 August they've managed to produce nearly 4,000 loaves in what was the German bakery in Ciepla Street, and the bread is being distributed to anyone who needs it. What's left over is transferred to the Quartermaster of the 'Chrobry II' group. Civilians get bread without paying for it, as the soldiers do.

The cookhouse—which produced 280 dinners on 2 August—now produces 450, and as many hot suppers for the civilians and soldiers in the Dering factory. The efficiency of the kitchens (which are run by some young girls from our street) really is amazing. The Quartermaster provides them with meat straight from the slaughter-house. Everyone who is useful has the right to meals from the kitchen. There are plenty of people, but many prefer to get their rations from the stores, and eat at home with their families.

Our transport column has just brought in stores of provisions from the storehouse in Ciepla Street, which is difficult to guard and also in danger from fire. The first of our stores has had to be moved to another house in the street, as the petrol stored there caught fire. Now the cans of petrol have been buried, and the food which has been saved is at our disposal.

When a heavy bomb fell near the western gate of the Mirowski covered market, it made a great hole in the road and smashed the main water-supply pipes so that the water has flooded the underground warehouses of the market. I allowed people to take away whatever they could save from the flood, to prevent it being wasted. Our Caucasian group worked in the water up to their waists and then up to their shoulders, fishing out tins, cases of eggs and tubs of herring. We were able to set up another storehouse with these things in the Dering factory. As a reward, the Caucasians each got a set of working clothes which we'd found in a tailor's shop, to replace their ragged and soaked garments of German make. They were delighted with their new 'uniforms'.

Other groups of men and girls are building up and strengthening the barricades and digging ditches. This is hard work, as they have to break through a thick layer of cement under the paving-stones that form the surface of the road, and we haven't any of the proper tools for this. Additional barricades are being erected, too, farther down the streets, just in case the enemy should break through our first line of defence. Tadeusz—who has time for everything—was arranging some heavy objects done up in paper and joined by a cable, then covering them with earth and marking out a path to be followed through the street.

'What are you up to?' I asked him.

'Laying mines,' he said.

'Where did you get mines from?'

'They're not real mines, only oddments of machinery. But I want to make the Germans think that the streets are mined. They know very well what is going on here, and they won't try to break through with their tanks.'

A tailor's shop has been set up in our street. We've got hold of a lot of German summer uniforms brought to Warsaw from the Eastern Front for repair. They'd already been mended, and now almost everyone in our unit is wearing the same uniform, both men and women. 'Clothes don't make the man'—but they can make him look a mess. I can hardly recognise Ola and Kasia in their patched overalls. Now volunteers are mending and patching the rest of these uniforms, as there are still more people to fit out, and they are all busy sewing. Next door to this shop more girls and women are making arm-bands and washing and mending our laundry.

The youngest of the lads are busy on tiresome but very important work, making anti-tank missiles. They sprinkle a thin layer of chloride of potassium in screws of paper, glue the edges of the paper lightly and stick them like labels to bottles, so that the powder is attached to the glass. Then they pour a little sulphuric acid into the bottles, top up with petrol, cork it tightly and the thing is ready for use. When you throw one, it spits flame in all directions as it bursts.

A thin middle-aged man called Grzmot, who keeps coming to see me with 'strictly secret' news of the 'dislocation of the enemy

forces' and of 'suspicious personages', has just told me that the
gendarmes have now quit the corner of Zelazna and Chlodna
Streets. I pretended to know all about this already, but I can't for
the life of me think what has become of them. Have they packed
up and gone, or have they been forced to quit by insurgents from
other units?

This same man went on to tell me that in view of this, he has
decided to join up, and has chosen my group because he likes
their leader. He claims to have been a lieutenant, but as a result of
more detailed questioning it turns out that he was never in the
army on account of his poor health. However, after enrolling
him I made him a 'civilian lieutenant' for matters concerning
civilians, as dealing with people who apply to me—as the local
government official, not to mention administrative authority
rolled into one—takes up too much of my time. And Grzmot
started work with a will.

All day the lads have been hunting down German snipers. And
in fact their mysterious shots have created an atmosphere of
suspicion among us. Rumours of German diversionists wearing
Home Army arm-bands have led to an increase of mutual
suspicion.

Jadzia came back from Area Headquarters to say she'd been
given permission to stay with us, and that she is to act as liaison
officer between Badacz at Headquarters and me. He is particularly anxious to establish direct contact with me on account of the
large stocks of food which the Germans have left in the area we'
hold. He has asked me to go and see him, and also to supply him
with bread, as there is no bread to be had in the Headquarters
area.

In the evening a column of us set out. Jadzia led the way, followed by me, and then, in single file, eighteen of the Caucasians,
each carrying a sack of bread. With them was rifleman Czortek,
armed, and Corporal Olgierd, a youthful, very tall partisan,
armed with a home-made machine-pistol. We crossed the deserted streets and, near the main Telephone Exchange, went down
into the cellars which were full of women and children. Then,

one by one, we crossed a low barricade of sandbags and paving-stones.

Here the streets bore traces of bloody fighting. The Area Headquarters building, formerly the Post Office Savings Bank, was packed with people, just as Jadzia had said. A number of German prisoners were sitting and standing about in the ground-floor hall, waiting to be interrogated. Some were wounded. One repulsive fat prisoner was looking about with an expression of animal fear on his face. Another was staring before him, sullen and insolent. But most of the prisoners looked quite indifferent, even apathetic.

I had to go down several flights of stairs to reach Badacz's room. After waiting for some time, he called me in at about midnight.

Sunday, 6 August

I am pleased with the result of our visit to Badacz, even though it took up a lot of time and didn't come off without a certain amount of argument. Badacz was under the impression that I've taken stock of every item in all the stores, shops and even deserted kiosks, that I have them under lock and key, placed guards on them, and will issue nothing without a written order from the Quartermaster of the area. This applies also to all other material and supplies, including cloth and so forth.

But I explained that I hadn't enough arms or enough men to do this. The Home Guard are to all intents and purposes without arms and completely occupied with dealing with the effects of air-raids. The Security unit in the police barracks is decreasing day by day, and in any case their main function at present seems to be to get tight 'in honour of the Fatherland and the Insurrection'. Of my three platoons, one which I'd sent to help in the attack on the railway post office is now fighting in the building of the Army Geographical Institute to the south of our sector; the second platoon is holding the streets leading from the Saxon Park; and

the third—as reinforcements—may have to start fighting anywhere at any time.

My administrative unit is of course fairly well up in strength,
but I can't use the fire-brigade, nor the working parties, nor the
kitchen staff, the bakery staff, the tailoring section, nor the
armourers to undertake the tasks Badacz demands. The only
possible solution, as I see it, is to collect everything we come across
which may be useful for the soldiers, hospitals or civilians without
any formalities—before these stores are buried in the ruins or go
up in flames.

In the end we reached a compromise. Badacz gave me a written order, with instructions to safeguard all stores in our sector,
and only to issue supplies on written authority from the Area
Quartermaster. We agreed that this order is to refer only to the
bigger store-houses, for which Badacz is to try to provide armed
sentries. I also have authority to issue food and equipment for the
hospitals and to provide stores for my own men and the entire
'Chrobry II' group. Also I have authority to deal as I think fit
with any stores which I consider in danger of destruction, whether
by fire or anything else.

I was given Home Army identity cards for all my men,
and was also authorized to issue similar identity cards to the
Caucasians. After all, the Home Army recognizes no differences
in nationality or religion, and indeed a number of foreigners
have been enrolled in its ranks already.

I also came away from Area Headquarters with something else.
Although no one specifically said so, I know now that we cannot
count on any help in our fight, either from the east or even from
the Soviet Army, at least in the near future. In fact, we can count
on nothing and no one—except ourselves.

It can't be helped. Now that this thing has started, we must see
it through.

Meanwhile, a large-scale German attack has started from the
western district of Warsaw. They are using all kinds of arms.
Their Stukas are flying low, placing their heavy bombs deliberately and sowing incendiaries by the thousand. Heavy

artillery is firing according to instructions from the aircraft. 'Big
Bertha' has been brought up by train and is firing shells. The
smoke and dust rising from crumbling walls provide cover for
the attackers, who are armed with flame-throwers. Any stiff
defence is smashed by Goliaths—small, strongly armoured tanks
without a crew but containing high explosive. And the Wehrmacht battalions and heavy Tiger tanks are moving in, under
protection of all this, slowly but safely and unchecked, towards the
centre of Warsaw.

We know that the partisan groups out there in the suburbs
cannot hold out. Patrols and runners keep coming in with increasingly bad news.

Meanwhile the Germans are growing more active in the Saxon
Park. Cannon are being brought up and dug in. Tanks have ad-
vanced to the Grzybowski Square. But they have not attempted
to break through our barricades—yet. The lads from Kilinski's
battalion have left the barricade in Rynkowa Street and cleared
off without even bidding us good-bye. Some ambulance girls
bring in a couple of wounded men and ask the way to the nearest
hospital.

Then two young men in Polish uniform ride up on a motor-
bike and order us to remove the barricades and clear our street of
mines.

'The General is coming this way,' they say. 'The road must be
cleared of mines.'

What General is going to visit a sector already occupied by the
Germans? And how did they know that our street was mined?
But although we disarmed and arrested the pair of them, neither
was able to explain who had sent them with this 'order'. All they
knew was that a senior officer had sent them on this important
mission on account of their having a motor-bike, and that it is
all very urgent.

Half an hour after this 'order' had reached us, the tanks started
their first big-scale attempt to break through—following the
'General's route'. But the two lads don't appear to have had any
evil intentions—they were just too eager and credulous. I sent

them off, under escort, to their Headquarters. We have gained two Sten-guns out of the episode.

Their entry into our street by motor-bike was possible on account of Captain Proboszcz, chief of staff of the 'Chrobry II' group, who uses a motor-bike himself. Narrow passages through the barricades have been left for his benefit, and there are planks for him to drive over the anti-tank trenches.

Refugees from the western district are appearing in increasing numbers. The town is in flames there.

People say that supplies have been dropped by parachute from a British aircraft.

Monday, 7 August

Yesterday the main body or refugees from the western district reached Elektoralna and Leszno Streets. And today at dawn they were on us. First singly, half running, their clothes torn, blinded with panic, men and women came along the streets. We had to stop them almost by force, threaten them. Then came whole families, dragging bundles containing anything they'd been able to save, bedding, with babies in arms, scurrying cautiously from one gate way to the next and beckoning one another on. Seeing our men, they started to ask what to do next, and they surged along, wave after wave of them, and, when we asked them where they were going, all they could say was:

'What do you mean? I'm following the others. . . .'

We set up sentry-posts to try to break up and halt the crowds. At the other end of our street they would come under fire from the Saxon Park. In the other direction they'd be under fire from the Cedergren building, which the Germans hold. If they go north, they will be mown down at the Iron Gates. More corpses, more wounded, for whom even now there aren't enough bandages or sufficient room in the hospitals. We could have sent them south, but what would have been the use? For there is already famine in the southern districts of Warsaw, which are the worst off of all for food. So it seems best to keep them here.

Soon something like six thousand refugees were crammed into the cellars and ground-floor rooms of the blocks of flats and two factory buildings in our street. Two army kitchens and all the civilian kitchens were serving out hot meals, to encourage and calm them.

I put a brave face on it all and assured everyone that the Germans will not break in, but I'd be glad if someone could convince *me* of this. Our Home Guard unit no longer exists, although a few local people are still here and have volunteered to join us individually. The police barracks are now deserted. The bombing goes on almost without a break. Someone has counted sixteen air-raids already today. The Dering factory is on fire again, and flames have broken out in the upper storeys. But we are trying to prevent the flames spreading by hastily blocking up the doors and windows.

I have not yet decided to move my own headquarters from the guard-room in the Dering factory as the big gateway forms some protection against fire and the fire in turns serves to protect us from bombs. No pilot would suppose this region of flames conceals the headquarters of our sector.

A brownish cloud of dust rose from No. 10 as the house collapsed. Then the first wounded to be dug out of the ruins were brought in. Clouds of flies swarmed on the fresh blood. Flakes of soot in the air settled on sweat-stained faces.

The Germans, moving along Chlodna Street, are fighting the last units of rebels as the latter retreat from the west. Some of these units have been driven into our street, and the scattered rebels, with their red-and-white arm-bands worn on German uniforms and wearing German steel helmets, mingled with the refugees.

I knew the leader of one of these units, who used to be commandant of an Underground organisation.

'Glad to see you,' he said, shaking me by the hand. 'Can you spare half an hour? We've got to decide whether all this is going to serve any useful purpose. I'd like your advice on our new position.'

I suggested he should man *our* position on the corner of Ciepla and Krochmalna Streets.

'You're joking,' he said irritably. 'I'm talking about the position as a whole—what's the latest from Moscow and London? We're almost certainly going to get out of Warsaw and take to the woods. I hope you won't regret what you're doing.'

I hadn't the time to listen to the radio since the fighting began in Warsaw. I didn't know what he was talking about at all. Then he and his men moved off. I couldn't help begrudging them their magnificent weapons.

Another air-raid and the shrill scream of bombs mingled with the heavy crash of explosions not far away. Everyone's nerves are on edge, and a shrill voice in the street was audible in my head-quarters shouting:

'All units are to withdraw to the Old Town. All units . . . to withdraw. . . .'

'What's his game? Shut his trap for him and bring him in here.'

Alexander brought in the man. But even he couldn't say who'd actually given the order or even what 'units' the order referred to. He'd heard that General Bor has issued some sort of order, but, alarmed by being arrested, he then denied everything.

'I don't know anything about it,' he protested. 'My command-ing officer probably knows. . . .'

'Where is he?'

'He's taken his unit to the Old Town.'

More stragglers, as they pass down our street, confirmed that in fact this order had been issued.

Still, we'd better wait for orders from our immediate superior officer at Group Headquarters. I send him regular reports, and he knows precisely what is going on here. All the same, Captain Proboszcz is hardly ever to be found at Head-quarters. He's usually out on patrol, or fighting somewhere at the head of a little group of men, wherever he's most needed.

Alexander reported the strength of our reserve platoon: they have one Sten-gun, two rifles, eleven revolvers of various makes and calibres, about a hundred home-made bombs and grenades and bottles of petrol.

The rumbling crash of steel caterpillars was audible from the direction of Chlodna Street. The Germans were drawing in to attack. They must have by-passed St. Charles Church and surrounded the men who were holding out there, for the first bullets now began to spray along Ciepla Street. But the main attack from the west is by-passing us, though only a few dozen yards separate the Germans from our barricades in Krochmalna Street.

Anxious people were peeping out of gateways.

'What's going to happen? Are you really retreating?' they asked me.

Among them I saw the doorman of one of the blocks of flats in our street. He spoke calmly:

'Lech, this is how I see it. If only you can hold the barricades, then we'll block up all the entrances from Krochmalna Street and place sentries on them. We've all got bottles of petrol and the tanks won't dare try to pass.'

'Can we hold out?'

'Why not? Anyhow, the main thing is for it to happen here and for us all to stick together.'

I sent a report on the situation to Group Headquarters, including details of the verbal order to retreat and our decision to hold out in our street in spite of it. I can see that the Germans will make an attempt today to drive us south—once they've linked up with the others in the Saxon Park. I asked urgently for support, particularly for them to send us Stefan's platoon.

The runner came back with a note from Captain Proboszcz, praising me for refusing to obey the order to withdraw and confirming my decision which, in any case, coincided with the orders of the O.C. City Centre, Colonel Radwan. He agreed to send support.

Soon afterwards, a reserve company led by Jeremy turned up, with orders to make a reconnaissance of the German forces in the area of Mirowski Square. They went along Ciepla Street to the square and fired some shots at the Germans, but were obliged to withdraw under much heavier fire from the enemy. However, they completed their mission. Then my observers, hidden in Krochmalna Street, saw a part of the German forces grouping to attack in our direction. Tadeusz has taken half his men over to the west side of Rynkowa Street and stationed individual snipers. Alexander has occupied the Ciepla Street barricades, and ordered his men to dig trenches at the Ciepla Street and Krochmalna Street crossings.

Three Stukas suddenly emerged from behind the towers of All Saints' Church and made straight for our position. As I hurried to Group Headquarters, I heard bombs hurtling down along our street. Captain Proboszcz was standing in the gateway of Group Headquarters, now in Sienna Street, waiting for Grzes and his platoon to arrive, as Grzes was to be sent to me instead of Stefan. A moment or two later Grzes turned up with some twenty men.

'Take them,' Proboszcz ordered, 'and go in to the attack, so that the Germans who are forming up in the square get what is coming to them. . . .'

We ran off into the ruins. But it was clear that with our solitary platoon of men we couldn't hope to throw out the German formation from Mirowski Square, as they consisted of very nearly a full battalion. The only thing to do was to prevent the Germans from attacking us, and by attacking them first we might be able to hold out till dusk. Since Jeremy and his men had attracted the attention of the Germans on the western side of the square, I decided to strike from the east.

On the way I put Grzes into the picture, and told him how I planned to act. When we reached our street I saw that the house in which my printing-press had been now lay in a smoking mass of ruins. Wiesia, Stas-the-Tailor's fifteen-year-old daughter, in tears, ran to meet me.

'Lech, people . . . buried in there! My father . . . Barbara. . . . Do something!'

'Get Tadeusz,' I shouted to her. 'If we let the Germans through now, we're all finished.'

Grzes is a first-rate N.C.O. and leader of men. But what Wiesia had told me left me unable to think properly. At times I was no longer aware of what was happening around me, as though I'd drunk too much. But what I'd told Grzes on the way from Headquarters sufficed, and he took command, leaving me to act as guide. I led the way into the crowded cellars of one of the houses in our street. Here I saw a number of men. I shouted to them to go and help dig out the people buried in the bombed building. But nobody moved. Then, behind me, Grzes said:

'The lieutenant's wife was in No. 17—she's trapped.'

How did he know that Barbara is my wife? But he must have known more about the human mind than I, for a moment later I heard the voices of women in the crowded cellar,

'Hear that? Then get moving, you men! Get out of here! Get out. . . .'

We hurried to the next house, where the ground floor was in flames, and again went down into the cellars. The smoke and flames made our eyes water. Then we went on, into Krochmalna and across the Janasz market-place. We must have got past the German sentries under the cover of the fire, for suddenly we saw before us what looked like a whole company of the Wehrmacht. Their rifles were stacked and the men were standing about 'at ease' in little groups, some sitting on the edge of the pavement or lounging against the walls. Our lads opened fire and before the Germans could return the fire the lads had all withdrawn, without losing anyone.

Grzes said we ought to do this again, but differently.

Then, through the thick smoke, twenty men slowly and soundlessly moved after him. A gust of wind drove aside the smoke for a few moments, and Grzes pointed out his position to each of his men. The narrow side-street separating us from the Germans was empty. Opposite, in the big covered market, Germans were lurking. We hurled grenades in.

'All right, that's enough,' shouted Grzes. The massacre was over.

Back at the Dering factory I wrote a short report. Marys,

Grzes' second-in-command, took it back to Captain Proboszcz. Then, as I went with Marys to show him the quickest way back to Group Headquarters, I came face to face in the smoking ruins with Barbara. Her hair, face and overalls were grey with dust.

'It's you. . . .' I said stupidly. 'You want a wash. . . .'

She was one of the first they had dug out, for they had seen her hand emerging from the wreckage. She had been standing with Stas at the bathroom window, when a single aircraft flew over. She didn't hear the bomb, but had *felt* it was coming down. She'd been able to cover her mouth and nose with her hand. Then, suspended between ground floor and cellar, her breast wedged between two rafters, she had heard groans and cries for help all round her.

'Quiet!' she had called. 'Don't all shout at once! Call out one by one, wherever you are.'

They all obeyed. Only one youth kept on bawling that he was being suffocated.

This infuriated Barbara.

'If you can shout like that, then you've got plenty of air! Why not go easy with it and be quiet?'

First they had dug out the people who, when the bomb fell, had been on the roof. They slipped down almost unhurt, with their heads showing out of the ruins. Then they got out my two assistants in the printing-works, Henio and Staszek. When the bomb fell, they had both been lying on the wooden bed in the cellar near the type cases. The wooden bedstead had somehow overturned, so that they fell under it, and this protected them from the walls that collapsed over them. Stas-the-Tailor was easily found, too; only bruised, for his bald head had gleamed amidst the bricks.

But there were still a good many people trapped. A young couple, who happened to be in the house at the time, are now trapped in the cellar under the bathroom, as though in a spacious tomb. Groans and cries can be heard from different spots. The rescuers are working at full tilt, but the digging is hard going, for careless moving of a brick or lifting a rafter may well mean a further collapse of the ruins and those still alive may be strangled.

Night has fallen. The electricity has been cut off in our street, though some volunteers are going to try to lay a temporary cable from Twarda Street. We lit candles in the guard-room of the Dering factory. Then Captain Proboszcz arrived on his motor-bike, in order—as he said—to find out for himself if Barbara is still alive. But he also brought with him two orders, hand-written on sheets of official notepaper, with big rubber stamps.

One of these appointed me in command of the northern sector of the 'Chrobry II' group, stretching from Graniczna Street in the east as far as Towarowa Street in the west, and instructing me to take charge of all rebel groups who are now in this sector and in the triangle with its apex in Group Headquarters. I am to organise the defence of this sector with these groups.

The second order is addressed to all group commanders and men in the sector now under my control. It requires unconditional obedience of all my orders, no matter what their rank or previous assignment.

I sent out patrols to search the sector for even the smallest group of men. Alexander set off with a patrol as far as Towarowa Street, to survey the German outlying posts in order to fix our line of defence.

The fire in the Dering factory is spreading. The women and our Caucasians, who had already taken all the beds from the Jarnuszkiewicz furniture factory to the hospital in Marianska Street, are now transferring stores from the Dering factory to the Jarnuszkiewicz building.

Some new faces have appeared in our cook-house—women representing the 'Soldiers' Aid' organisation. They asked me if they could be of any use, and I said that everyone is useful, and they thereupon took charge and set about reorganising the place, much to the disgust of the women and girls who had been running the cook-house previously.

I asked one of the 'Soldiers' Aid' girls where her commanding officer Regina had gone?

'To Area Headquarters, to get an order to set up a kitchen for the men in your street.'

'But the kitchen has been working for days.'

'Yes, but unofficially. We have to have official authority.'

But one of her colleagues, Janka, was already bringing in bread from the burning factory—without waiting for 'official authority'.

Tuesday, 8 August

Soon after midnight I held a parade in the guard-room of the Dering factory, which, by the way, is still on fire. Captain Hal arrived first; he is O.C. of a battalion which was fighting in Plocka Street and who managed to get a few platoons over to Twarda Street. Then came Janusz, who is in command of some forty ill-armed men whose company has been driven back by the Germans into our street, then Lieutenant Jan, in command of a fairly strong and well-armed platoon which has had to withdraw from their strongholds to behind our barricade, and finally Alexander and Sergeant Grzes. They are all prepared to accept the orders which have been given me.

We agreed upon the details of our plan of defence. The length of our sector is about 2,000 yards. Our defence is based on the strong barricades which close all the streets in the direction of the enemy, and on a number of scattered observation-posts and patrols. We decided who was to man the various barricades. I have kept back Grzes' platoon as reserves in the ground-floor rooms facing into our street at No. 20. I have transferred my headquarters into a shop at No. 18.

Work on strengthening and building up the barricades went on till early morning. Then Captain Proboszcz sent me Jeremy and his company. I sent them to man the barricade in Zelazna Street, and told them to take over the Haberbusch brewery, part of which is already burnt down. We have also come across another little group of men, led by sixty-year-old Lieutenant Wislanski, who has reported to me as 'Officer in charge of motorised column No. 48'—without, needless to say, any motors.

By the time the Germans moved forward to the attack, at about ten o'clock, we were ready for them. Their main blow was made along Rynkowa and Graniczna Streets in the direction of Grzybowski Square. The attack was made by troops of the Wehrmacht, but without tanks. Our lads lay in wait without firing. Not until the first Germans crossed our street did they open fire, shooting at them obliquely, from the barricades and from the windows of Rynkowa Street.

People crowded into the gateways to see for themselves as runners brought us the rifles, grenades, ammunition, steel helmets, packs, papers and army badges which have been seized. A light machine-gun, the first in our sector, was greeted with a cheer of triumph.

But there was one critical moment, which might have led to disaster had it not been for Wanda. She'd been dismissed by Alexander from the barricade in Rynkowa Street, which was under fire from the Germans, and was coming back in the middle of the road when, passing No. 8, she caught sight of Germans in the inner courtyard of the house. She raised the alarm, and we hurried there, while Alexander came up on the other side. We reached the gateway just as a number of hefty German gendarmes were about to emerge into the street. They drew back hastily in the face of our fire.

Once again I had occasion to see the remarkable rapidity of action and decisiveness of Grzes. He indicated the balcony of the first floor over the gateway to the lads. Giving each other a hand, the lads climbed up, and I, from below, tossed them some grenades, which they caught like balls. They then ran with them into the house and, from the windows overlooking the inner courtyard, tossed the grenades down. After the first explosions, Alexander and Grzes went into the yard. Then I heard a single shot. Going in, I saw two gendarmes lying dead on the cement paving.

'How did you do it?' I asked Grzes. 'Two men killed with one shot?'

'Never mind,' Grzes replied with a gesture. 'I had one bullet left, and Alexander's rifle wouldn't fire, damn it. We couldn't retreat, of course. So we finished them off with our boots. Unfortunately, the rest of them bolted and took with them the men we'd wounded with our grenades.'

I eyed Grzes' hard face and thought that he wasn't human. But immediately I realised that I myself was incredibly happy as I looked at the papers the Germans had in their pockets, and found a photograph and a lock of curly hair among them. The yellowing photograph showed a young woman and two boys in the uniform of the Hitler Youth.

Two new Mausers and ammunition which we acquired in the gateway of No. 8 were divided fairly between Grzes' and Alexander's groups. But the heroine today was Wanda—if it hadn't been for her we'd have lost the barricade on the corner of our street, and would have had a good many men killed.

They told me that the Germans used ladders to clamber over from Krochmalna Street into the yards at the back of our street. Thus the sentries I'd posted at the entrances were not sufficient to protect the street from an unexpected attack by the enemy. It was just as well to know this, and I went along to check our defences. Unfortunately I was a little too late. In the cellars of the rear part of the Dering factory I found the scattered belongings of the refugees from the west, but there was no one there. Water was boiling in a kettle over a Primus stove, a canary was chirping in its cage and some thin stew was steaming in a tin dish. The steel sheet which had blocked the entrance from other cellars off Krochmalna Street had been removed. I can only suppose that the Germans broke through and had driven the refugees out.

In the afternoon I was appointed commander of the second battalion of the 'Chrobry II' group. The commander of the first battalion is a captain with the same name as myself—Lech. A reserve company was being formed at 'Chrobry II' group, but as they had no weapons, they armed themselves with sticks and were drilling with these.

On the way, I saw an elderly major drilling volunteers in saluting at attention and on the march.

Now I am in command of a battalion. The only thing is that the battalion must first of all be formed. Then, with it, I shall have to defend a sector over a mile long.

Wednesday, 9 August

Reports have been coming in since dawn. Tadeusz considers that rescue work in our bombed house is now ended. Nine people have been rescued. The tenth, an old lady who lived on the second floor with her sons, died as she was being taken to hospital on a stretcher. No trace can be found of Stas-the-Sailor, who was talking to Barbara in the house just before the bomb fell. It is difficult to make out who— if anybody—is still in there, but by this time there is no hope of anyone surviving.

By morning Jeremy and his company had cleared the Haberbusch brewery of German patrols and made the area safe. Similarly, there are no more Germans now along our side of Krochmalna Street from Rynkowa to Wronia Streets. However, they are holding out on the strong barricades they have built on the street corner.

The fighting in our sector, which has hitherto been sporadic and scattered, has now taken on the character of a battle from firmly held positions. The northern districts of Warsaw are cut off from the rest of the city. But the inhabitants—and not only civilians—still do not realise the change that has taken place in the situation as a whole. From time to time we have to stop Boy Scouts who still want to try to get through to the Old Town in the north. We have to argue with N.C.O.s who insist on trying to get through to the storehouses in the covered market, to obtain food for their units. One sergeant who didn't want to go back empty-handed tried to get into our stores, but I showed him the order signed by Area Q.M. Badacz.

'That doesn't mean anything,' the sergeant retorted, significantly shifting his rifle from one hand to the other.

In addition, he showed me a piece of paper, with an elaborate rubber stamp on it, signed by 'C.-in-C. of the Sikorski Regiment'. But to put an end to any uncertainty, he started to call one of his pals 'Colonel'. The 'Colonel' was very strict, and the sergeant went off with as much butter, eggs and tinned food as his men could carry.

For the first time some War Correspondents came to me for news of what is happening in our sector. They brought the latest issue of the 'News Bulletin', which have reports on their front page of the fighting in our sector. When the lads read a report with the head-line 'Poles counter-attack near the Mirowski covered market', someone jokingly commented that the 'Bulletin' has an excellent German source of news, for it can only have learned from the Germans how many were killed the day before yesterday in the fighting there. None of us counted the dead and no report was made on our side, so that the figure of forty dead given in the newspaper strikes us as nothing more than a guess.

The journalists, also jokingly, retorted that the 'Worker' evidently has still better reporters on the German side, for in today's issue of their paper they claim that our group killed about 150 S.S. men.

'It's almost impossible to check', I put in, 'which source is the better informed. All the same, the "Worker" has a better system of distribution. We get it regularly, every day at the same time.'

This is so. The newspaper is delivered by an elderly actor, who isn't in the least bothered by the firing he encounters on the way. He doesn't simply deliver the paper either, but also likes to read it aloud to the lads. So the 'Bulletin' reporters promised from today we'll get their paper regularly as well, and that their reporters will check their news with the individual commanders of sectors.

But the journalists themselves turned out to be better sources for news than the newspapers they write for, for we learned from them that Colonel Radwan is now in command of the entire City Centre District, that my sector is part of IV Region under Major Zagonczyk and that the whole 'Chrobry II' group is regarded as being politically 'Nationalist'.

'Yet I have recognised several of your men as Socialists,' one of the journalists commented. 'How do you explain that?'

'I don't know anything about what is happening at Group Headquarters or in the first battalion,' I replied, 'and in any case it's of no consequence. Besides, as far as I know the only former Nationalist among my men is the Quartermaster.'

The 'Bulletin' reporters then went on to say that no one now has any illusions as to the intentions of the Reds, who have deliberately suspended all military activity on the right bank of the Vistula since the Insurrection started in Warsaw. Since this is clearly dangerous from a purely military point of view and could prove costly both for them and for us, it is obvious that the reason for this attitude is political.

This made me think. It almost seems as though—apart from their evil intentions in regard to Poland—the Reds are concerned lest the Germans capitulate too suddenly. For once Hitler has surrendered, nothing would justify the Soviet Army advancing into liberated Europe.

The Germans have again begun an attack along the side-streets from the direction of Krochmalna Street. But today they have a clearer picture of our defences and know that they must reckon with our resistance. They precede their attacks with heavy fire against our barricades, and support their infantry with mortar and grenade fire. But now the aim of the attack is clearly different. Yesterday they tried to penetrate the sector held by us in the direction of the Telephone Exchange building and the Central Railway Station. Today, on the other hand, they are trying to drive us back along the whole of our defence line. This isn't surprising, for their only road across Warsaw to the Vistula is under fire from us in many places. I gave the order that ammunition was to be used very sparingly, but it is hard to prevent the lads from firing when a German column is moving only a few dozen yards away, and individual Germans often approach even closer to our positions.

After the victories of yesterday the lads are in fine form. Even the men who retreated from Wola in the face of what seemed like immense German superiority in man-power have now re-gained confidence in our strength. Meanwhile the Germans themselves encourage our resistance and stubbornness by their acts of savagery.

People were ready to swear yesterday they'd seen German tanks with naked men tied to them. The Germans have also set fire to all the houses in Chlodna Street, as they did last year in the Ghetto, and all the civilians driven out in this way are split up on the spot into groups—the women and children are marched off to the west, while the men are forced to work on German fortifications. Anyone unfit for work or refusing to obey is shot.

Some of the lads on our barricades have been wounded, but the German attack was thrown back as soon as they came within range of our grenades. Our home-made bombs never fail. But the defenders are poorly armed, so that I and Sergeant Grzes have to go from one barricade to the next. I've only known Grzes two days—but already I'm fond of him and we get along very well together.

'I'm not going to let them transfer me from your sector,' he told me at one stage. 'I've picked on you as my commanding officer. And do you know why? Because you didn't give way when your wife was trapped in the bombed house. I like to know that my C.O. isn't likely to give way.'

So the two of us insisted to Captain Proboszcz that Grzes and his group should stay in my sector for good. He agreed, but I've had to make do without Stefan, who has been transferred with his platoon to another sector.

A young student, with a babyish face, told me something of Grzes. In World War I he obtained the Cross of Valour. During the Occupation he worked in the Warsaw power-station and commanded an Underground unit. With his men, he took part in the successful assassination of General Kutschera, Himmler's son-in-law, known as the 'hangman of Warsaw' on 1 February last year. His men are fanatically devoted to him—and now I understand the force and competence of his men during the attack the day before yesterday.

Thursday, 10 August

The organisation of my battalion is now complete. The main difficulty was that I haven't been able to include all the individual groups which were put under my command when I took control of the sector. Captain Hal's unit—or what was left of them following their withdrawal from the west—would have made a good company, well armed and with good officers. However, Captain Hal still hopes to re-form his own battalion, and claims that he agreed on this with his cousin, Major Zagonczyk, O.C. IV Region. But it seems to me that the man who settles the organisation and the distribution of man-power in Warsaw ought to be the officer commanding the area.

As far as Jan is concerned, things look rather different. He belongs to another group, neighbours of ours on the far side of Grzybowski Square. The order laying down the boundary of the sector assigned to me was issued when Jan was by chance within this area. Jan therefore accepted the order, knowing that it was necessary, and has since remained in his position in Rynkowa Street within my sector. He likes being here, although he is continually being ordered by his own commanding officer to return to his original group. Now, in agreement with me, Jan has replied that the question of his return to his original group must be decided at a higher level. I can't do anything about it.

Jeremy and his company in the Haberbusch brewery are under my command, and they are included in the strength of my battalion, on condition that officially he is still a reserve of Area Headquarters and, if needed, may be recalled. I have to take this into consideration and consequently cannot send them any replacements; as a result, the fighting strength of his group is relatively small, with a high proportion of officers. Among these officers is Second-Lieutenant 'Goliath' who, with some of his lads, made a name for himself on 4 August by cutting the Warsaw-Berlin telephone cables.

Consequently, my battalion officially consists of only two companies, Grzes' platoon and the administrative personnel.

The first of these companies has been strengthened today by the arrival of a new assault group, 'Blyskawica'. This company has only two officers: Alexander is in charge, his deputy is Tadeusz. At the same time, Alexander is my deputy as commander of the whole sector and of our battalion. The fighting core of this company consists of the men who took part in the guard of our secret printing-press and of a party of volunteers, mainly working men and craftsmen who live in the sector and know the ground like the palms of their own hands.

The second company—under Janusz—also has only one officer in addition to Janusz himself. In order to complement the strength of this company, which is holding the barricades on the north-west side of the sector, Alexander has transferred some men from his own ever-increasing company to them. Janusz has shown a good deal of ingenuity in providing his men with arms. The Quartermaster complains that Janusz refuses to hand over any boxes of butter, even though he's got more butter than his whole company could use in months. Our stock of butter from the battalion stores was taken by men of the Sikorski Regiment, and now there isn't any butter, even for the hospital.

'What do you want butter for?' I asked Janusz. 'Share it with us.'

'I can get guns for this butter,' Janusz then confided.

'Where?'

'Military police. I've already got two rifles in exchange for butter. And they've promised to try to get more.'

'But that's indecent.'

'Yes, but useful. We can manage without butter, and they can get along all right without rifles.'

So I let him keep his stock of butter, and gave instructions to the Quartermaster not to let this valuable source of arms be cut off.

'Why didn't Janusz tell me?' he countered. 'I can try to get butter somewhere else.'

I have not included Grzes and his assault group in either of the two companies, as I can foresee having to create a third company should Jeremy and his group have to leave. Besides, Grzes and his lads can now take the place of either company in case of need.

The two companies exchange ammunition, particularly for their revolvers, in view of the great variety of types and calibre of our revolvers. Some revolvers, in fact, are useless, as there is no suitable ammunition for them. The only use we can find for them is to ornament our sentries.

I kept Wislanski, the commander of the 'motorised column', for my own use. Other men from this 'column' have been posted to Janusz's company. As for the two assistants in the printing-works, one—Henio—who has a degree in economics, has been put to work in the stores, as he has weak eyes and flat feet. Staszek, the other printer, is training as a soldier in the first company.

A very valuable addition to our unit was the three qualified nurses—Zofia, Maria and Alicia. The Germans captured them in the Malta Hospital, with the rest of the hospital staff. But wounded German men and officers in the hospital came to their defence, and had them freed on account of the care which the Polish personnel of the hospital had shown them. Somehow the three girls have reached our sector. They say that things are much quieter in the Powisle district, on our bank of the Vistula, and that there are even a few shops and little cafés open. But there is confusion everywhere.

The German attacks are growing stronger. They have been launching attacks almost without a break since early this morn-ing. Tanks support the infantry as the latter move in to the at-tack. Jeremy's company, on our northern barricades, have thrown back the strongest of these attacks by decisive action from the Haberbusch brewery. This resulted in an important capture—two machine-guns and about 800 cartridges. But they have lost one man.

While the fighting is going on, the civilians in our street have had a respite from bombing. The Germans cannot bomb our street when their own units are attacking us. All at once a single aircraft came over and dropped leaflets.

'ULTIMATUM TO THE INHABITANTS OF WARSAW!
The German High Command wishes to avoid unnecessary bloodshed, particularly that of innocent women and children, and has
issued the following appeal: You are urged to leave Warsaw in
a westerly direction, carrying white flags or handkerchiefs.'

This is followed by a promise that no one will be punished,
that those who are fit will obtain bread and work; while those
who are sick, the old, women and children will be given medical
care, billets and medical attention.

'The Poles know,' continues the anonymous writer, 'that the
German Army is fighting Bolshevism. Anyone who persists
in allowing the Bolsheviks to make use of him, no matter
under what slogan, will be held responsible. This ultimatum is
urgent.'

As though to confirm the good-will of the Germans and their
wish to avoid the bloodshed of innocent women and children
and their offer to care for them, we now saw German tanks
moving along Ciepla Street, driving before them a large crowd
of civilians: men, women, old people and children. Driven by
the rifle butts of the S.S. men concealed behind them, these people moved up to the first barricade and began to dismantle it.
Our men withdrew without firing a shot.

When I was told this, I took Grzes with me, and we hastened
to the second barricade on the corner of Ciepla and our street.
Under cover of the civilians, German tanks were already moving
past the police barracks towards us. Our lads lay in their positions,
as if paralysed.

'Why don't you fire? Fire!'

Nothing happened.

'Fire!'

Two of the lads had rifles. Grzes leapt to one of them, and
grabbed at his rifle. The lad fired. A young woman with a baby
in her arms fell to the ground. The crowd scattered like a pane
of glass shattered by a stone. The machine-guns of the tanks
opened up.

Friday, 11 August

Fighting has been going on in our sector for five days without a break. Some of us call it the 'defence of our street', others the 'battle of Krochmalna Street'. Day after day the Germans have been moving up to the attack, firing at the barricades, sending over a hail of shells, spreading flames and driving us from house to house. Night after night, our lads move out into the ruins armed with bottles of petrol, revolvers and single grenades and, by the light of rockets, creep up to the German defences and drive them back beyond Krochmalna Street.

A week ago we were counting by hours. But now we count by whole days. How many more days can this go on? Two days ago the barricades were crowded. Now they stand unmanned. We stand guard over them from the ruined houses, in which we have built positions and defence works with sandbags. Most of the positions are now held by lads with bandaged heads or arms. Light wounds don't count. The hospitals can only take in people if they're seriously wounded.

The lads don't come into the mess any longer. Instead, the girls take food and hot coffee out to the barricades and positions. The lads don't wash themselves for days at a time. There's no water. It has to be brought up from a well between our street and Twarda Street, which, however, is under fire from the Germans.

Platoons of 'Cossacks'—a German formation consisting of prisoners-of-war formerly in the Red Army—move up one by one along Zelazna Street. But their attack yielded under fire from the light machine-guns we 'acquired' yesterday. A shell from a tank has killed Second-Lieutenant Goliath, and his command has been taken over by Lieutenant Karol. Jeremy's lads have reached the limits of their endurance after fighting for seventy hours. I have sent a handful of men to Janusz so that he can relieve Jeremy's company. On the way back to their billet, Goliath's men gave him a decent burial in a little grass plot in an inner courtyard in Ceglana Street, where he now lies in the shade of a couple of green trees.

The first platoon of Alexander's company has had a bad time with German tanks as they attacked along Rynkowa Street. German mortars were firing at our barricade. One shell shattered the leg of Rifleman Zelazny, and it was amputated in hospital. I had to go and tell his sister what had happened. She and her husband, a Spaniard, and two of his friends, have been living in Halina's flat, just behind my headquarters. These Spaniards are all Republicans who came to Poland after the Civil War. All three Spaniards at once volunteered to take the place of their friend. They know we are short of weapons, but begged me to give them at least one grenade each. I did, and they at once set off for the barricade. Later they reported one by one for Home Army identification papers and red-and-white arm-bands.

I had a tricky moment at this same barricade. It is built across our street; to the left are houses wrecked in 1939, and to the right more ruins, surrounded by a low wall. The ruins are under fire from three sides, and they make a sort of no-man's-land which we patrol, mainly at night. The only way in is through the barricade and a little gate in the wall some yards from it.

We had to get into the ruins to attack a German machine-gunner who has been in support of the Wehrmacht attack. I told off two lads for the job, one with a machine-pistol and the other with a rifle. I explained the situation and told them to go ahead. They did not budge. I looked at them more attentively and realised that they were afraid. I explained that there wasn't much danger, as the gate is not far away, and it would only take them a couple of seconds to reach the shelter of the wall. But neither said a word.

Who among us doesn't know the meaning of fear now? Each of us has been afraid, is afraid and will go on being afraid. To conceal and master fear requires a tremendous effort of will. I wanted to help these two lads. If they haven't enough will-power to conquer their fear, I must do it for them. So I repeated my order in a firmer voice, which brooked no argument. Still they didn't move.

Fear and poor discipline are catching. I remember, on an

officers' training course, hearing that when a soldier refuses to obey an order in battle the officer has the right—and indeed it is his duty—to make him obey by force of arms. But what was I to do in this case? Shoot them? Was it to be like yesterday, when I had to give an order for the lads to open fire on women and children? Seconds passed in silence.

Then I grabbed the rifle of one of the two lads, jumped over the barricade, and a moment later was crouching behind the little gate. German bullets crashed into the wall, and then I found one of our N.C.O.s at my side, armed with a light machine-gun.

'You on your own?' he gasped. 'We can't have that. . . .'

Then, a few seconds later, both the two lads came over too. I grinned at them, and handed over the rifle I'd grabbed. They went ahead and carried out their mission smartly. The N.C.O. remained crouching there behind the low wall until both the lads got back to our side of the barricade.

In the evening the tanks withdrew as usual into Chlodna Street, and halted there, forming mobile block-houses for the defence of the street. The 'Cossacks' fight far worse than the gendarmes, Wehrmacht or S.S. Our strongholds have moved forward from our street to Krochmalna, and are digging themselves into position.

Back at my headquarters, Wislanski has brought in some 'clients'; but he made them wait while I gulped down some herrings and drank some coffee. There was a glass of vodka to go with the herrings—herrings because today is Friday.

Our Quartermaster Strzelczyk has informed me that he kept his real name and rank secret up to now, and that in fact his name is Waclaw, he's a lieutenant, and he went on to add that he has taken charge of a second German bakehouse in Twarda Street, where things are quieter. A supply of flour has also been brought up. There's no shortage of meat, for their owners have themselves offered us cows and horses. Waclaw showed me a long list of foodstuffs he has issued, but it did not interest me much. I was more interested to hear that a big store of clothing has been un-

earthed in the police barracks. Our stores of overalls have come
to an end, at night the lads shiver under the open sky, and the
position with shoes is still worse. Tomorrow we'll take over the
storehouse.

Our sector armourer has been having difficulties too. When
the house in which the armoury was situated was burned down
the day before yesterday, he started work again in a cellar in
Marianska Street. The arms and machine tools were saved; but
he now needs more silver for soldering, and so we've had to start
making a collection of all silver coins.

They told me that there was an incident today in Janusz's
company when a prisoner was shot. Apparently he was caught
looting, but even that is no excuse.

'You don't have to take prisoners. But if you do, then you
must send them back to me. I won't tolerate murder.'

The lads didn't seem sure that my decision was right. They all
agreed, however, when I put it to them rather differently.

'We have to interrogate all prisoners. They can provide us
with plenty of useful information.'

'We didn't think of that,' they finally admitted.

The lads brought in three civilians and a few minutes later two
more. All were in a state of complete exhaustion, both physical
and mental. They were from Mirowski Square, and were sur-
vivors of a mass execution by the Germans. A sixth man has
turned up, too, whom our patrol rescued from a heap of burning
corpses. He was terribly burned, and was taken to hospital at
once.

Saturday, 12 August

Two of the men rescued yester-
day have already applied to join the men responsible for saving
them. One is apparently a university man, and has chosen to call
himself 'Igra'. He has been able to show me on a map new German
bunkers and positions which Polish civilians have had to build in
the area. He has also given us a report on the strength and dis-

tribution of the Germans, their armament and also of crimes they have committed and of which he was a witness.

He says that yesterday the Germans shot at least 200 men in the market. The executions took place in groups, and the Germans shot their prisoners down with machine-guns. Then the dead and wounded were piled up, drenched with petrol and burned. Just before our patrol rescued him, Igra managed to hide under a booth against one wall of the market. Not that this would have helped much, had it not been for our patrol, which opened fire on the Germans from the ruins surrounding the market-place.

Today we had more visitors—this time film cameramen from Area Headquarters. Intrigued by what they had been told by newspaper reporters who visited our sector, they have decided to take some pictures of what is going on. They admired our barricade, which they passed on the way to my headquarters, but it was deserted, for the Germans are now on the other side of Krochmalna Street. But the cameramen asked me to station a few of the lads on it, and they picked out the smartest, who put on steel helmets and ammunition belts. Then the lads ran along the walls, jumped over trenches, climbed up and made as if to throw their grenades.

'Splendid! But couldn't they really throw a few grenades, so we could take pictures of the explosions?'

I agreed to let them sacrifice one grenade.

'Excellent! It will make a wonderful documentary shot.'

Then I grew angry. A few dozen yards away, Grzes and his lads at the next barricade were under fire—while these fellows were staging a battle scene.

So I suggested that we'd show them something really interesting, and they agreed to this willingly.

So I led them through the cellars to the corner of Krochmalna and Rynkowa Streets. Here we found Jan, and I told him in an aside what was up. He led us into a building, then up by ruined stairs to the fourth floor and finally into a tiny room where two snipers were stationed behind a hole in the wall. These lads handed me a scrap of paper on which they had noted down the times when German columns crossed the square. Their list included all units, tanks, cars, horse-drawn wagons and even single ambulances and runners on motor-bikes.

We invited our visitors to look down through our observation-holes. To the left, as far as the eye could see, was a monotonous landscape of smoking ruins, with black chimneys rising here and there, fragments of shattered walls with empty holes of windows; from the direction of the Saxon Park a line of horse-drawn carts was moving. On both sides of this string of carts we saw long lines of women and old men, shuffling along with their hands on the shoulders of those in front, forming a living shield. This would have made a good 'documentary film shot'. Then, opposite, we saw German soldiers, stripped to the waist, washing in buckets or drinking from their tin mugs, unaware that from above the high, strong walls which sheltered them they were being watched.

'Why don't you fire at them?' one of the cameramen asked.

'We've no ammunition,' Jan replied. 'We must keep what ammunition we have for when the Germans start to attack. Anyway, if we were to fire at them, we'd have to quit this post, for they'd open up at us with their howitzer.'

The cameramen took a picture of the scene. Then I suggested they stay here until an attack started. They might be able to take pictures of women and children being driven along in front of the attacking tanks. A picture like that would be worth waiting for.

There are aircraft overhead again. This time, however, the pilots are not bombing the houses but are trying to hit our barricades. This time, too, German artillery has joined in, bombarding our street from the west. The shells land in Ciepla Street, and burst in the walls of the block of flats on the corner.

Now mortars have started firing. Runners come in with reports that the Germans are attacking again, that ammunition is running low. The second company hasn't a single round either for their rifles or revolvers. Besides, the ammunition we 'acquired' yesterday has been taken by Jeremy's group, who had a right to it.

I have sent an urgent message to Captain Proboszcz. But his reply is that he hasn't a single round. He has asked Regional Headquarters to send some.

The next runner brought in a message from Janusz, to the effect that his company now only has a few grenades left. I sent him the last of our store and informed Proboszcz. He has replied that he'll soon be sending more, as they are just 'being made'.

Yet another runner brought me a brief note from Janusz. His men are holding out on the corner of Zelazna Street, but if they do not get ammunition or grenades at once, they will have to withdraw in the face of the next German attack, and quit the barricade. This would mean that the Germans could penetrate our street.

When Proboszcz himself and four other men arrived with two heavy sacks containing grenades, it was 12.30. These are the first grenades made in our Sienna Street workshop. They are contained in little bags of thick, dark cloth with metal attachments. Proboszcz showed us how to use them, and some of the lads chosen to act as grenade throwers loaded their pockets and packs with them. I led them at a run along the right side of the street towards the most threatened of our barricades. Proboszcz followed us.

I reached Zelazna Street first, with one grenade: the lads, who were weighed down with grenades, came up more slowly. I know this barricade by heart. Shielded by a pile of paving-stones, I crossed to the other side of the street and leaped into a deep ditch in front of the bombed shop-front on the corner. There was no one there. I looked round. Beyond the high wall of earth two bayonets were sticking up, and I caught sight of a dark blue cap with red edging betraying the presence of 'Cossacks'.

I jumped out from the ditch, hid behind the paving-stones, and wrenched off the head of the grenade, counting as I did so.

Then, without looking to see what was happening on the other side of the barricade, I hurled the grenade over.

It went off. It shook the whole barricade. But I still couldn't see my lads. Then, suddenly hell broke loose on the other side of the barricade. One explosion thundered after another in an unbroken roar. Proboszcz must have seen me at the barricade and, realising what I was up to, he led the lads through the gateway from our street and up to the window of the first floor of the block of flats on the corner.

It was hardly a fight this time—more of a massacre.

Janusz appeared. After firing his last bullet and throwing his last grenade, he had to withdraw his men from their position. He sent a runner with a message to this effect, but as he sent him by another way we missed him.

At one o'clock, Jeremy and his men took over the first barricade.

The store of uniforms in the barracks has been moved safely despite German attacks.

One of the lads from a civil defence squad has just come up. A woman is giving birth to a child in one of the cellars. She wants help, so I've sent Maria, one of our ambulance girls.

Sunday, 13 August

I didn't expect such a find in the barracks. Waclaw has already counted our 'winnings'—600 dark blue police capes, 350 uniform blouses and 250 pairs of trousers, as well as 2,000 pullovers, 600 linen sheets, 600 bed-covers, 400 pillow-cases, 200 towels, 150 pairs of ammo pouches and 400 summer uniforms, not to mention 15 bales of blankets, 12 bales of grey overall material, 18 bales of artificial silk and 100 pieces of soft leather. Unfortunately, we found no shoes, nor any leather for soles and heels.

There are also some heavy fur coats, but Waclaw said that they're of no use.

'Take them, lads,' Grzes said, nevertheless. 'We don't know but what we may have to spend the winter here. I remember 1919, during the war with the Bolsheviks—all through that hard winter. . . .'

But the lads didn't take his words seriously.

The bed linen was transferred to the hospital, where it will be useful for the beds we took there from the furniture factory. Now the whole battalion will be able to dress alike and every man will get a pullover. I ordered a thousand pullovers to be distributed among the civilians, particularly those who have been bombed-out and to the refugees from the west. Our tailor's shop will be able to make underwear from the artificial silk and light uniforms for other units from the grey material. What is left over of the pullovers and uniforms will be transferred to the Quartermaster of Group Headquarters, and in exchange we'll be able to ask for boots, since more and more of the men are having to go about barefoot.

We're beginning to feel the effects of the shortage of cigarettes. Personally I can't complain, for people are always offering me one and giving me a few to keep me going. The civilians have distributed their cigarettes generously among the lads. But there's no question of our buying more, as money has lost its value. Someone has started to organise the exchange of vodka for cigarettes.

Second-Lieutenant Pszczola has come up from the communications unit of 'Chrobry II' with orders to extend the telephone line linking Group Headquarters with mine. He took the opportunity to congratulate me on my distinction, but I didn't know what he was talking about. So he told me that yesterday, after the recapture of the barricade in Zelazna Street, Captain Proboszcz put my name up for the Virtuti Militari Cross.

'Proboszcz was talking about nothing else all day,' he said.

I felt startled, embarrassed. In the first place, I'd no idea that anyone in Warsaw now is thinking of military honours. If any medals are to be handed out, then they ought to go to many of my subordinates. Then again, I'm certain that if we hadn't happened to miss Janusz's runner yesterday and I'd realised that the barricade was deserted, I'd never have gone there. I'd have brought up a suitable number of men and staged a counter-attack. The success of the operation was conditioned by nothing more than a series of accidents and lucky coincidences. Besides, I had no choice, nor time to think of what I was doing.

Proboszcz has now asked us to send out strong patrols to make as accurate a reconnaissance as possible of the strength of the enemy, their defensive positions and the direction of their line of fire. This is a difficult task just now, since we ourselves are having to hold back continually renewed attacks against our main defence positions. Proboszcz then explained that tonight a special assault group is to be sent out from our street, consisting of seven picked platoons under the command of Major Wola, whose mission is to break through to the Old Town. Our task will be to provide cover for this attack from the west and to ensure the break-out from our sector.

Towards four o'clock the platoons, consisting of men from various groups and battalions in the City Centre, began to appear in our street. I have to give them cover till nightfall. But how am I to conceal so many men, each platoon in a different kind of uniform, almost every other man armed with machine-pistol or rifle? Some even have feathers in their hats or caps. Compared with my lads, they looked like hussars.

The girls from the 'Soldiers' Aid' organisation are doing their best. Since the refugees from the west reached our street, these girls have been providing up to 900 hot meals a day—and today they have to feed another 200 men. Moreover, everyone in Warsaw knows that there's no shortage of food in our sector, and as a result none of the men has brought any food with him.

No one knows, of course, that an attack is being planned in the direction of the Old Town. The civilians and our lads think that the new arrivals have been posted here for good, and a feeling of increased strength cheers everyone up. The atmosphere is like the first days of the Insurrection, and for two pins many people would start to put out Polish flags again. No one is afraid of the Germans now!

The two men in charge of the civil defence came up with three local ladies to present me with, of all things, a sabre.

'This is a small token of regard from the civilians,' they said, 'in memory of the defence of our street.'

Someone told me that the officer commanding the area,

Colonel Monter, was in the sector. I went out of my headquarters and at once spotted Colonel Antoni Chrusciel as he approached from the other side of the street. I knew him before the
war, and had seen him several times in our street during the past
year. He didn't recognise me, and it dawned on me that he is
'Colonel Monter', the officer in charge of the Insurrection.

He was dressed as a civilian and wore no arm-band. In my
sector we have not kept strictly to army etiquette, but when the
officer commanding the area is concerned, then it's another matter. I sprang to attention in the way I was taught as a recruit,
clicked my heels and saluted.

He interrupted impatiently. 'Don't give me away,' he said.

I was amazed. It hadn't occurred to me that there was still any
need to maintain the secrecy of the Underground. But Monter
at once started to talk. He wanted to know how we'd come to be
fighting in our street and how our battalion had been formed.
He was interested to hear of our secret printing-press and two
Gestapo raids a few months ago. Now was a good time to
straighten out a number of things with him.

But it was soon time for the operation to start. Everyone was
ready. It was growing dark.

First to go in was the covering group from the Haberbusch
brewery, under Captain Lech. Major Wola waited. Then reports
began to come in. Lech and his men have cut across Wronia
Street, opposite the brewery, but have sustained a good many
losses and have now been brought to a halt.

The second covering attack from the west is led by Captain
Proboszcz who, with some of the men from Jeremy's group, has
cut across from the brewery through the ruins to Chlodna Street.
At the same time, Grzes, with some of his own men and others
from Alexander's group, is attacking between Walicow and
Zelazna Street. Major Wola, with his seven platoons of picked
men, is still hanging on.

More reports have arrived. Proboszcz and his men have now
reached Chlodna Street in two places, destroyed one armoured

car and are strengthening their position. Grzes reports that he has cut through Chlodna Street at the crossing with Zelazna Street, and is in position in the undertaker's shop on the corner. The Germans dare not show themselves in Chlodna Street, and Grzes is awaiting further orders.

Major Wola now leads his men along Ciepla Street in the direction of Mirowski Square. Fierce firing goes on for a few minutes in Ciepla Street, and Major Wola returns with his men into our street. Then each of the seven platoons clears off—back to their own units. The break through to the Old Town has been cancelled. I have no idea why.

Shells started to fall into our street. After midnight, I was ordered to withdraw Grzes' and Jeremy's assault groups from Chlodna Street. Jeremy's men were to go back for a short rest, while Grzes and his group hold the barracks.

Monday, 14 August

The north-west wind is blowing thick smoke and soot over us from conflagrations along the far side of Krochmalna Street, for the Germans are burning and demolishing the blocks of flats where, last night, our lads were in position. German tanks are standing at a safe distance and firing at us unceasingly. The artillery fire is getting heavier.

Janusz has sent back the body of one of his men who was killed by an artillery shell near Zelazna Street. The man's wife came to collect his body. She will see about his burial herself.

More volunteers are turning up from among the civil defence squad, fire-brigade and rescue workers as well as from the refugees from the west. Men from other streets in the district appear, too, as the units fighting there refuse to let them join in on account of the shortage of ammunition and arms. We work on the assumption that a weapon goes with its position, while it is the men who change. For each weapon we need three men.

A couple of Boy Scouts have volunteered to start a workshop to manufacture anti-tank petrol missiles. They already know all about the various types used, but have suggested a slight improvement. Instead of carrying the bottles about with the packet containing inflammable material stuck to them, the Scouts suggest that the men need only carry the packets while bottles of petrol can be distributed along the barricades, in windows and wherever necessary. So instead of being weighed down with bottles, the lads will have greater freedom of movement, and this will also prevent the risk of the bottles accidentally breaking in their pockets. Besides, it will be easier to protect the paper packets from getting wet if it rains.

The boys gave a demonstration, and the experiment went off well. The paper packets, when stuck on the bottles, minimise the scattering of the glass, so that the flames are more concentrated. The young inventors did not want anyone to help them, but enrolled more Scouts for the job. I gave instructions for a supply of petrol, potassium chloride, sulphuric acid and bottles to be issued to them, while someone has found a good store of suitable paper in a deserted shop.

'What made you decide to bring me your invention?' I asked the Scouts when their workshop had been set up.

'We heard that the Germans have most of their tanks massed in this sector. Besides, we've been working as messengers in Warsaw, and we soon saw that here we wouldn't have to wait long to come up against tanks. Besides, we haven't as much to do now as messengers as we had at first.'

Regina, of the 'Soldiers' Aid' organisation, and Zofia, one of the ambulance girls, came to see me about tomorrow's celebrations.

'Celebrations?' I echoed.

'Tomorrow is the 15th of August,' said Regina, rather shocked by my ignorance. 'It's Soldiers' Day. And even if you've forgotten, *we* remember it.'

'What can we do in conditions like this?'

'We must get a priest to celebrate Mass,' Zofia suggested.

But Regina had more elaborate plans.

'There's a suitable hall in the furniture factory, where we can set up a chapel. We can decorate the men's mess too. We must give them a special dinner and invite representatives of the civilians to come. Then you must make a speech.'

'You can manage without any speechifying from me. . . .'

'Then we'll arrange a concert for the men. There's a concert party at Area Headquarters. We can also ask them to send some-one to make a speech to cheer us all up and encourage the men. Don't forget, after all, that this is the first Soldiers' Day which we'll celebrate after the years of occupation!'

'All right, do as you think best, get a priest, a concert party and speechifiers, but remember that meals must be sent out to the men in their positions as usual.'

Our conversation was interrupted by Janka.

'Sir, I think you'd better go to No. 16. I don't know what's going on there, they told me to take thirteen dinners, but when I got there I saw only one man alive . . . The others are dead!'

'Go and fetch Alexander! Zofia, you bring the stretchers! Wanda, come with me,' I shouted at once.

In the inner courtyard of No. 16, planks laid across the ground-floor windows led into a ruined inner room in which positions for snipers have been made with paper sacks filled with earth. A dead man was lying under the window. Another lad was groan-ing with pain, blood gushing from his mouth and nose. But young Zbik, an eighteen-year-old youth with blue eyes and fair hair, his face blackened with soot, was coolly in position, gaz-ing down the barrel of his rifle.

'What's going on?'

'Everything is under control, sir. The Germans have with-drawn. I couldn't get away to let you know, as I was on my own.'

Alexander ran up with a handful of men, followed by the ambulance girls with stretchers. I went on to take a look at the other positions. They'd had a rough time in the barracks too. The Germans had winkled out our lads from the front rooms and set fire to their bedding, while tank shells smashed in the façade so that the lads were forced to withdraw to the rear part of the building. And the Germans were moving about the yard as though the place belonged to them.

'All the same, we put up a good show,' the lads told me. 'They won't be so anxious to come over again.'

Cadet Puchacz, a rather silent young White Russian, does not share our enthusiasm and has asked to be transferred to another sector.

'Why? Other men want nothing better than to join Grzes' men and you want to leave.'

'I've nothing against Grzes, but his lads are fools and quarrelsome.'

'That's no reason for a transfer. The lads are the same everywhere. Besides, I'll have to talk it over with Grzes. I can't transfer you without him.'

So I went to see Grzes.

Grzes was amused. He told me that Rola and Joe managed to get hold of some big red silk handkerchiefs and tied them round their necks. The other lads admired the look of these scarves so much that half an hour later the whole crowd of them turned up wearing red scarves. They wouldn't take the things off, and insisted that they 'looked real smart', and that in any case they now stand out from everyone else.

'It's their idea of looking smart,' said Grzes, laughing. 'But the trouble is that the scarves make a good target for the Germans.'

'What's wrong with Puchacz?' I asked Grzes. 'Have you any idea?'

'Yes, I know what it is,' said Grzes, looking worried. 'It's a silly business and it all started on account of a civilian. You told us not to let anyone into Krochmalna Street, but you know what the lads are, they're easy-going when it comes to our own people. This civilian said he wanted to get over to his home on the far side of the street, see whether the Germans had looted the place much and get some food for the children. So they let him go through. He was there a long time, but in the end he came back. No one checked what he brought with him. A little later, he came back again and wanted to go through once more. But this time the lads wouldn't let him. Puchacz warned the chap that if he tried to get through without permission, then the lads would shoot. But the chap didn't listen and ran for it. So Puchacz shot him.'

Grzes stood looking thoughtful for a moment, then went on, 'I couldn't say anything. Puchacz was right, officially. He was on duty, he warned the chap. . . .'

'So what's wrong?'

'The other lads think there was no proof that the chap meant any harm and that Puchacz should have had a better reason for shooting him. They made this clear to him in their own way, and Puchacz has taken offence.'

'Rather a stupid business, wasn't it? What do you suggest?'

'I'll be sorry to lose him, as he's a good man. But there's nothing else we can do. He's stubborn. I think you'd better transfer him to another unit and transfer Zbigniew as well, if he wants to go. It will be better if there are two of them. Besides, they're friends, and friends ought to stick together.'

Just before dusk, runners brought in reports that the Germans were moving in to the attack again. Our ammunition is running out. Group Headquarters have no ammunition left either. Twenty minutes later, Jeremy's company reported to me armed with one light machine-gun, two hand machine-guns, only one machine-pistol and nine rifles. None of them had much ammunition. But the Germans withdrew after firing only a few shots, so it looks as though all they wanted was to reconnaissance our positions.

The bombing went on till twilight. Artillery fire kept up unceasingly. But the girls in the basement of the furniture factory were working with a will, getting ready a splendid dinner for tomorrow and decorating the dining-room.

Tuesday, 15 August

At five o'clock this morning, the Germans threw in everything they'd got. Wave after wave of Junkers and Stukas flew over, Tiger tanks and Panzers moved towards us along all the surrounding streets. The din of bombs and shrapnel, the roar of engines, the thunder of hundreds of tons of metal crashing down, all mingled with the rumble of falling walls and roofs, the rattle of machine-guns and the shriek of bullets overhead, like a storm gone mad.

Begrimed runners hurried along in the shelter of walls with messages from officers on the barricades. They all told of what they had seen. In one street tanks had smashed through one of our barricades. Then Captain Proboszcz appeared as though he'd risen out of the ground, he hurled in a grenade at a tank and, immediately after the explosion, he leaped on to the tank, wrenched open the lid and shot the German driver at close range with his revolver. Then he grabbed the German's gun and hurried on. This lad also saw Rola and one of his pals drag out the dead German and get hold of some grenades from inside the tank.

Another runner told us how he'd seen Corporal Iwanski killed by a shell from a tank, which hit him at close range in the stomach. His shattered body fell to the roadway where it was crushed by the tanks that rolled over it and trampled underfoot by his own men. There was nothing left of him for burial.

Four barricades have already fallen to the Germans. Jeremy's unit was sent up as support, but has been driven back, step by step, from Wronia Street towards Zelazna Street. He has lost nineteen of his men, six dead, ten wounded and three badly burned. But Slaz and his lads have burned out three tanks so far with their petrol bottles. All the officers are begging for ammunition.

Just before midday, a messenger ran up, out of breath, asking me to go and see Captain Proboszcz. I found him waiting for me on the corner of our street and Ciepla Street.

'What's going on in your sector?' he shouted as soon as he caught sight of me.

'We're holding all our positions from Rynkowa Street as far as Walicow Street. But things aren't so good beyond Walicow Street. The tanks that got through into our street have got as far as Zelazna Street.'

'What the devil does Jeremy think he's doing? You've got two whole companies up there.'

'Jeremy's doing more than we've a right to expect. But he can't fight "Goliaths" with a bottle of petrol. And his men are having to deal with them for the first time. I haven't heard from Janusz. I don't even know if he's still alive. His company are still in the ruins.'

'Let's get over there.'

We could not go along the street as it was under heavy fire from machine-guns. But by going through the Pluton building and across courtyards full of rubble, we were able to get almost as far as Walicow Street. The first German Tiger tank was approaching, without its accompanying 'Goliath'. In a few minutes it would be able to attack the defenders of the barricade on the other side of the street from the rear.

'Are they deaf or blind or what?' Proboszcz shouted, trying to make his voice heard above the uproar. 'Go and liven them up, Lech.'

Proboszcz underlined his order by flourishing a German grenade.

To do so, I had to get obliquely across a fairly wide street. The Tiger tank wasn't more than thirty yards away. It was ploughing up the pavement with bursts of machine-gun fire. In the din, I tried to catch a momentary break between bursts of firing. 'Death comes once only,' I thought—and jumped for it. In the middle of the roadway I skidded on something wet and landed head-first on the pavement opposite. A burst of machine-gun fire blazed over my head. I tore on and leaped into the trench behind the barricade. I knew the men holding it. They must have caught sight of the tank and were deliberately letting it come up, for at this moment a fierce burst of air threw me backwards into the trench again. Tongues of flame and thick smoke whirled up round the tank. Three short bursts of firing followed and cut down the Germans as they leapt from it.

Good work, I thought. This will please Proboszcz. I looked round for him and saw the traces of my long skid in the roadway,

amidst what I now saw to be scattered human entrails. Near them
I saw scraps of human bodies and uniforms, and the heads of
two young girls with long curly hair.

'Our ambulance girls,' said one of the lads who was standing
by me, as he guessed my thoughts. 'If it hadn't been for them,
you'd be in heaven by now. They were trying to cross the street
with a wounded man on a stretcher.'

'Did you see which way Proboszcz went?'

'He didn't go anywhere. They've just pulled him into that
gateway.'

And in the gateway I now saw Proboszcz's driver, kneeling
down and unfastening his jacket.

'How did it happen?'

'In the usual way. He followed you, but came out straight
along the street. He must have wanted to get to the next gateway.
There were two bursts of firing before they got him. Once in the
stomach, then higher up, in the chest.'

The rumbling was increasing in the direction of Zelazna
Street. Three Panthers were rolling up. A 'Goliath' preceded the
first of them, and I saw it carefully avoiding the larger piles of
brick and tangled girders. In the uproar, the sound of bombs
falling in the distance was no more than the bursting of puff-
balls when you tread on them. The explosions farther away
couldn't be heard at all; only reddish brown, sinister plumes of
smoke rose above the ruins.

As I went back to my headquarters, I caught sight of a little
group of men approaching our street through the ruins. It was
the 'Harnas' group, coming up to lend a hand to the men on the
barricade. But I wondered if they could help, after all. Other
tanks will move in, and behind the tanks are the German infantry
and gendarmes.

Hal reported that he had thrown in everything he had and
had no more men. Alexander sent a message to say that he only
had one section left in reserve. I still had the assault group under
the command of Sergeant Grzes. But how could I expend the
rest of my men in a hopeless attempt to resist tanks?

I ran across to the furniture factory. In a big basement room the girls had set up a soldiers' canteen, and the long bare tables were covered with clean white paper. Festoons of leaves had been hung on the walls, with white and red ribbons twined among them. A big eagle, with paper wings outstretched, was hanging on one of the walls. The girls were setting out plates of biscuits. There were some crates of beer. I remembered that it was 'Soldiers' Day'.

The concert party, consisting of a handful of actors, was sitting about near the windows.

'You're not very hospitable,' said one of them, jokingly. 'We're here as arranged, but no one's at home. Where are all the men? We can begin the concert as soon as you like.'

Ziuta and Regina stopped me at the exit.

'The stew is getting cold,' Ziuta said sadly. 'Wouldn't you like just to taste it?'

'Don't bother him with the stew,' Regina broke in. 'Don't you understand? Should we get ready to retreat?'

'No, keep calm. I'll send a runner if that becomes necessary. Have you seen Sergeant Grzes?'

'He's upstairs, in the chapel. The priest is saying Mass for the people who couldn't attend earlier.'

In the 'chapel' I found everyone kneeling. The Elevation was just being sounded. Grzes was kneeling by the altar, but he caught sight of me at once and nodded to indicate that he understood. Then he gently nudged his neighbours and pointed almost imperceptibly to the door. Singly and in twos the men tiptoed out. As the priest elevated the Host, aircraft came over and the walls shook. Grzes emerged last. The bark of cannon as it drew nearer almost drowned the sound of a silver bell.

Alexander and Tadeusz were waiting at the gate. The barricade on the corner of Krochmalna and Ciepla Streets has fallen to a 'Goliath'. The tank has broken through. We are about to play our last card.

'Alexander, your last reserves will man the barricade on the corner of our street and Ciepla Street. Tadeusz, you take com-

mand. Strengthen the barricade and dig trenches for as long as
you can. Take the Caucasians and anyone else you can get hold
of from the fire-brigade. Grzes, you take your men to the other
side of Ciepla Street, but don't bother about the tanks and don't
fire at them. Then attack as far behind the German infantry as
you can. Not enough ammo? I'll try to send you some. I'll be
waiting for you to report back.'

Barbara and some other girls were sitting in my headquarters.
Major Zagonczyk, C.O. of the region, had just telephoned.
He wanted to know whether it was true that Proboszcz is
dead. He also said he had some ammo for us and had already sent
it over.

The tanks in Rynkowa and Ciepla Streets were moving along
behind a crowd of civilians, who were being driven ahead to
provide cover for the Germans. They were mostly men. I gave
the order to fire. Some of the civilians were hit and left lying on
the pavement. Then Grzes sent in his first message. He had
already come into contact with the enemy in the Krochmalna
Street area, and he wanted more ammunition. Fortunately
the ammunition sent up by Major Zagonczyk had just come
in—four cases altogether. Alexander is to have one, the
other three must somehow be got to Grzes. But German
machine-gun fire is coming almost unceasingly from Walicow
Street, along our street and from Krochmalna Street along
Ciepla.

Who will volunteer to try to get through?

Young Adam was first to step forward. Bent under the weight
of two cases, he reached the opposite side of the street before he
was hit. Orlinski tried next, with one case, but with only a couple
of paces still to go he too fell. Rifleman Lech followed. He
lifted the cases and went on. But he didn't make it. The ammunition still had to be got through.

'Next man—Oscar.'

Oscar was fourteen years old. He ran to the far side of the
street and dragged the cases lying on the pavement. Good lad!
Then he tried to help Adam. By this time both were out of

range of the machine-gun fire, but a shell suddenly burst near by. Oscar was covered with blood. Orlinski and Lech slowly dragged themselves towards us, and Marta and Halina went out with stretchers, under fire, to meet them.

The tanks were nearer still. The barricade of Walicow Street has been jettisoned.

The men in their position at No. 13 Krochmalna Street sent a message to say that some women there were trying to persuade the men to change into civilian clothing. The men want to know what to do.

'Don't do it.'

'We know that. But what are we to do with the women?'

'Send them away.'

The tanks moving from Walicowa Street must by now be very close to Tadeusz's barricade, for we can hear the whistle of bullets as they smash into the walls through the open doors of the shop.

'We'd better go over to the other side of the street,' Barbara suggested, 'otherwise we'll be cut off.'

She was right. Two men took the telephone and carried it over, carefully unwinding the cable line. Jadzia and Wanda collected papers and oddments. Basia grabbed the typewriter and hurried across.

It wasn't until this moment that I realised that all the houses in our street were empty. Signs of hasty flight were everywhere. Shells from the cannons of tanks burst against the façade of the furniture factory. The telephone operators reported that they had set up the telephone in the doorway of No. 19 and were in contact with the commanding officer of IV Region. Then Major Zagonczyk asked for me.

'I know you're in trouble. I'll do what I can to help. But you've got to hold your street. You've got to. Can you do it?'

'We'll hold out, sir.'

The shells were coming closer. I looked round and saw young Kajtek, one of Alexander's runners, without any weapons. The two telephone operators were unarmed too. I hadn't a single grenade left. When the ammunition arrived from Zagonczyk I'd forgotten to keep any for myself.

Then Ryki spoke up.

'What about your sabre? You've left it in the shop.'

'You know what you can do with my sabre!'

I had just reached the gateway of the furniture factory when a powerful blast deafened me. A shower of bricks was falling. A 'Goliath' had blown up the last of our barricades. What had become of the men who were there?

I ran through the factory. It was deserted. There were still a few plates of cake in the canteen, and the paper claws of the eagle had folded up grotesquely. In the chapel, the chairs and benches were overturned, the walls were spattered with bullet-holes.

I started along the street. The smoke had died down a little. To my left was a deserted barricade; then, immediately below the corner block of flats, the corpse of a tank half buried in a trench was smouldering. The firing had died down. I crossed the street and cautiously went up to the barricade. I looked over the top, and saw a powerful Tiger tank snarling half-way down Ciepla Street.

But I could hardly believe my eyes. It was retreating.

Another tank stood near Krochmalna Street, motionless. Its caterpillars had been ripped off. And down there, near the barracks, I saw a third tank dead, with its covers open. I looked to the west, along our street. The sun was shining in my eyes as it sank across the distant suburbs enshrouded in red mist. Then I saw that it wasn't mist but a storm of dust. Everything was covered in dust—walls, fences, the heaps of brick and rubble scattered across pavements, the shattered roadway, the motionless iron tanks—all were the same dull reddish colour. Only here and there dim outlines revealed the presence of the dead, lying in this valley of death.

From across the battlefield two of the lads appeared, clumsily scrambling past the smouldering tank. I hardly recognised Tadeusz and Puchacz, for they looked as if they'd dug themselves out of a heap of cement. Somehow they'd survived, hidden by the heavy balustrade of a balcony on the first floor immediately above the barricade. They'd let the tank come up to the barricade so that they couldn't miss, for although they were half buried in rubble their arms were free.

I reported back to Zagonczyk by telephone.

'We've held our street. The Germans are retreating. We ought to send patrols out after them and try to man the barricades again. We ought to bring in the wounded and bury the dead. But there are only six of us left. We haven't a single bullet or grenade. As far as I know, only half of Alexander's company is still holding out in their position between Rynkowa and Ciepla Streets. We must relieve them, or they'll fall asleep at their posts.'

Meanwhile more and more people started to come in. Some began digging in the big factory yard behind my new head-quarters. Women with stretchers appeared in the gateway. Someone brought a bucket of water. Barbara was there too. She told me that the battalion office had been set up in Sienna Street, and that the girls were fixing up a kitchen in the same building. The hospital in Marianska Street has allowed them to make some coffee there. The stores have been transferred. But I still hadn't heard from Janusz or Grzes. Two new telephone operators, girls this time, have been sent to take over night duty. Camp-beds have been set up in the gateway, beside the telephone. Mattresses for runners and the ambulance girls have been laid out along the wall.

It was growing dark when we lowered the first bodies into deep pits. Janka and Alina brought hot coffee and poured it into our mugs. People paused in their work, and leaned on their spades, above the open graves, to drink greedily.

'Please drink this,' said Janka, giving me a mug of coffee. 'You ought to eat something too.'

Our spades cut into the ground, and the earth fell softly and very quietly on shattered bodies and bloodstained uniforms.

Wednesday, 16 August

We are still trying to count up our own losses and estimate those of the enemy. It is simplest to add up the number of tanks destroyed. Five wrecks stand between Towarowa and Walicow Streets, one near Pluton building, two more in Ciepla Street, and the ninth is at the barricade on the corner of our street and Ciepla Street. Over a hundred Germans were killed in these streets. We have buried about thirty of our men, but these are not all who died, for many were taken away by the soldiers of units which came up as reinforcements. But some men were wiped out, and no traces of them for burial can now be found. I don't know how many Grzes took with him, but only one section of his platoon has come back.

I continue to get telephone messages from Major Zagonczyk as I have done since the death of Captain Proboszcz yesterday. But I haven't seen him and don't even know where his headquarters is. He has notified me that as from today the commanding officer of my sector is Captain Hal.

'I've got complete faith in you, of course,' Zagonczyk told me. 'After the fighting yesterday and for holding out in your street, I'm recommending you for the Virtuti Militari Cross. On the other hand, Captain Hal is a Regular Army officer, and he's quite properly pointed out that it wouldn't do for him to be subordinate to a younger officer of the Reserve. We must maintain seniority in the army. And we must also bear in mind the actual state of affairs. Hal has two full companies of men and every chance of being able to reorganise a battalion, while what's left of your men can't be considered as a battalion any longer. The best thing for you to do will be to try to make up some sort of a company out of the men you have left.'

However, Major Zygmunt, C.O. of the "Chrobry II" group, had other ideas.

'They'd be only too glad to do away with the whole "Chrobry II" group,' he told me when I told him over the telephone what Zagonczyk had said. 'Still, we won't give in to them. I'll send over more men at once from my company of reinforcements, and you'll get enough officers to re-form your battalion.'

So the manoeuvring at highest level, which I found baffling, turned out to our advantage in the end, as we have been able to strengthen our sector. There will now be two battalions to defend our street.

When I went to report to Captain Hal, as the commanding officer of the sector, he greeted me very cordially.

'It's all nothing but formality,' he told me, smiling and gripping my hand forcefully. 'Let's have a drink on the strength of our brotherhood of arms, which is far more important than rank. I've recommended you for a decoration. No, don't thank me. You deserved it. Where's the wine?'

When we'd finished off a couple of glassfuls, Hal took me by the arm.

'We needn't stick too closely to seniority. Our sector is big enough, we can divide it out—unofficially, of course. You shall hold Rynkowa Street, Krochmalna as far as Ciepla and both sides of Ciepla Street. My men will take over Grzybowska Street from Walicow Street to the west. The only thing is that you'll have to send reports and statements through me. All right?'

A surprise was awaiting me in our street. Grzes had turned up with all his men. He reported that he'd carried out his orders and had attacked the Wehrmacht troops several times from the rear, and he'd caused them heavy losses. Then he'd been cut off and surrounded. They were sure that they'd never get out alive.

'Not a single one of us would have survived if it hadn't been for our Wojtus. It was he who managed to find a way through the Germans surrounding us, and he got us all out without the loss of a single man.'

Wojtus is eleven years old, the youngest soldier of our battalion. He's been fighting in Grzes' group since the first day of the Insurrection, and already has a fine record. On the second day of the fighting, he got through the enemy lines to the main railway station which was strongly held by the Germans, and three hours later came back with a report on the strength, armament and distribution of the enemy. He brought up ammunition wherever it was needed during the heaviest fighting. I decided to recommend him for the Cross of Valour.

My first reinforcements have arrived from Group Headquarters, and Alexander has divided them out fairly between his own company and Grzes'. Jeremy has brought in his men, who have also been joined by reinforcements, and they have been reorganised. I gave him instructions to occupy the furniture factory and the near-by buildings.

Four lieutenants posted to me by Major Zygmunt were waiting at the new battalion office in Sienna Street: they were Grzymala, Wojtek, Czarnecki and Remigiusz. Wojtek asked to be sent into the line, so I sent him and Grzymala to join Alexander. Now at last his company will have its proper strength of officers to take command of his platoons. Czarnecki, who was dressed in an elegant pre-war officer's uniform, stood puffing out his chest and frowning fiercely, but didn't evince any desire to join the men on our outer positions, and made it plain that the command of a mere platoon wasn't at all suitable to his rank. So I have made him my deputy in charge of administrative matters. He can sit in the battalion office, and will relieve me of having to worry about rations, billets, stores and workshops.

Remigiusz announced that he didn't know whether he'd be staying in my battalion. He had to think it over and discuss the matter with his superior officers.

'Isn't Major Zygmunt your superior officer?'

'Officially he is, as I belong to the "Chrobry II" group. But I've been transferred to you without the knowledge and permission of my superiors in the Underground movement. Their orders are more important, as far as I'm concerned, than the orders of anyone else.'

'In that case, I'm afraid that even if your superiors in the Underground tell you to stay with my battalion, I shan't be able to agree. I'd never be sure whether my orders are going to meet with the approval of these mysterious superiors of yours.'

My men have been tremendously impressed by the news pub-

lished in today's newspapers that General Bor has issued an order
addressed to all units of the Home Army outside Warsaw, in
which he asks for an intensification of the armed fight against the
Germans.

'This means that the Insurrection has started throughout
Poland,' the most excitable lads exclaimed. 'About time too.'

'Just a minute!' said someone more level-headed than the rest.
'Read it carefully. It goes on: "Well-armed units must make for
Warsaw as quickly as possible, attack the German positions on
the outskirts of the city and break through in order to take part
in the street fighting in the centre of the city".'

The lads who have joined us from partisan groups in the woods
have a good deal to say about all this. In contrast to most, they
listened to the news very sceptically.

'Every partisan knows that he's most useful in his own district, where he knows every footpath and every cottage. He can
strike where he's least expected and where the enemy is weakest.
If they stay where they are, they could seize the nearest small
towns, get hold of arms, start recruiting. . . . As it is, they'll come
rushing up to Warsaw and get themselves in the soup altogether.'

But not many of the lads would agree.

'Don't you try and be clever! Bor knows more than you lot
will ever know! You just wait and see what we'll do to the
Germans when the other lads join us. They've got plenty of guns
and ammo.'

Thursday, 17 August

                    All our platoons have been in
action since six o'clock this morning. The Germans are attacking
again, mainly in Grzybowski Square and Kazimierz Square, as if
they wanted to drive a wedge into our street from the rear, but
we're not worried. Kazimierz Square is defended by a strong
company of men, all hardened fighters, and although Lieutenant
Ned, their commanding officer, was wounded the day before
yesterday, Ned's place has been taken over by Second-Lieutenant

Kos, a tough, forty-year-old man like a bear at bay, who will show the Germans no mercy. The far side of Grzybowski Square between the Central Telephone Exchange, which the Germans still hold, and the Saxon Park, is strongly occupied by Romanski and his men. Romanski has already made a name for himself in the defence of the 'fortress' at No. 16, Krolewska Street. He's a dashing cavalry officer, with a colourful imagination.

We have held off the attack on our street without any great losses. Only one of Karol's men was killed during the fighting with German tanks in Ciepla Street. A German tank has been destroyed. One man has been wounded in Alexander's group. But the strength of our battalion continues to grow. The reinforcement company has sent us up a number of hastily trained volunteers under Cadet Smigly.

Our battalion office and the cook-house have been installed on the third floor of No. 44, Sienna Street. Henio is now listing the stores in the little front room, and has shown me with unconcealed delight a new 'acquisition' consisting of a case of good champagne sent over by Hal from the cellars of the Haberbusch brewery. All the same, we haven't a single pair of shoes, apart from the boots which we've taken from corpses, both German and our own. Nobody is buried with his boots on, but even so there are more people who want boots than there are corpses. We're short of belts too. The Group Headquarters has, however, promised to let us have some leather for repairing boots if we can fix up our own shoe-repair shop.

My office has been installed in the room next to the stores. Jadzia 'borrowed' one of Regina's girls who can type, and is now dictating a lengthy list which Group Headquarters require. Among the papers waiting for me to see was one called 'Instructions relating to the use of shoe-leather', which requires us to keep a 'Ledger' showing the amount of leather used, with the following columns: No. of Home Army identity card, rank, sex, date of birth, place of birth, unit, duties, type of boot, kind of repair required, amount of leather required, date issued, date repair started and completed. The last column is for the signature of the man whose boots have been repaired.

'Where is the leather for these boot repairs?'

'In the Group Headquarters stores.'

'Is there much of it?'

'We're supposed to be getting about two kilos of leather for repairs.'

I'm not much of a soldier when it comes to this sort of thing, and I wrote in red pencil across the 'Instructions': 'I forbid the keeping of this kind of ledger'.

The 'Soldiers' Aid' girls sleep in the third of our rooms, where there is some straw on the floor. In the cook-house next door it was as hot as a furnace. Dinner was cooking in big saucepans.

'Wasn't it more comfortable in Grzybowska Street?' I asked the girls, recalling our decorated canteen in the factory there.

'It's all right here,' said Bogda, 'only a bit of a tight fit. We girls have to wash in the kitchen and there's always someone coming through. We were rather shy until one of the runners said, "Fat lot that matters! This is the Insurrection and no one bothers about that sort of thing." But it's not so good in one way, because we have to bring all the water from the well beyond Twarda Street and it's farther when meals have to be delivered. Still, it can't be helped—the buckets and pails must be carried, and that's all there is to it.'

Our conversation was interrupted by a pudding-faced little person of indeterminable gender.

'I'm a sanitary inspector,' this person squeaked. 'I'm going to give you a lecture on hygiene.'

'I'm afraid I'd forgotten that you were coming, and I'm sorry to say that all the men are on duty.'

'Never mind. I see there are some young ladies cooking. I can talk to them about hygiene and not waste any of my valuable time.'

I turned to Regina.

'Get your girls together if you can. I know Major Zygmunt
attaches a lot of importance to these talks.'

'Very good, sir.'

I went back to the office.

'Drop work and go to the lecture,' I told Jadzia, as I sat down
to sign the papers she'd got ready. I could hear every word
through the half-open door, since the lecturer was speaking
clearly and precisely.

Suddenly the lecture was interrupted by a stifled murmuring.
'This is a waste of time! Let's get out of it!'

Before I could reach the improvised lecture-room, the pudding-
faced lecturer was already hurrying off down the stairs.

After dinner I went back to Grzybowska Street. On the way I
passed a procession of ambulance girls and our Caucasians carrying stretchers. They were taking wounded to the hospital—two
of our riflemen and one girl newspaper reporter, all of whom
had been wounded by the same shell from a mortar, which
dropped unexpectedly near my headquarters in Grzybowska
Street. On the way, the little procession had been under fire from
the Telephone Exchange, but no one was hit.

The lads have found a German soldier hiding behind a dustbin
in one of the yards between our street and Krochmalna Street.
He's half out of his mind with pain and exhaustion. One hand,
his face and half his body are swollen, and his uniform is burned.
Two days ago he jumped from a burning tank and went into
hiding, for he was afraid we'd shoot him. His officers had told
him that we don't take prisoners.

After giving him first-aid, Ola and Helenka were about to take
the German to hospital, when a group of inquisitive people
gathered round his stretcher and one spat, and said:

'Why bother with him?'

'Yes, why?' said another, backing him up. 'As it is, there's no
room in the hospital, and yet here they are bothering about this
rat, instead of looking after our own men.'

'The Huns don't look after our men. He isn't worth wasting a
bullet on. Let's stone him.'

Horrified and angry, Ola put herself between them and the German.

'Leave him alone. Please go away and leave him alone!'

Some of the civilians had already picked up stones. At this moment one of them suddenly stepped back. Little Premier had all at once appeared in their midst, his revolver drawn.

'Clear off, you bastards,' he said between clenched teeth. 'You seem to forget that this is Poland, not Deutschland. If you want to fight Germans, then get out there to Krochmalna Street. We're not going to tolerate the murder of unarmed men here.'

The air-raids went on until evening. I saw a heavy bomb fall on the block of flats on the corner of Twarda and Marianska Streets, where one of Hal's groups is stationed. After the explosion, the upper part of the façade slowly crumbled down into the street, then was hidden by a thick cloud of black smoke that rose into the air. A few minutes earlier, I'd seen men in the windows of the first floor of this building, getting ready to turn in for the night.

Grzes and his platoon have occupied the police barracks. After inspecting all our defence lines, I stayed the night in the gateway of No. 19. Olga was on telephone duty. Our link with the 'Chrobry II' group has been cut, and a patrol has gone out to try to locate the breakage in the line.

All Saints' Church in Grzybowski Square is on fire.

By the flickering glow of a lamp, our old actor-cum-newspaper boy, who was very late today but who has never yet failed us, is reading aloud a poem printed in today's issue of 'Worker'.

Friday, 18 August

Jeremy has reported a big attack by tanks in Ciepla Street, though his men are holding out. Grzes and his men, hidden in the barracks, have not yet opened fire. I went over to the Ciepla and Krochmalna crossing with a group of reinforcements, so that Grzes and we could then get at the Germans from two sides.

A tank was moving along the far side of Ciepla Street under the cover of the houses. Evidently the Germans were unaware that our men were on the opposite side of the street. Then I caught sight of our lads moving swiftly at the first-floor windows, and a grenade exploded beside the tank, while bottles of petrol burst in the roadway. The flames missed the tank and it continued to move on towards Grzybowska Street. Immediately above it I recognised Rola, outlined in a window. He was holding a heavy fragment of masonry above his head with both hands, and then hurled it down on to the tank.

'What the devil is he doing?'

Grenades started to explode at the crossing of Krochmalna and the entrance to Ciepla Streets, and from Grzybowska Street I could hear Jeremy's light machine-gun barking. Then the tank began to withdraw, undamaged, into Krochmalna Street. A moment later I was able to run across into the barracks. Rola had come downstairs.

'What were you trying to do, Rola? Smash a tank with stones?'

'No, sir—it's just that I lost my temper because I missed him through being in too much of a hurry, and the lad who was with me missed too. We hadn't another bottle or grenade. It's maddening when you've got nothing to throw.'

'You've just missed getting a medal.'

'Who'd have given it to me?'

'An order has just been issued saying that any man who destroys a German tank is to be recommended for the Cross of Valour.'

'And Rola deserves it, sir,' put in one of his friends. 'When we were cut off three days ago, Rola put up the best show of anyone. I saw him shoot and kill three Germans.'

'What happened, Rola?'

'Nothing much, sir. I was having a look round and three of them were crossing that little space beyond Krochmalna Street. So I fired and got one of 'em. As he dropped, I gave the others a shout, "Your mate's had it!" Then I shot the second of them, and the third one still hadn't got out of it—he was trying to get his mate away, carrying him. So I shot him too.'

'Didn't you feel a bit bad about shooting the third of them?'

'No. No, I didn't. Because, don't you see, none of us thought we'd get out alive. I'd a right to shoot him. But I felt a bit rotten about the other one.'

'Which one?'

'There was another of 'em. There's what used to be a dentist's surgery in that block. It wasn't ours and it wasn't the Germans' either. Things were quiet, so I nipped in to get myself some iodine and have a look round for anything else that might come in handy. So I looked out of the window, and there was a German sitting on the grass outside, a good way off. I fired and the bullet got him in the temple. I felt bad about killing him. He didn't know I was watching him, so our chances weren't equal. I don't know if I'd a right to shoot him.'

The girls brought up dinner: thick barley soup, horse-meat and bread. They said that it's quieter and safer out in our front line than it is in Sienna Street, for the Germans are systematically blowing up the houses in the surrounding streets with heavy mortars. People's nerves are on edge from the terrifying whine of these shells, with a pause before the first explosion and the five shells that come over in rapid succession afterwards. The effect is worse than air bombardment. This weapon hasn't much range, but we're as powerless before it as we are before aircraft or artillery. But from today we shall not be as helpless as we have been in the face of the German tanks. Group Headquarters has sent me two anti-tank pistols which have been dropped to us by parachute from British aircraft, and, with them, a crew of our own trained men under Lieutenant Wir. It was the first time I'd ever seen this type of weapon, and at first sight it didn't arouse much enthusiasm. But Wir swore that it is both accurate and effective. But the trouble is in that the shell must hit the tank directly, and to be sure of hitting a tank you have to fire from a distance of not more than a hundred yards away. Anyhow, a shell fired into a tank's tracks will rip it off. We were soon to see this for ourselves.

Captain Hal has had a new company of reinforcements posted to him, and has volunteered to relieve my men. For the time being, only Jeremy and his men are up in the front-line, and they spent a night in billets two days ago. Now Alexander and his men have gone for a rest period to our new billets in Sienna Street—their first relief since 7 August.

I looked in at the hospital in Marianska Street, where the doctors and nurses welcomed me as though I were someone important. They wanted me to visit all the wards.

'Everything we have has come from you,' said one of the doctors, an elderly man in a white linen coat. 'The beds, linen, towels, food, candles, lamps and even catgut. . . .'

'And most of the wounded have been sent to us by you too,' said one of the younger doctors, with a grin.

The beds were packed close, one next to the other, in all the wards. I saw Adam, who was feeling better. But I could hardly recognise Lech; apparently he has several dozen fragments of shrapnel in his body. Orlinski's wounds refuse to heal, tomorrow he is to be X-rayed. Oscar is very ill, although at first sight there seems to be nothing much wrong; however, the doctors see symptoms of brain trouble. The most severely wounded have already been sent to a hospital in Sliska Street, where there is a proper operating theatre.

Back in Sienna Street, I found that the lads and girls had already settled down and were having supper. I gave instructions for a tot of vodka to be issued to each man, and wine to the girls, if they wanted it. Then someone brought out a little mouth-organ and began to play; someone else had a mandolin, and finally a civilian turned up with an accordion. The lads pushed back the bedding which was spread on the floor, and one or two couples began to dance.

I had to go and see Major Zygmunt in his headquarters on the opposite side of the street, and found a number of other officers already there. At least ten of them have various jobs at Headquarters. Among the rest, I saw Captain Sek, who is in command of a reserve company, and Silkiewicz, O.C. an administrative company.

Standing round the walls in a crowded, smoky little room, we listened to speeches by several officers installed behind big desks. Captain Twardy, for instance, had a good deal to say about the keeping of records, including reports on promotion and awards; while Captain Adolf, of the Quartermaster's department, told us that it is our duty to transfer all stores to the Group Quartermaster, and then to take them back again in the form of daily issues. Major Mecenas, of Security, spoke on the lack of proper co-operation between officers in command of men in the front line and the Security and police authorities. Still others talked about improper requisitioning, the importance of burying our dead deeper, applications for leave and the use of passwords.

'Has anyone any questions?'

Captain Lech Zelazny came forward. He is O.C. No. 1 Battalion in the 'Chrobry II' group.

'What about ammunition?' he asked.

A painful silence followed. Through the open window I could hear the sounds of music and cheerful singing.

'We'll discuss that when we've got some,' said Major Zygmunt. 'In the meantime, I must mention one thing more. In some units I've noticed a good deal of lax discipline. The men behave in a way that isn't at all in keeping with the seriousness of this time and with the sacrifices being made by the people of Warsaw. I've heard loud singing, dancing, even laughing. When you go back to your units, gentlemen, I want you to make it clear to your men that this sort of thing really cannot be tolerated.'

He rose, indicating that the meeting was over. The officers who had been seated all rose to attention. Then everyone looked at me. They all knew that it was my men who were enjoying themselves and singing out there.

Then for the first time I spoke.

'Sir, my men have been fighting in the front line up till to-night. They all fought bravely, and tomorrow they're going back to fight again, perhaps to die. For the last five years they hadn't been allowed to sing or dance. But they're young, they want to enjoy this freedom which they've fought for themselves. I'm not going to stop them, or to talk to them about the "seriousness of this time".'

Major Zygmunt didn't say a word. Then Captain Zelazny took a step forward and stretched out his hand to me.

'Thanks,' he said, in a clear voice. 'We'll have plenty of time to mourn—afterwards. Let's go.'

Back at my own headquarters, I couldn't help smiling at the sight of the ambulance girls all in their men's uniforms. Some had tied bits of string round their waists, others looked as if they'd be engulfed at any moment in the outsize pants they were wearing.

'I think you've had enough fun,' I said presently to a couple of lads who were standing near the door. 'You must get some sleep.'

The music died away. The girls went off to their billets and the dance-hall once again became a dormitory. A few minutes later there was silence everywhere. The runner on duty, a twelve-year-old boy, the son of one of my N.C.O.s who was killed the day before yesterday, was on guard at the door. Two more sentries were on duty below, at the gates.

I realised then that I wouldn't exchange my men for the best-trained and smartest regiment in the world.

Saturday, 19 August

After a night's rest, all our men have returned to their positions in the line. But the men are pleased, for the front is now more or less fixed, and the tanks are keeping back, as though the Germans know that we now have British anti-tank pistols. Our ramparts and barricades, which have been reinforced and banked up with earth, give us a feeling of comparative security, while heavy mortars and bullets spread death and destruction in our rear lines, two hundred yards away. People have come back to our street, though not the refugees from the western districts. However, the people who used to live in the street are almost all back in their ruined homes and cellars, which they are tidying up, clearing out the rubble, sweeping up broken glass and scrubbing the floors, as well as fastening up sheets of cardboard in the window-frames, and strips of black paper to serve as black-out coverings. Stas-the-Tailor's wife has ironed a pair of curtains and hung them in the broken windows of their ground-floor flat. Someone has made it his business to tidy the graves of the dead, and has placed sods of earth over some of them.

The heat is troublesome. There's not a cloud in the sky. The sun glares on the walls and buildings and burned-out heaps of ruins. The pavements are soft, so that our heavy boots leave heel-prints in the melting asphalt. The unburied dead, or those in shallow graves, are quickly decomposing, and the street is full of the odour of corpses. But it is the flies which torment us most. They settle in clouds, buzzing, greenish-blue in colour and fat, on anything that attracts them. Millions of smaller flies hover in the air, they get into our eyes, our nostrils and mouths.

Lieutenant Remigiusz has reported to me after three days' absence; not, however, that he wanted to join us, but instead he had to tell me he's been called back to his headquarters for a special job. He has asked me also to provide him with a detailed account of the death of Captain Proboszcz. I learned from him that Proboszcz was not a Regular Army officer, but a high-school teacher of mathematics. Remigiusz has also warned me to look out for a visit from some senior officers, and asked me to get ready a suitable reception for them in my headquarters.

'If you make a good impression on them,' he added in confidence, 'and can come to an understanding with them, then you can be sure of quick promotion and a good job to go with it. I've tried to prejudice them in your favour.'

Curiosity got the better of my feeling of distaste, and I agreed to fix a time for them to visit my headquarters in Sienna Street.

Then I went for the first time to see Major Zagonczyk to whom, as my superior officer, I had to report in any case. I cut across Wielka and Zielna Streets under the cover of low ramparts of paving-stones, and couldn't help feeling some amusement at the way these ramparts are described by sentries as 'barricades'. 'Barricades' like these provide cover to passers-by against distant rifle-fire, but would not constitute any defence against tanks or artillery attacks.

Two sentries were standing at the entrance to a shop in Marszalkowska Street. I gave the password and went through the shop into the courtyard behind. Armed men showed me the way through cellars, joined up by holes in the dividing walls going parallel to the street above. Suddenly I found myself in a brightly lit underground room, where officers were sitting at big desks. All kinds of metal and wooden boxes stood along the walls.

A young lieutenant with a black moustache came over.

'You'll have to wait,' he told me. 'The Major is very busy today. . . .'

At that moment the ceiling of the room shook under half a dozen successive explosions.

Finally, an officer in uniform, with highly polished boots and spurs, emerged from behind the blankets which served as a door. Carefully shaven, his chin up, narrow-waisted, smiling, probably not much over forty, and clearly a cavalry officer.

This, then, was Zagonczyk. Optimism, self-assurance and satisfaction were written all over him.

Eyeing me from head to foot, he said:

'I'll never forget that first telephone conversation of ours on 15th August. Everyone assured me that it was out of the question to hold Gryzbowska Street, and yet you told me that you'd do it. And you did.'

'My men held the street, not I. I think I ought to admit that it was nothing but a piece of bluff.'

'I, too, know that now, but at least you got away with it, both as far as I was concerned and as far as the Germans were concerned too. And that is the only thing that matters. All the same, I wouldn't care to play poker with you. . . .'

Before I left, Zagonczyk said:

'How are you off for ammunition? I can let you have 300

rounds for your machine-pistols and revolvers, but they'll need sorting out, as they've been buried and some may be damaged. You must come and see me more often. For my part, I'll try to ensure that you don't go away empty-handed.'

Corporal Deska was waiting for me in Grzybowska Street. His wounds have not yet healed, but he prefers to be on duty rather than in the crowded hospital. I gave him the ammo which Zagonczyk had let me have, and appointed him N.C.O. in charge of our arms and ammunition, and told him to draw up a list of the arms and ammunition which the men hold and to report to me every day on the state of our armament.

Rifleman Czortek has been killed in Ciepla Street. A patrol sent out by Jeremy engaged a German patrol in Krochmalna Street, and in the fighting one of our men was killed.

The telephone girls told me that some ladies' shoes have been unearthed in the Headquarters Stores, but that the Quartermaster refuses to issue them. So Alexander went off with Maria and Wanda to sort it out, and they returned soon afterwards with a couple of dozen pairs of the shoes. Apparently the Quartermaster tried to quote rules and regulations for not issuing the shoes, but had to give way in the face of a flood of curses and threats from Alexander.

Sunday, 20 August

An army chaplain is celebrating mass at a little altar which the girls have erected and decorated with greenery in the yard of No. 44, Sienna Street. I don't altogether like to see so many people gathered in this small yard, for the Germans are not observing this day as a holiday, and their aircraft are patrolling the sky, looking for targets and observing the results of their mortars in position in the Saxon Park. Fortunately, the yard has two exit gates, which will make it easier for the men to scatter if necessary.

Czortek's wife has just come to my headquarters, to take away her husband's belongings. One of my most painful duties is that of talking to the widows of any of my men who have been killed. If only they'd cry or make a fuss, then at least I'd know how to try to comfort them with some commonplace remarks. But they are all so calm, inexorable; they never seem to want a word of comfort. They know everything and never have to ask any questions. So there's nothing for me to say, and these moments of silence seem worse than bombs exploding.

Corporal Deska has just brought me the first report on the state of arms of Alexander's company and Grzes' platoon. His list includes 1 light machine-gun, 16 rifles, 10 machine-pistols, 28 revolvers of all sorts and calibres, not to mention some dozen bayonets, daggers and knives.

'But the list isn't complete,' Deska explained, 'for the lads are deliberately keeping quiet about their weapons, not only to H.Q., but even to their own mates. If anyone manages to get hold of a weapon without anyone else seeing, then he'll hide it for fear of having to hand it over or give it up to someone else. Of course they can't hide a rifle for long, but several men have got hold of revolvers, and still pretend to be unarmed, as they hope to be issued with something better. And they do the same with ammo.'

As I went across from Twarda Street I took cover, as usual, on account of the German machine-gunners in the Telephone Exchange building, but soldiers I met on the way told me I needn't trouble. They pointed out a yellow flag which was hanging on the Telephone Exchange building, the significance of which escapes us all. Does it indicate that the Germans in there are short of food? or infection? Or is it some kind of signal for German aircraft? People are saying that they heard explosions during the night which must mean that our men have blown up the Central Telephone Exchange, but this can't be so, for we'd be able to see worse damage over there. All the same, something is happening, for the Germans haven't been firing into our street since this morning.

As if out of sheer spite, the Germans have changed their tactics since we obtained our anti-tank pistols. Their tanks no longer come up to our barricades, but stop out of range to provide mobile block-houses, from which unceasing firing is able to demolish our resistance. Very nearly 500 shells have been fired into the façade of the furniture factory. But as the thick outer walls facing the street fall in, the reinforced concrete ceilings sink and provide further covering for the interior of the building, where Jeremy and his men are still holding out.

Everyone is excited to see clouds of smoke rising out of the Telephone Exchange building. Evidently our men have decided to smoke the Germans out of their fortress.

But the bombing is growing heavier, and the German offensive from beyond our street is increasing.

Both Alexander and Grzes are irritated by the frequent in-accuracies of official communiqués and newspaper reports of the fighting in our sector. Whenever Captain Hal and his units relieve my men in one of our positions, we always hear afterwards that Hal has 'occupied' the barricades—giving the impression that the barricades were previously held by Germans. It so happened that a sergeant was killed when his unit relieved a barricade which Grzes and his men had been holding; next day we read in the paper that this sergeant had been killed during a 'counter-attack' which ended in the 'capture' of this position.

And now, taking over new outposts, Alexander and Grzes are up against more trouble. Some of their lads cleared off without permission as soon as they heard of the Telephone Exchange building being captured, in the hope of being able to 'acquire' some arms and ammo.

The field hospital in Marianska Street has been hit by a bomb, and the wounded who have been carried out of the shattered building are now lying in the open air—some in beds, others on stretchers or simply on the ground, wrapped in blankets. Those who can walk have wandered about trying to make their way back to their old units. But no one knows where to take the others.

Someone has indignantly reported that unarmed and exhausted German prisoners-of-war, captured in the attack on the Telephone Exchange, were stoned by angry women as they were being marched across Dabrowski Square.

Monday, 21 August

         The Telephone Exchange build-
ing has finally been cleared of Germans. Cadet Bohun, a young
newspaper reporter, who has taken up with Grzes and his men,
told me how we set the building on fire, spraying petrol through
firemen's hoses up as far as the third floor, how the Germans
tried to break out to the Saxon Park, and how in the end they
were mopped up in the cellars in which they'd barricaded themselves. Several dozen were taken prisoner. One man was carrying
a pocket diary, in which he'd kept an account of what happened,
Bohun had had copies of this diary made, and distributed them
among Grzes' lads, to keep their spirits up. When things are bad,
it's comforting to know that in fact our enemies are still worse off.

Kurt Heller's Diary [1]

1st August. Street fighting began this afternoon in Warsaw.

2nd August. We're surrounded.

3rd August. Ulrich has been killed. Still no help from outside.
Hollweg has been seriously wounded.

5th August. Rudolf killed, as well as several others. We've reached
the limit of endurance.

6th August. Got a little sleep this morning. Dinner was coffee
with sugar. Death everywhere, but I want to live. Three men
have committed suicide.

7th August. Our own artillery fired at us this afternoon, but no
one was killed. An attempt to break out failed—one man
killed, four badly hurt. We buried 14 of our men today at 8
a.m. in the yard. The air smells bad.

8th August. Our positions are 300 metres away, but the bandits'
resistance is still strong.

9th August. Food very short.

11th August. The police have taken what food we had, including
our cigarettes. We're in no condition to resist longer.

12th August. Hungry. Some soup, 6 cigarettes. The police have

---

   [1] Kurt Heller, a German from Stettin, was taken prisoner in the Warsaw Telephone
Exchange.

seized everything, even what was left of the jam. When will this end?

13th August. Heavy tank fire against the Poles so that our Tower is being hit, but no casualties. A tank has brought in food supplies for five days. I can hardly stand. When will they get us out of here?

16th August. Hunger. The men are afraid at night. When I saw the first star I thought of my wife and the boy, lying in the earth in Stettin. Can't stop thinking of them, am in the same position myself.

17th August. The Poles are trying to smoke us out with petrol bottles. More men have lost their nerve and committed suicide. The dead smell horrible, lying in the streets.

18th August. Cut off entirely from the outer world.

19th August. No hope. The Poles are surrounding us.

I spent last night in Grzybowska Street as usual. Despite the many graves there, I have grown to like these nights spent in the open air in the ruined gateway of No. 19. It's quieter than in the day-time and sometimes quite silent. The ruins don't stink as they do in the sunlight, and the flies are no longer troublesome. A sentry is on duty at the entrance, which is protected by sand-bags. One of the girls is on night duty at the telephone. A group of lads on guard duty doze fitfully on mattresses spread along under the walls, each man with his rifle or revolver within reach. In the intervals between inspecting positions and receiving reports, I can lie on my back on my camp-bed and doze off under the starry sky. The outlines of the lofty ruins all round look like fantastic cliffs and towers.

In the morning, more reinforcements arrived from Group Headquarters, and at the same time I heard that eleven-year-old Wojtek, our youngest soldier, has been killed. He was shot in Ciepla Street bringing in a message from Sergeant Grzes.

The heavy mortars have been bellowing since dawn. They fire six shells in rapid succession, either explosive or incendiary. But we can't distinguish by the sound what is coming. I inspected the fragments of one incendiary; is consisted of a brass tube about a foot in diameter.

Whenever a shell is fired we wait for it, in our third-floor headquarters in Sienna Street, listening intently, to see whether it is our turn. Every explosion is like a respite. It isn't our turn—yet.

But at last our turn came. There was an explosion on the ground floor as if two giants had collided. Before my eyes a crack opened up in the wall. I felt the floorboards rise. I threw myself towards the door and tried to steel myself for the five following explosions.

But they didn't come. The building is still standing. A cloud of dust rose into the air, fragments of glass and plaster were scattered over the floor.

From below I heard someone shout.

'Bring a stretcher! Where's the doctor?'

I ran down. The gateway was dark with smoke as I made my way out blindly into the street. A great gap had appeared between the ground-floor windows of the house opposite, which contained the Group Headquarters. Wounded men were being helped and carried out. One of the girls has been killed. I could see her in there, but she was unrecognisable.

Dr. Leopold has asked me to intervene on his behalf, for he had taken over a ground-floor flat in Komitetowa Street as an operating theatre and battalion sick-bay. Then, after he'd put the place in order, a priest tried to turn him out, claimed that the flat was the most suitable place for the ambulance station of his own battalion. I have tried to argue with this priest, but it was no use.

Going back to Sienna Street, I found the floors of our billet and the office had already been swept. The walls are cracked, but it looks as if we shan't have to vacate the place. The main thing is that the soup was saved, for the girls were able to cover the saucepans before any plaster from the ceiling fell into them.

Then Remigiusz brought up the visitors he promised. They were both colonels, both accepted my invitation to have a drink, and we sat down with a couple of officers who have just been posted to my sector and whom I wanted to get to know better.

We talked about the fighting, about the supplies which have been dropped by British aircraft in the City Centre but which we haven't yet seen, and the position on the Western Front; and finally about how different things would have been if we'd had more ammo and anti-tank guns. When we'd finished off a few bottles of the wine, tongues loosened and we all spoke more freely. It turned out that the two colonels have no contact with District Headquarters, nor do they belong to Monter's staff officers or to General Bor.

'We're only concerned with the men who're actually fighting, for they're the ones who will decide one way or another,' said one of them.

Tuesday, 22 August

'Vive la France!'

An insurrection has at last started in Paris, the people have risen and thrown up barricades. Now both the capitals of Freedom are fighting! Tadeusz couldn't help grinning when he reported to me that all is well in our street and one girl was humming the *Marseillaise* as she poured out coffee for the men.

Then a girl came running across from the position opposite the furniture factory, to say that they'd caught a civilian who was trying to get through to the German lines. He refused to say who he was or what he wanted to get through for. Then he asked to see the officer in command of the sector. However, they couldn't send him over to me, as an armed soldier would have had to accompany him and this would have weakened the position. So Alexander went back with the girl and a few minutes later brought him in. He was a solemn middle-aged man, not tall, with an intelligent and rather absent-minded expression. I had the impression that I'd seen him before somewhere.

I went out to meet them as Alexander brought him in. Then Alexander introduced me to him.

'Sir, may I introduce Lieutenant Lech, who's the officer in

command. Lech, this is Kazimierz Baginski, chairman of the
Polish Peasant Party and a member of the Underground Polish
Government. I've already apologised for the misunderstanding.'

'No, it is I who should apologise. I didn't realise that I'd reached
the front line. A few days ago I was able to get to the corner of
Grzybowska and Ciepla Streets quite easily.'

'That's the way things are. As a matter of fact, there aren't any
Germans there now, but we haven't been able to hold out in
those houses on the corner. Might I ask where you were going,
sir? Perhaps we can help you get through.'

'Thank you—as a matter of fact, I wasn't going anywhere in
particular. But as the Director of the Department of Internal
Affairs, I thought it was my duty to see for myself what conditions
are like, what people need and how they are holding out in
various districts of Warsaw.'

'Was it you, sir, who issued the proclamations and announce-
ments signed "Dabrowski"?'

'Yes. Of course, I'm telling you this in confidence. . . .'

'Thank you, and I'd like to be equally frank. You're the first
representative of the civilian authorities we've had the honour of
seeing up here. Up to now, all we've known of the existence of
any civilian authorities in Warsaw has been from the newspapers. Unfortunately many of the proclamations can't be carried
out here, but they're useful as giving us some idea of what is
going on. Now, tell the truth, sir—can they be carried out in the
City Centre?'

'As a rule they can, though of course much depends simply on
the good-will of the inhabitants of Warsaw.'

In fact, much depends on good-will, fair-play and a sense of
responsibility among us in our sector too. It is all right if someone takes a shirt from an empty apartment or if a soldier takes a
battery for his torch from a deserted shop. It is all right if a fit
civilian is used to take the wounded to a hospital. But it is not all
right to force civilians to build barricades, or if someone hides
in his own home more food than he needs. even if he rescued the
food himself from a fire.

And yet today there's been what amounts to nothing more than plain robbery in our street, when a group of civilians started to ransack some shops. But what could we do? Arrest or shoot them? The only sensible method turned out to be a way that is quite illegal. One of these civilians, who was carrying off a gramophone from one of the shops, had his teeth knocked in by a blow from Alexander. I went for another looter who was making off with four bottles of vodka, looted from the shop belonging to Stas-the-Sailor's widow.. Then we made it known that anyone else caught like this would get the same rough handling.

Order again reigns in our street.

Wednesday, 23 August

Yesterday's visit from Director Baginski and our talk with him has led to some rather harmless joking. Coming in from a patrol, Wojtek announced to me that he'd been studying the needs and spirit of the civilian population in the little area between Krochmalna and Ciepla Streets. In his opinion, 'the civilian population' of this area should be evacuated, and he asked me to send out a girl and a couple of men.

'The civilian population', however, turned out to consist of one solitary old lady, whom Wojtek's patrol found in a little space under some half-ruined stairs in Krochmalna Street. She's almost paralysed and starving, unable to move but fully conscious. She says that the Germans have come across her several times, but that they didn't disturb her. She is not at all sure how many days she's been there.

I sent Zofia and two men to bring her in. Half an hour later Zofia returned.

'We've brought in the old lady,' she announced.

'So what?'

'What am I to do with her?'

'That's your business. I haven't time to be bothered with matters of this kind.'

'But she isn't wounded and she isn't a soldier, she's as deaf as a post, and she must be at least eighty.'

'Don't bother me. There must be a civilian hospital somewhere or a shelter.'

It was still early, and I took advantage of the warm weather to wash properly and shave, which I hadn't been able to do for several days. I bathed my feet in cold water. Then they brought me a clean shirt (which used to belong to Miecz) and a pair of socks (formerly the property of Stas-the-Sailor).

After I'd inspected all our positions, I met Zofia in the gateway of No. 19.

'What's become of the old lady?' I asked her cheerfully, in an attempt to soften my earlier irritation.

'Everything is under control now, though to begin with I thought I'd have to spend the night with her in the street. Nobody wanted to take her in, and I was afraid to bring her back here. Then I heard that a little clinic for expectant mothers has been opened in Zlota Street, and I thought I'd try there. It was a fine place, with whitewashed walls and beds with clean linen, and there was even glass in the windows.'

'Don't try to tell me they took in your old lady! She was eighty. . . .'

'They didn't exactly take her in, but I was lucky, as there was a bombing raid at the time and I managed to tuck the old lady into a bed and clear off. As we were making our get-away I couldn't resist shouting to one of the nurses, "She had a baby—forty-five years ago".'

'So I see you coped with the situation. I'd never have thought of that. Do you think they'll keep the old lady?'

'They can't put her out into the street.'

Shells from the tanks which have moved up on the far side of Ciepla Street, and which have not yet been able to reach No. 19, have now battered a way through the protecting walls and houses and have started to hit the archway above our gate. So I instructed the men to clear out the rubble from the cellar below and make

an entry into it direct from the gate. We have moved the telephone down there, as it will be a little safer.

We have all been impressed today by a message in the newspapers which has also been broadcast by Warsaw radio, addressed
by the Polish Socialist Party to British workers:

'Why is help not forthcoming for us as we fight Hitler in the
most forward line? Who and what is preventing us from getting
the arms which are desperately needed by the Insurrection? What
is going on behind our backs while we are bleeding in the fight?
How is it that our pilots were able to fight in the defence of
London but are not allowed to fight over Warsaw, and that we
have no defence in the air, even though there are American air
bases not far to the east of Warsaw?

'One wish alone inspires us all. We want to be free. We are
paying for our freedom with our own blood and we believe that
the peoples of the world are with us, but they must try to force
the politicians to stop acting like Pontius Pilate.'

'Do you remember that prayer of English sailors?' I asked
Barbara, who was sitting thoughtfully reading this appeal. 'It was
quoted in a life of Queen Elizabeth which I once read to you. The
sailors prayed before setting out against the Spanish Armada.
They prayed for victory and that the least possible English blood
should be spilled.'

'I was thinking of a prayer too,' Barbara said, 'when little
Andrzej was saying his prayers one night, I overheard him
whisper, "Please, God, let all the children have ice-creams, but
the kind we used to have before the war, with chocolate, on a
stick. And if the Germans try to attack you in Heaven, don't be
afraid, for England will help you".'

Thursday, 24 August

With yesterday's appeal still in
my ears, I looked through a copy of 'The Week' which someone
brought in. We printed about sixty issues of this paper on our

secret press before the Insurrection, and although I didn't always agree with the statements of these spokesmen of the ex-Pilsudski party, we could always rely on them for accurate news and bold criticism of Polish-Soviet relations.

Now I read.

'Forsaken, we are nevertheless fighting on for freedom. There is much that is tragic in this, yet at the same time there is consolation and even joy too. Both our enemies, as they fight, are nevertheless in agreement on one point and that is—Poland. In conditions like these, our fight cannot end in a victory over the Germans. Yet the battle of Warsaw and the whole country has become the expression of our will to make Poland a state independent of any other power and not shamed by any agreement to losing any part of the lands which constitute our Republic.'

On page 3 I found an 'attempt to evaluate' the situation.

'It seems that two possible solutions exist in Poland today: either the Soviet Army will enter Warsaw in the footsteps of the retreating Germans or Russian troops will cross the Polish republic to occupy a part of the German Reich after the Germans have surrendered.

'The first alternative requires no comment and in fact we have already done as much as we can to minimise its moral and political effects. For, once the German threat has been destroyed, the entry of the Russians as "protectors and an occupying force" would be nothing less than a catastrophe for us Poles. Our politicians would at once find themselves in the hands of the N.K.W.D. supported by our own Communists. They would do everything possible to destroy those elements in our society which would prevent Poland being surrendered to Russian imperialism.

'It is the other alternative which seems more probable as time passes. This is based on the British victories in France where, it seems, the final stages of the war are taking place. The situation in which the German armies now find themselves, surrendering *en masse*, fleeing in disorder, is no longer that of a battle but of defeat and unavoidable catastrophe. It makes the surrender of the Reich within the next two weeks something which is really at hand.

'When the Reich surrenders, the Russians will cross our territory to occupy a part of Germany. But the Russian forces would not enter Warsaw as victors responsible for the defeat of Germany. In a situation like this, America and England will not leave us at the mercy of the Russians and will certainly find a way to regain their political and military superiority.'

If only this comes to pass! We have held out for twenty-four days and can hold on for another fourteen. Now that we have seized the Telephone Exchange building our men are attacking successfully on all sides. The Germans have been cleared from the central police station in Nowy Swiat Street, while the district Telephone Exchange on the far side of Jerusalem Way has also fallen. We have driven the Germans from the Polytechnical College, while the Germans in the Mokotow suburb have surrendered to units of the Home Army who reached Warsaw from outside the city.

Friday, 25 August

Last night our patrols laid mines along Grzybowska Street between Ciepla and Walicow Streets, but this time they were real mines, which we'd made ourselves. The mines have been ready for the past three days, but we postponed laying them in the hope that we'd be able to drive the Germans out and get back to the positions we held before 15 August. But we've had to give up this idea due to lack of ammunition for our light machine-guns and machine-pistols. Some of the shells for the anti-tank pistols which Lieutenant Wir has must be put by for a 'rainy day', and we're now obliged to stand and watch as the German positions grow stronger every day before our eyes.

Lieutenant Jaskolka, in the armoury, has shown me his log-book, containing over fifty items repaired.

'We'll accept work from any unit and also from individual soldiers on condition that weapons sent in by you get priority,' he explained. 'Also we make it clear that we have to put aside repair of lighter weapons should anything larger come in.'

'There isn't any kind of work we won't take on,' his colleague added, showing me a gleaming Browning; 'look, we had to manufacture all the trigger mechanism for this by hand.'

'Most of our time is spent cleaning weapons which people have unearthed, and we also waste a good deal of time manufacturing pieces lost by careless stripping.'

Back in No. 44, Sienna Street, soup was being got ready for distribution to the men out in the line. Two of the Caucasians were holding a cauldron on a long stick between them, near a temporary stove in the open air, and one of the girls was pouring out the rations. Two other girls were driving away clouds of flies, while a fourth was scooping them out of the soup in a big ladle. But it's hopeless to get soup out to the men without flies. However, the girls try hard to keep out as many flies as possible.

'Soup is nicest with dried berries in it—then you don't notice the flies,' one of the girls said, laughing.

'It must be easier for you to take the dinners round, now that the Germans are no longer holding the Telephone Exchange building.'

'It's easy enough for a "tich",' Janka complained. She's a tall thin woman with a sharp tongue in her head. 'Even if a tall person keeps her head down getting past a barricade, her behind sticks up. Then if she's hit she can't say she was wounded on the field of glory.'

Ola came out just then, and I called to her,

'What have you been doing with yourself lately? I haven't seen you or Kasia about for a long time.'

Apparently Kasia is very ill, and Dr. Leopold, unable to diagnose her complaint, decided that she has 'taken refuge from reality in a nervous disorder'. She has a high temperature and is in our 'new hospital'.

'What new hospital is this? I haven't heard of it before.'

'It came into being more or less by chance. After the hospital in Marianska Street was bombed, we decided we couldn't leave the lads in the open air, so I took them into my flat in Zlota Street,' Ola explained. 'We had to move them down into the cellar, and now we're gradually taking over more and more of the cellars. It's a hospital of a sort, after all. The convalescents can come and sit about upstairs.'

Ola has taken charge of this hospital and is helped by her mother.

'How about doctors?'

'Dr. Leopold visits us, but the chief surgeon is my cousin Mieczyslaw.'

Then Tadeusz came to fetch me. Sergeant Brzeski, senior N.C.O. in Alexander's company, had just been killed in Grzybowska Street.

Saturday, 26 August

The bombing continues. Houses collapse and the burned-out shells of buildings damaged earlier are going up in flames once again from incendiaries. The flames lick over graves heaped high with rubble. It's strange to think that there are living men and women in this blazing inferno.

I have had to go from one end of Grzybowska Street to the other giving urgent instructions, transferring men to new positions in an attempt to make up our losses and supervising the ambulance squads. No. 18, the last block of flats left standing in our street, has just been hit. It was crowded with people, no one knows how many have been killed. The injured are now being brought out.

Alexander's men are holding on in Krochmalna Street. Lieutenant Wojtek has just been brought in; he was hit by firing from a German bunker, and he is dying.

'Take him to the hospital in Sliska Street!'

Women with babies, who have been driven out of bombed houses, come seeking shelter, and they crowd together into dark recesses, where they try to shelter their little ones with their own bodies.

Another man wounded: then three more: then another. . . .

People call along from gate to gate for stretchers.

Three men were standing in one gateway just staring as two ambulance girls struggled by with a stretcher. Then Barbara ran up, red-faced, her lips pale. She went straight up to the three men with her fists clenched.

'What are you standing about for, you . . . . ?' she shouted.

The men gazed at her as if they'd just woken up. Then, without answering, they hurried out of the gateway, two of them seized the stretcher from the girls while the third looked round anxiously, wondering how to help.

Things are no better in Sienna Street. The mortars are concentrating their fire on the building in which Group Headquarters is situated. The officer in command, Major Zygmunt, has been wounded. Barbara, who has gone there from our street, seems to have gone out of the frying-pan into the fire. A string of high-explosive shells has just crashed into the billet at No. 44, Sienna Street, and the two neighbouring houses. None of my men have been wounded, but the buildings are now out of action. Covered with a thick coating of dust, the girls came running out with a cauldron of soup they'd been able to save; then started to dish it out there and then. I hungrily ate hot pea-soup from my mess-tin.

We've had to transfer Alexander's billets, the cook-house and out stores to No. 52, Sliska Street. On the way it was often difficult to recognise the narrow streets, for they were heaped with rubble, often up to the first floor. New pathways through this formerly heavily built-up area are beginning to appear.

I went into the hospital, and was taken up to the first floor, then was admitted to a little room at the end of a long corridor, where I found Lieutenant Wojtek on a bed under the window. A girl in a white linen coat was smoothing his pillow.

'I'm his commanding officer.'

'I'm his fiancée.'

But Wojtek didn't recognise either of us. Now and again he would raise his head, while his hands gripped the bedclothes convulsively. There was no doctor. We could do nothing.

Sunday, 27 August

For some days past I've noticed an outsider in our street. He's rather conspicuous on account of his dark beard, though it isn't the beard of a young man who wants to look impressive or the beard of someone trying to disguise himself. It's a 'respectable' beard, an Orthodox beard, and a beard you feel you could trust. We've got used to his frequent visits to his flat in Ciepla Street, which has not yet been bombed or looted. None of us minds his show of interest in what is going on in our sector, and he's always ready to pass on to us anything he notices in the German lines.

The block containing his flat is not held either by us or by the Germans, and it lies in a wide strip which is patrolled by both sides. The bearded chap goes out there on his own, refusing the cover we offer him.

'I'm armed,' he assured the lads, patting his heavily weighted pockets.

But today he asked for our help. He had no ammunition for his revolver, and this morning, in a raid on the 'Café Club' on the corner of Nowy Swiat and the Jerusalem Way, he used up his last grenade. If I'd let him have two of our newly-made grenades, he said, he'd feel safer when he goes over to his flat to fetch some clean linen for a wounded comrade. Besides, he'd be able to warn us if by chance he came on any Germans.

So I gave instructions that he was to be issued with two grenades. These are the only weapons of which we have plenty. I've heard that three of our workshops are now turning out these grenades and that production isn't likely to be interrupted.

In the afternoon I went to Lieutenant Wojtek's funeral. During the ceremony a string of shells burst along Sosnowa Street, like a farewell salute.

Towards evening, as the Germans were withdrawing their tanks to Chlodna Street and the firing had died down a little along the front line, Zenek went out with a patrol of three men along Ciepla Street. A quarter of an hour later, a runner came in and reported that there were Germans on the first floor on this side of Ciepla Street, opposite the northern wing of the police barracks. Zenek was watching them, but asked me to send him more men. At once an idea struck me.

'You know that bearded chap?' I asked the lad.

'Yes.'

'Do you know where his flat is?'

'Yes. It's where the Germans are.'

'Have they found him?'

'It doesn't look like it. Zenek says there's something fishy about the whole thing.'

I managed to get together five men.

'Go ahead, but be careful,' I told them. 'Don't fire unless Zenek gives the order.'

It was dark in my billet when Zenek appeared, to report that he'd brought in the bearded chap, his mate and two women. Then he put a loaf of German bread, some ham and papers on my table.

'What's this?'

Zenek told me that to begin with he'd heard someone talking loudly in German. He sent his runner back to me, then moved up to a window near by, but couldn't understand or make out how many of them were there. But one thing at least was clear— they were drinking. Before the runner got back with reinforce- ments, four Germans came out of the house. Zenek let them pass without being seen, and continued to watch. When the rein- forcements arrived, he stationed them in the yard and went in with two lads, up to the first floor. He could hear women giggling and drunken cursing. They knocked at the door. The people inside fell silent, and Zenek knocked again. Then some- one approached the door on the other side.

'Wer da?'

'It's a patrol. Open up!' Zenek replied in Polish.

'Was für eine Patrolle?'

'From Lieutenant Lech. Open up immediately!'

'Ich scheisse auf ihren Leutenant Lech!'

Zenek and the lads were just about to smash the door in when they heard muttering inside, a key turned and the door opened to reveal a frightened girl in a torn blouse and grubby skirt. The bearded chap wearing top-boots was leaning against the opposite wall, drunk, with his trousers unfastened and his shirt open.

Zenek and the lads searched the flat, but found nothing. They took the papers, bread and ham from the table, amidst empty bottles and half-finished glasses of vodka.

'Send the four of them with a good escort back to the military police, and have them locked up and watched until further orders. Then search their flat thoroughly once more, at dawn. I gave the bearded chap two grenades this morning, and I want to know whether they're in the flat or not.'

By the light of my carbide lamp I examined the big sheet of paper, which had been used to cover the table for their spread. It wasn't difficult to see what the various crooked lines, marked in pencil, stood for. This was Grzybowska Street, a square indicated the furniture factory and these little circles were our positions. Even my telephone was shown.

Clearly they were spies and should be executed. But I tried to figure out what had made them do it and what lay behind their activities. I wondered whether they were embittered for some reason, or merely puppets, under the influence of some uncontrollable and primitive emotion? And what about the two girls? Surely they could have found a safer place to ply their trade for the sake of vodka, ham and a few cigarettes. Either they were in love or else just fools.

The arrival of Lieutenant Pszczolka interrupted these musings. He brought in and introduced to me his deputy, Lieutenant Danuta, and we talked about the replacement of the telephone line out to my sector, and how to protect the cables from breakages. At that moment, 'Partisan' brought in a receipt from the civil police for the four people we'd arrested and sent over. He mentioned that the escort had had no supper, as they had been forgotten when the suppers were given out, so I gave them the bread and ham that were still lying on the table.

'See that?' said Pszczolka to Danuta. 'There's an officer for you! Gives his own supper to his men and he's going without himself.'

My own supper. . . .? I let it pass.

Monday, 28 August

Mr. Czerwonka, who owns both the shed in which our first-aid post is and the workshop which the Boy Scouts use for producing the paper bags we use for our combustible petrol bottles, is a real Warsaw character and, like all war-time black-marketeers, he's fond of holding long conversations over a bottle of vodka, providing he can find someone who is his intellectual equal. He talks sensibly and with a good deal of philosophising about everything—the war, the Insurrection, bombing raids, fires, destruction, death. When he's quenched his thirst and given us all his views on these topics, he's inclined to drop off and to snore dreadfully; but when he wakes up again, he's very active, and Zofia can get anything she wants out of him.

A deep trench has been dug in the yard of Mr. Czerwonka's property, and a long plank placed across it, thus doing away with the need for building a latrine. By ill-luck, however, Mr. Czerwonka was making use of this plank when a whole string of mortar shells burst round about. When the last explosion died down Mr. Czerwonka emerged from the cloud of smoke and dust, covered with blood but still holding up his trousers self-consciously with both hands. He'd been wounded in the face. Zofia had an opportunity of showing him her gratitude, but I'm sorry to say that no one else seemed to remember that we should never laugh at the misfortunes of others.

When a military police patrol came up, I was sure they'd come about the four spies we arrested yesterday, and was about to have Zenek and his lads brought in, when the N.C.O. in charge of the patrol explained that they'd come about something else. They'd received a complaint that some of my lads broke into a locked flat in our street on 15 August, looted the place and made off with a Zeiss camera. And he asked me whether I knew anything about the episode or whether I can help identify the lads concerned. The flat was the first-floor flat with the balcony from which Tadeusz and Puchacz destroyed a tank.

The shell of this house has been under fire almost constantly for some days, while what was left of the furniture has been thrown out of the windows and used for reinforcing one of the barricades that we hastily built there.

'Have you inspected the flat where the robbery is alleged to have taken place?' I asked. 'You ought to start with that, preferably taking the owner of the property along with you.'

As far as the four spies are concerned, the military police are not going to go into the matter, since the four are civilians. Explanations were forthcoming, and since there is no reason for holding them any longer, they're to be set free. I couldn't believe my own ears when I heard this. To think that they're to be let loose without hearing any evidence from us! The first thing to do was to prevent this. So Alexander set off with some men to bring in the four while I got in touch with Group Headquarters, and obtained an order to deal with them as I thought fit and as quickly as possible, i.e. appoint three men to try them and, if they're found guilty, to carry out sentence.

The matter was dealt with very rapidly, in the open air. Everyone knew that they were guilty, and there was no hesitation about the sentence—death by firing squad. I had to pronounce sentence.

The Caucasians dug a trench along the wall behind No. 17. Three picked men stood waiting with their rifles, each loaded with four bullets, making a total of twelve. We had to be economical with the ammo. So the men were to fire at close range, aiming between the eyes of the prisoners.

I took my place on a little heap of earth, and signed to the girls who had just come out of the first-aid post that they were to look away. Then I looked at the condemned people a little below me, who were watching the preparations, fully aware of what was going to happen.

'Have you anything to say?' I asked.

They said nothing, but only looked at me, and in their eyes I saw a plea for mercy, but I resisted it.

The first of the four was a dark-haired young man in a black suit and white shirt, without collar or tie. His face was sunburned. He came forward obediently, moving like a labourer tired from working in the fields. They tied a handkerchief round his eyes, and Alexander lifted his hand. I knew I ought not to turn away, so I stared fiercely at a solitary white cloud that was moving across the blue sky. The men fired. Dr. Leopold leaned over the prisoner and nodded. Two of the Caucasians dropped the corpse into the pit.

I have always been opposed to the death penalty. One of the arguments I used to put forward was that if those who passed the death sentence were also obliged by law to see the sentence carried out, then there would be no more death sentences passed.

And yet already twice in the past year I've had to execute men with my own hands.

'Next!'

I stopped the bearded chap as he came forward.

'Where are the grenades I gave you?'

He didn't reply.

'Go ahead. . . .'

The men fired again. Twice the doctor leaned over the man, twice he shook his head and twice Alexander had to fire point-blank at the man's temples.

I wanted to stop it, to get away, out of it. Then Igra suddenly appeared in front of me, his lips white, trembling;

'Enough!' he exclaimed. 'You can't shoot the women.'

'Sentence must be carried out.'

'I know, but. . . .'

Suddenly I remembered how Igra himself had been saved by what was almost a miracle from mass-execution.

'All right, you can fall out,' I said to the man who was standing guard with his rifle over the two women. 'We don't need you any more.'

Then:

'Get out of it!' I shouted to the girls.

They stared at me blankly, as if they hadn't heard.

'Get out of it!' I repeated, in a louder tone.

Both burst into convulsive sobbing.

'Shut up, for heaven's sake! I won't tell you again—be off. And don't let me set eyes on the pair of you again, or I'll . . .'

I stared after them as they scrambled along a pathway between the ruins, stumbling blindly over the rubble.

Tuesday, 29 August

Czes has been and told everyone that today is Barbara's birthday, and already before breakfast several of the lads asked for permission to withdraw from Grzybowska Street in order to wish her a Happy Birthday in the name of the entire company and also to give her a little present.

'What have you in mind?' I asked.

'Nothing much, it's only a little thing.'

But I insisted on seeing the present, and one of the lads produced a superb gold Swiss watch.

'Where did you get that from?'

'From those Germans we buried yesterday.'

'I see. In that case, you'll leave the watch with me and think up something else for a present. You know perfectly well that no one is allowed to keep any gold or money.'

The lads looked sulky, for my decision didn't strike them as at all reasonable.

'But Barbara lost not only her watch but everything she had when she was buried in No. 17 that time. It's *owing* to her.'

'Don't try to be clever. In the first place, she never had a gold watch, and besides, you can't make up to everyone what they've lost. Anyway, gold must be handed over to a higher authority and we can't make exceptions.'

'Suppose it was a nickel watch, then?' one of the lads asked, unstrapping a watch from his own wrist and showing it to me.

'Do you want to give away your watch?'

'What do you mean "*mine*"? I got it off a dead body and I can get myself another one. But if we don't give one to Barbara, she'll never take one for herself.'

It has been decided that we are to prepare for action on a large scale, which is to take place tomorrow. Attacks are to be made both from the Old Town towards the City Centre, and also from the City Centre towards the Old Town. I am to be in command of units which will go in to attack from between Rynkowa and Ciepla Streets, and am to be told the precise time and details of the attack tomorrow. Today I am to make a thorough reconnaissance of the German defence lines and positions in my sector.

I know the German fortified positions and lines very well by this time, but still have to be sure that they haven't made any alterations in the last twenty-four hours. Our attack is to be launched at night, so I waited till dusk to go out with two lads, Olgierd and Turek, to see what I could see.

Wooden stairs heaped with a thick layer of crushed plaster led us out of some cellars into a long, deep inner courtyard. The ruined and long-since-deserted side-wings of the building were five storeys high, though only a line of small shops separated us from Krochmalna Street. Something was burning in one of these shops; from time to time the flames leapt up brighter and green tongues of fire flickered against the upper edge of the wall, while orange-coloured sparks flew up from them. Then we saw a black helmet gleam in the light of the flames at the far end of the inner yard.

Olgierd caught sight of this helmet at the same time as I did. We drew back a pace, into a doorway. It was very quiet, only the flames crackled, like resinous logs just lit in a stove. We were able to get nearer the gate through a dark passage, and looked out cautiously through a shattered window, our machine-pistols ready. And there the man was, motionless, his two eyes staring at us from beneath his helmet. I could see his hand raised above his head. Moments passed. He didn't move. Then Olgierd whispered:

'Fancy letting a dead man frighten us. . . .!'

He was evidently one of us, with a red-and-white arm-band, but I didn't recognise him, and in any case he'd probably altered. . . . Anyway, Olgierd went through his pockets, took his revolver and some ammo, as well as two grenades. A third grenade was gripped in that uplifted hand.

'Don't touch him,' Olgierd warned Turek. But Turek was already pleased with the helmet he'd acquired.

Then we heard the murmur of voices somewhere in the depths of the yard, and again we retreated hastily into the passage and looked for a way into the rear part of the building. But we could still hear strange shuffling sounds and whispering which came from the floor above. There was only a skeleton of wood where the staircase had been, but Olgierd spotted a ladder in the yard. As usual, he wanted to go up first, but as he was our best shot, I made him wait below to act as cover, while I climbed the ladder slowly.

The shuffling noise stopped, but I could still hear whispering. I reached the top of the window-sill, held my breath and looked in. Against the opposite wall I saw a battered old wardrobe, with a bit of cracked looking-glass, and a rifle leaning against it, with a man's uniform cap hanging on the barrel. The floor was scattered with plaster and half the ceiling had fallen in. I looked closer and saw a mattress on the floor, where it had been pulled from an iron bedstead. An almost naked girl lay on it. Her face was hidden in the thick curly hair of a youth, leaning over her. . . .

Quickly and silently, I retreated and signalled to Olgierd to put down his rifle, with which he was covering me. Fortunately the pair hadn't heard me, for I wouldn't have known what to say to them. I couldn't, for instance, have told them that this sort of thing isn't done. . . .

It was only when my excitement had calmed down and we'd regained the gateway that I became aware of the unbearable stench in the ruins. It was made up of the smell of decaying human bodies and of scorched flesh.

The gateway out into the street was barricaded with paving-stones and all the ground-floor windows in the opposite line of houses had been bricked up. It was too dark to make out the German bunkers which were situated a little farther on. I whispered to Olgierd to stay where he was with Turek, and I'd find an observation-post. When I was ready I'd whistle to him. Then either he or Turek was to push a few of the paving-stones down from the barricade and stick out the helmet, so that we could see where the German fire came from.

Turek begrudged the helmet, but Olgierd comforted him, 'The bullet won't go through it, and besides, you'll look as though you'd really stopped a bullet. You'll be a hero.'

So Turek obediently stuck the helmet on the barrel of his rifle.

'What are you up to, half-wit?' Olgierd protested. 'If they shoot off the barrel of your rifle, you'll never be able to get it mended. Find a stick or something.'

I was able to find a convenient place easily enough near by on the second floor, and gave the signal we'd agreed on. I heard the rumble of the paving-stones as they were dislodged, but they fell with only a dull thud, for the barricade was heaped with earth and it was not until five seconds later that I heard the first shots open up from their position to my left and could see both the source and direction of the fire. The shots ricocheted, and one, a tracer, flew up and expired in the abyss of the black sky. Three seconds later another gun opened fire to the right and tracer bullets gleamed below me.

A red rocket shot up from behind the wall and curved above my head, to be followed at once by a white one, which burst into a whole chandelier. By its light, the street looked like a stage-set. I kept trying to count the seconds. Twenty seconds later the first hand-grenade exploded on the pavement, and a shell fell near it. Then shells began to come over thicker, and machine-gun fire started from both sides, like roused dogs along a village street.

Before the chandelier of lights went out, I tried to estimate as accurately as possible how far it was to the opposite positions, and to fix in my mind as many details of the scene as possible.

When I got back with the two lads to Headquarters, Captain Jerzewski, the new Chief of Staff of the 'Chrobry II' group, rang me up.

'What's going on over there?' he demanded. 'Zagonczyk is worried, and I've told the reserves to be on the alert.'

'You can call them off, nothing is happening. Just that the Germans have too much ammo and are getting nervous. All that noise was on account of nothing more than one helmet on a stick. But we've been able to get a good idea of the German positions. I don't think they'll be able to alter them much between now and tomorrow.'

This was true enough, but we couldn't make any alterations either. I ought to have got some sleep, but couldn't. Tomorrow I had to lead an attack against that barrage, and I was trying to work out how to do it with as few losses as possible.

Wednesday, 30 August

At a conference held by Captain Rum, who is deputising for Major Zagonczyk, we have been discussing how to tackle the attack planned for tonight. The attack is intended to support the units which are going to break out of the Old Town and make for the City Centre, and also to provide cover for the evacuation of the Old Town against counter-attacks by the Germans from the east and west of their route.

I put forward my plan. After opening up and capturing a way through the barricades between us and Krochmalna Street, our anti-tank patrols are then to silence the enemy machine-guns in the German bunkers. This will be the signal for sappers to get across the street and lay explosive charges under the opposite walls, then set the fuses and withdraw before the Germans can open fire. As soon as the charges have exploded and under cover of the smoke, the first two assault parties will penetrate the German defences and start hand-to-hand fighting. All this is to take only a few seconds.

However, it turned out that the sappers only have enough explosive for two charges, so we finally decided to blow gaps not at street-level but at window-level, where the walls are not so thick. We shall have to prepare portable scaffolding of some kind for this, and in addition the difference between street-level and the height of these gaps will make things more difficult for our infantry. The anti-tank patrols only have two shells for each anti-tank pistol, and after breaking through Krochmalna Street, they'll only have one shell left to blow up the German positions in Mirowski Square, and to attack the tanks should the Germans bring them into action. There's very little ammo, particularly for our light machine-gun, and we have no rockets for signalling purposes. However, I am to get one home-made flame-thrower, with a range of fifteen to twenty yards, and some smoke-bombs.

I went back to our street. The Germans are not attacking to-day, but they are not sparing their ammo in an attempt to destroy our forward positions and in bombing our line. Rifle-girl Kubus, who lost an eye ten days ago, but who has already returned to duty and insisted on going back to her former position, has just been wounded again. Her forearm has been damaged so badly that her right hand will have to be amputated. Several wounded men have stuck to their positions after first-aid.

Janusz and Grzes have been getting together the assault platoon for tonight's attack. It consists of forty-two men, not counting the machine-gun crew.

Dr. Leopold is getting the ambulance squad ready. The officers in command of the sappers, the anti-tank patrol and the telephone patrol have already studied the area and made a thorough reconnaissance of the German positions. Three volunteers from Janusz's company have been transferred to the sappers. Some women have also come up in order to get to know the sector, as they are to help when the people from the Old Town start arriving, so I have taken them out to the position at No. 5 in our street. Just at the moment some Junkers came over and dropped bombs, and No. 11 (a four-storeyed house) has collapsed and a soldier has been buried in the wreckage.

Night is falling. Korda and Stefan and their platoons are already in Grzybowska Street. Captain Zelazny has sent me over a platoon under Second-Lieutenant Danek, with a hand machine-gun. The officers in charge of platoons and their deputies are meeting in my billet in the ruins at No. 19 for a final word. Captain Rum has come, too, and his presence is encouraging. The well-trained parachutist from England and quick-witted and decisive officer is to stay here all night.

'Carry on, Lieutenant,' he said, taking a seat. 'I'm only here as an observer. If necessary, I'll co-ordinate action on the spot as Major Zagonczyk's deputy.'

The attack is to be launched at 1 a.m., and we have had time to talk over in detail our mission, the positions of our own men and of the Germans, as well as the actual carrying out of the attack, so that all contingencies have been foreseen. My place is with the men on the left flank, with the telephone patrol. I am confident in the men on the right flank; they know the terrain, and once they're across Krochmalna Street their task will be easier. In any case, Grzes can be relied on whatever happens. We shall have to keep in touch with one another by runners, and have arranged a code of single words, which are to indicate that the various stages of the attack have been successfully carried out—first the crossing of Krochmalna Street, then the capture of the covered market and penetration into Zimna Street.

11 p.m. Officers are going out to their men, giving brief instructions to the men in charge of sections and groups, and then, very quietly and cautiously, they lead their men forward into position.

Superstition forbids us to wish anyone luck.

'Hope you'll break a leg in those f—— ruins!'

Thursday, 31 August

All our preparations are over. The men, their weapons at the ready, grenades in their hands, the runners, the ambulance girls with stretchers, telephone operators with lengths of black cable, sappers with their mines—everyone is waiting for the signal, gazing out into the darkness at the vague outlines of the German positions and at the walls behind which, we know, the Germans are waiting.

Then at last a green flare goes up. The silence is shattered by an explosion, and a second later by another. The sappers have hurried out. A blinding flash and deafening roar echoes between the dead walls. Men running, shouting, cursing, single shots, everything is drowned in the crash of the explosions that follow.

Before I got out of the gateway, all the men had gone ahead. Stefan and his men had reached the other side of Krochmalna Street, and the flares the Germans were sending over lit the scene up as though it were daylight. A big gap in the walls a little to the left enabled a number of men to get through at the same time, while the rubble of the wall made it easier to climb up.

We made our way through the gap and into the ruins beyond. The first grenades began to burst behind us. There were no Germans. Somewhere in front a grenade exploded. Then I heard someone shouting my name. It was a young lad with a message from Janusz.

'Fortress!'

This meant they had got through.

We went ahead, into a yard where we could hear firing. Some of our men were lying on the ground, taking aim.

'Who are you firing at?'

'Germans—they're firing at us!'

'Where? Fire again! Can't you see? Your own bullets are rebounding from the wall. Come on!'

We reached the square beyond, which was divided from the covered market only by a low wall and a narrow side-street. A little group of men were lying at the gateway, taking cover in the face of fierce machine-gun fire. The bullets sprayed along the pavement.

'They're firing from the watch-tower!' called Stefan. 'We can't get through the gate, even though some of our lads have already got into the market.'

Korda then let me know that he'd reached Mirowski Square two houses farther east and had sent some of his men into the market itself. But he didn't think it would be possible to get through to the positions which he'd been instructed to take in the face of this machine-gun fire.

I had a glimpse of Korda as I ran along the south wall of the western market. Hell had burst loose inside. Shells and bullets were being fired and throwing up fragments of shrapnel from the skeleton of what had been the glass roof. By the light of flashes and sparks, we could see men running in all directions trying to find cover and looking for weapons. Two wounded men were lying at the entrance, but we couldn't get them away.

I hurried back to find Stefan. Nothing more had come in from Janusz, but I knew they must be in the square too. Maybe his runner had been killed.

Then seventeen-year-old Olga ran up from the direction of Krochmalna Street.

'Olga, what are you doing here?'

'I've brought a note—from Captain Rum.'

She was radiant with joy and pride.

The note said that Rum had just been told that we'd driven the Germans out of the market. To our right only a few of Janusz' and Grzes' platoon had crossed beyond Krochmalna Street. Janusz's men have had many losses. Jeremy has seized the police barracks and crossed Krochmalna Street, but was not able to get the Germans out of the watch-tower. Our attack in these sectors was to be renewed. In the meantime, I was to hold the market and wait for the flanks to come forward and level up the line of attack.

I scribbled a report under cover of one of the market stalls, by the light of an electric torch. In it, I asked for another machine-gun, as ours had jammed, more ammo, and at least a few shells for the anti-tank pistol. What matters most to us is that the firing from the watch-tower should cease.

Olga went off with my report. As we were not firing, the Germans also gradually lessened their fire. Time passed slowly. We could hear fighting farther away, and tried to make out what was going on. But there was total silence from the direction in which we'd expected the men from the Old Town to come. Meanwhile the sky grew grey over the Saxon Park. Dawn was coming.

Wanda managed to make her way through to us from our street, with the news from Captain Rum that all our attacks on the flanks have collapsed. Jeremy had had to withdraw from the police barracks. We would not get any arms or ammo, not to mention the machine-gun I asked for. There is no word from the Old Town, not a single man has broken out to our sector. I was to decide for myself whether we could hold out any longer in the Mirowski market.

It was growing lighter and the absence of any counter-attack from the Germans was beginning to puzzle me. I could understand that they would not take the risk in the darkness, but already it was quite light.

At 7 a.m. a runner came up from Alexander, to say that the Germans were taking the positions they had occupied yesterday in Krochmalna Street from Ciepla and Rynkowa Streets. They had brought several tanks into action, and the whole of Krochmalna Street was under fire from their machine-guns. We might be cut off and surrounded at any moment.

So we had to withdraw. Korda busied himself with the wounded, while I stayed behind with a group of men to provide cover.

At half-past seven we fired our last shots at the German positions and pulled out.

Krochmalna Street was crammed. The Germans were still holding out in their positions, which we had not been able to blow up. Olgierd was standing on the opposite side of the street, with his rifle; he leaned forward slightly from a gap in the wall, calmly took aim and fired; as the bullet hit the firing aperture of the nearest German bunker, a few of my lads darted across to the other side of the street.

'Good for him!' exclaimed one of the lads, indicating Olgierd. 'If he hadn't been there, half of our lads wouldn't have been able to get across.'

Stefan and Korda inspected their men; each had two or three wounded, but nobody had been killed.

Then someone said that there was still one wounded man in the little shop immediately opposite the German bunker. The only way into the shop was from the street, so we couldn't get in to him. I called up some of the sappers, who still had a little dynamite left. They eyed the wall, calculated rapidly, then placed the charge and exploded it. The ambulance girls were then able to get through the gap and bring the wounded man out without very much difficulty.

By eight o'clock I was back in our street, and reported to Captain Rum at No. 19. In the gateway I came face to face with Colonel Monter.

'Sir,' I said, 'I have to report that I've withdrawn my men from the Mirowski market, without completing our mission. I withdrew . . .'

'On whose orders?' Monter interrupted sharply. 'You wanted your morning coffee, I suppose.'

I felt the blood go to my head and bit my lower lip.

'Well, never mind. Thanks,' he went on.

He thrust out his hand and looked me straight in the eye. I could see anger and at the same time dejection in his look.

'By the way, you can call yourself captain now,' he added after a moment.

The ambulance girls were carrying wounded men past us on stretchers. They were stumbling from exhaustion. There was a dead officer and six wounded men in No. 30, and there were dead and wounded men lying here and there along Rynkowa Street, but they couldn't be brought in on account of the heavy fire.

'What a nightmare it's all been,' one girl whispered, wiping sweat from her face and trying to straighten her forage cap with blood-stained hands.

I tried to make out what had happened in our sector from fragments of what various people said. Jeremy and his men had been able to get hold of two machine-guns and some ammo during their first attack, but at dawn they'd had to retreat from beyond Krochmalna Street and quit the barracks for fear of being cut off by German tanks. He had two men killed and three badly wounded. Janusz and his men were mown down as they tried to break through Krochmalna Street from No. 13. Janusz himself and Sergeant Grzes were both seriously hurt and were taken unconscious to the hospital in Sliska Street. Marys and his fiancée Krysia, Corporal Marian and Czapla, Joe, Mrowka and Kazik were all killed.

Nobody could explain how all this happened. But one of the ambulance girls claimed she'd seen Janusz in our street, telling Monter that he was unable to get across Krochmalna Street. Then she heard Monter order him to go back immediately and attack. Iran saw Janusz just before he led his men in to this attack; he was worried, full of foreboding as though he knew that death was waiting for him.

German artillery and aircraft bothered us all day, preventing us from digging graves. A common grave had to be dug at No. 19.

Janusz and Grzes have both died in hospital.

I tried to snatch a few minutes' sleep without even taking off my helmet. German tanks were standing in our street and firing unceasingly at the façade on the Jarnuszkiewicz factory. And the factory building is already so damaged that it no longer provides any cover for my headquarters. Some of the German shells have smashed the archway of the gate over our heads.

Then the telephone girl on duty woke me. Captain Jerzewski had come in. He turned out to be very different from Proboszcz, his predecessor: direct in manner, he listens carefully to whatever is said to him, is quick in making decisions, so that he inspired trust and liking at once. This was the first visit he'd paid to my sector.

After questioning me about what happened last night, he told me that Monter has ordered my promotion to rank of captain, and that I am to take this rank without waiting for it to be published officially

But my first job as captain was very disagreeable. During my round of inspection I found one of the officers recently posted to my sector very drunk, staggering about and unable to utter a word. I relieved him of his command and had him sent back to Group Headquarters.

Friday, 1 September

The bodies of the dead from Rynkowa Street have had to be brought in under cover of darkness and under fire from the Germans. The bodies of men from other units were to have been brought in by their comrades, who came over to our street specially to do this; but my lads and ambulance girls couldn't just stand by and watch. I couldn't say for sure which was more important: the dead bodies or the weapons they had on them. Anyway, it was always the weapon which my men brought back first. Maybe there was some sense in this, for a corpse on the pavement can at least provide a crawling man with cover against bullets.

Many of the bodies were unrecognisable, charred by flames. We buried them in the yard of No. 5 in our street.

There's a rumour about to the effect that one unit was able to break through from the Old Town last night, but nobody knows anything certain. We listened to the news rather doubtfully, the more so as we'd have heard something of the fighting from that direction.

Captain Jerzewski looked in again this morning, with unwelcome news. Captain Hal is to take over all my sector from Rynkowa Street to Walicow Street, while my men and I are to withdraw to the west beyond Walicow Street.

I tried to protest.

'We've been here since the very beginning! It's like being thrown out of your own home.'

'I can sympathise,' Jerzewski replied, 'but it's the only solution to the administrative chaos we're all in. Nobody knows who is responsible to whom and for what. From today you won't come under Captain Hal's orders, even technically.'

Fortunately I know my new sector well. It is probably one of the most difficult sectors of all to hold, particularly now that the Germans have consolidated their positions in the ruins of the Haberbusch brewery. There will be Germans to the north and west of us, though we shall not have a single strong position for defence. The Haberbusch warehouse, in Ceglana Street, is to remain in what is now Hal's sector. After their losses last night, the group that was formerly Janusz's is now very short of men, while Grzes' unit hardly exists any longer. Only one of the officers transferred to my sector a couple of weeks ago is left, while the only unit which is up to full strength is that of Alexander.

'I'll see that you get reinforcements,' Jerzewski promised. 'You can then deploy them as you think best.'

In addition, Captain Hal now claims that all his men are in the front line, so that he hasn't a single man to help relieve Alexander's company until my men have occupied the western end of our street. So to begin with I had to take out what was left of Janusz's company into the new sector.

I found these men in Twarda Street in a state bordering on revolt. Following the death of their leaders and over thirty of their comrades in the course of a single night, they are now embittered and discouraged. The only officer of this company still alive, Second-Lieutenant Iran, though intelligent and brave, has not been able to enforce any discipline. His efforts to persuade them had no effect, nor did threats. The main topic of their excited argument was 'who is to blame for the defeat?—Grzes or Janusz? But they're both dead. So was it the sappers, or Monter, or General Bor?'

FRIDAY, I SEPTEMBER   137

Cadet Hrabia, who had taken over after Grzes' death, gave me a list of the men who had 'deserted' from one platoon alone: it contained eight names.

'We can't call them deserters yet,' I said, to calm down Hrabia.
'Why not?'

'Better put down that they've gone of their own accord. After all, we don't know where they've gone and what they're doing. They may come back. Besides, we've taken on people from other sectors without getting permission from their previous commanding officers. Some of them have turned out to be fine soldiers. Let's just forget about those who've gone and concern ourselves with those who are still here.'

'All right, but I still want to find Rifleman Czarny—he's gone off with a Sten-gun.'

After a short conference with Second-Lieutenant Iran and Sergeant Hem, I ordered the men to fall in. Then I told them that as Janusz is dead, I myself was taking command of his company as from today. Second-Lieutenant Iran was to be my deputy and Sergeant Hem was to continue as senior N.C.O. I then put cadets Olszyna and Dabrowa in command of the two platoons. Hrabia took over the assault group formerly led by Grzes.

I looked at my watch.

'In an hour from now,' I went on, 'you will take up positions in the sector between Zelazna, Grzybowska, Wronia and Lucka Streets. You have an hour to get ready. But no man need stay in the company unless he wants to. Anyone who doesn't want to stay can go—now.'

An hour later the company was ready. Not another man had gone. Then, clambering over the ruins, we set off in single file, across what used to be Panska and Sliska Streets, until we reached Walicow Street. Then we cut across behind what was left of the barricades, which gave some cover from the German tanks less than a hundred yards away.

When we reached our destination, we found a company of men already there. It appeared that the Germans in this sector are now holding both sides of Grzybowska Street. In Wronia Street the distance between our positions and the Germans amounts in some places to only a few dozen yards.

We relieved the company from their position and they went off, to relieve Alexander and his men in Rynkowa and Krochmalna Streets. I still had to man the sector between Zelazna and Walicow Streets, where the Germans are only holding the north side of Grzybowska Street. One strong position here will have to suffice, based on the Makowski factory building at No. 16, Ceglana Street. In the yard of this building I came on the grave of Lieutenant Goliath.

On the opposite side of Ceglana Street was the desert landscape of the 'Little Ghetto' razed to the ground. And yet beyond this landscape I saw four almost undamaged four-storey blocks of flats still standing, and we could see the sunlight reflected in the glass of some unbroken window-panes.

A hefty, sun-burned man of about fifty was standing in the gateway of one of these blocks. He introduced himself to me as Tabaczkiewicz—a Regular N.C.O.

'As I've got a bad hand and can't use a gun, I've taken on the job of air-raid warden for this region and also intelligence officer for the district.'

I tried to interrupt, but he went on, unruffled,

'My job is also to keep down looters and people of German sympathies, who act in a hostile way towards the Insurrection. I am in constant contact with all military authorities in the entire area. When I was a lad at school, I ran away from home to join the Polish Legion and ever since I've been working for my country. . . .'

'You can tell me all this some other time,' I broke in again. 'Now, please try to find me a suitable billet for the H.Q. of the sector and my men.'

'There are no empty rooms in this area, but all the flats are at the disposal of the Polish forces. The people living in these houses will be pleased to have you as their guests. . . .'

'Where can we find a billet?'

'The best will be No. 65. I'll give you a billeting order.'

'What number is this one here? 69? I think we'll take this block, and I'll install my H.Q. on the ground floor.'

'But. . . .'

'I shall also want billets for a platoon of my men.'

'The civilians will be glad to remove their furniture.'

'Thank you, Mr. Tabaczkiewicz. I'll be back within a couple of hours and hope to find everything in order. Good-bye!'

Saturday, 2 September

So it was true, after all! Sixty men, under Lieutenant Jerzy, were able to break out of the Old Town and reach the City Centre nearly twelve hours later. But by this time no one expected them any longer and our men fired on them. And to think that only sixty men have managed to break through—when 6,000 were expected.

People from beyond Marszalkowska Street are saying that small groups of the defenders of the Old Town have been able to reach our side of Warsaw via the sewers. They look terrible, and what they have to say makes the last days of the defence of the Old Town and the withdrawal sound like scenes from hell. Down there in the sewers they have been making their way along in the darkness and stench, with open wounds, stumbling over the bodies of the men in front, exhausted from hunger and thirst and deafened by hand-grenades thrown into the sewers from above. No one yet knows how many have got through—or how many are still down there.

Many of my men are asking for leave, as they want to try to find friends and relations among the men from the Old Town, but I can only let one man from each platoon go.

For some reason the Germans have not yet made any attempts at large-scale action in response to our attacks on the Mirowski market, but they seem to be strengthening their defences against any further attacks from our side. They have been laying mines carefully and putting up a still stronger defence line of bunkers and barbed-wire. Alexander has been able to occupy a position at

No. 16, Ceglana Street, and after establishing firing-posts and sentries along the street, he has sent the rest of his lads out to dig deeper anti-tank ditches beyond the barricade in Zelazna Street. This is our only link with No. 5 Company, and so we have decided to dig a tunnel under this street as well.

I didn't really expect to get much help from Mr. Tabaczkiewicz, but I was mistaken, as he got all the billets ready and then asked for further instructions. I told him to find a suitable billet in the building for a first-aid post and to collect volunteers for digging the tunnel and a well. The volunteers will be paid for their work, either in food or supplies.

I went into the yard to inspect the reinforcements sent to me by Captain Jerzerski. They are young lads, but that is all to the good.

Then, in a corner of the yard, I saw a little group of civilians gathering. They were very disturbed by the news that Zygmunt's Column, in Castle Square, has fallen down.

'It's seen so many wars and occupations,' one of the men said mournfully. 'Warsaw isn't the same without Zygmunt's Column.'

'Never mind,' said the caretaker of the house. 'That's nothing to shed tears over. I'm sorrier for the lads—and besides we'll put up a lovely new column. And the Chopin Monument will be put up again too. . . . But the Germans will never rebuild their Goth's Line in Italy, which our allies have smashed. . . .'

Sunday, 3 September

         The sky is covered with heavy clouds and long-awaited rain has at last started to fall. There are no German aircraft to be seen, and the fires are dying down; the ruins smell less foul. Even Hitler's faithful allies—the flies—have stopped attacking us and our saucepans, and have taken refuge in cracks and holes best known to themselves. Only the German mortars continue to throw over their shells in series of six at a time.

We've still got plenty of good new bread from our own bake-house, much to the dismay of the ambulance girls, who try in vain to keep it out of the hands of the men suffering from dysentery. Common sense doesn't enter into it when a man wants to satisfy his hunger or thirst, and to make matters worse the latrines which have been put up beyond the dividing wall of a block of flats which we occupy are only protected from the rain by a sheet of metal, and the wooden walls contain an increasing number of gaps and spaces as a result of German shells. Consequently, even the most sanitary-minded of us are inclined to use less comfortable but safer places.

Tabaczkiewicz has made himself very useful in finding and arranging more billets for the lads, but he has not managed to get together enough civilians to undertake the essential digging of a tunnel and well. Of the men who were tempted by the prospect of getting some of our rations and who started work, only about half were still there a few hours later. Tabaczkiewicz is very sore about this 'decline in civic responsibility' among his fellow-countrymen, and has suggested that we should improve it by force, quoting an order concerning the duties of civilians towards the army.

'No, we won't try that—it's the line of least resistance,' I replied. 'These people have got to understand that the tunnel and the well are as necessary to them as to us.'

'They *do* understand that!'

'Then let's go and talk to them.'

Tabaczkiewicz took me down into the cellars. At first I could only make out the feeble little flames of some oil-lamps. Then faces began to emerge from the obscurity, and a line of daylight from the half-open door let me distinguish two old ladies, squatting on an upturned bale and fingering rosaries in dry old hands as they muttered prayers.

'How long have you been here?' I asked them.

They gazed at me with dull, dim old eyes and said nothing.

Tabaczkiewicz repeated my question.

'Who? Us? This makes it the fifth Sunday, sir. . . .'

'Have you anything to eat?'

'Good people won't let us die, and the Lord Jesus is merciful. . . .'
They went back to their prayers.

In one corner I saw a piano and plush sofa, on which four kids
were scrambling about, while a woman, bending over a little
iron stove, was frying something in a pan. A full-blown aspidistra
plant was wilting in a big flower-pot on top of a heavy chest. Beyond, four men were playing cards by the light of a flickering
tallow candle.

'So you weren't able to dig the tunnel under Zelazna Street?'
I asked them at a venture.

They didn't stop their game.

'Nor a well, either? And yet the air-raids have stopped.'

They behaved as though my questions didn't concern them.

'Hey you, it's you I'm talking to—not the walls,' I went on,
going closer to their improvised table on a wooden box.

'Nothing doing. . . .' muttered a big youth, with tousled hair.

'What do you mean? Everyone wants water.'

'That's just it! They'll all drink it, so why shouldn't everyone
dig the well? We've been digging five hours while the others
have been doing nothing but picking their noses. What do you
take us for?'

'If everyone talked like that there'd never be a well. My lads
could talk like that too—they could say, "We won't man the
barricades unless everyone does!" '

'Well, so what? Nobody would take me when I volunteered.
Five years ago, in September 1939, I went from one H.Q. to
another, and it was the same this August. If they don't want me,
all right—I'm not going to go on asking.'

'I don't know where you tried to volunteer, but you hit on the
wrong places. I took on everyone.'

'That's easily said.'

'And I still do.'

Silence. The players had paused in the game and were eyeing
me searchingly.

'Are you pulling my leg?'

'No. I'll take any man.'

'Into the army?'

'Yes.'   .

'Well, in that case . . .' said one of the men, 'why didn't you
tell us that at the beginning instead of carrying on about the well?'

'Let's go,' said the youngest.

'Not like this,' said his companion. 'You'd better shave and
have a wash first.'

So I 'acquired' seven more soldiers, and I hadn't finished
issuing them with identity papers when an eighth appeared. He
was a hefty, blue-eyed, middle-aged man with a low forehead,
high cheekbones and heavy jaw. He asked, in broken Polish, to
talk to me in private, so I took him out to an empty shop intended
for the battalion armoury.

'You—Russian?' I guessed.

Then, recalling a Russian phrase, I asked him to sit down and
indicated a bench.

He sat down and looked at me searchingly before coming to
the point. His name was Buzunov, and he was a captain in the
Red Army. As officer in command of a rifle battalion at Stalin-
grad, he was seriously wounded and taken prisoner by the
Germans, who transferred him from one hospital to another,
each time farther west. Then, somewhere near Ploskirov, Soviet
aircraft bombed two German motorised transport columns, one
of which was carrying wounded prisoners-of-war, while the
other was bringing civilians from Russia for slave labour in
German factories. There were a great many casualties. Buzunov
was wounded again. The drivers, Ukrainians, all knew the fate
that was awaiting the Soviet prisoners-of-war and managed to
transfer Buzunov and a few of his companions to the civilian
column and had taken an equal number of dead bodies to replace
them. Buzunov had then gone on as a wounded civilian 'volunteer' to work in the Reich. When his wounds healed, he worked
in an arms factory in Lower Silesia, and had later been transferred
to another factory in Warsaw. When the Germans pulled out, he
had got away and hidden himself among the Poles.

And now he was sitting there before me, and neither of us

spoke for a minute or two. I had no intention of cross-questioning him in order to find out whether his story was true. It may well have been a lie. All the same, I should have liked to know why he'd come to me and why he'd told me all this. I couldn't make out whether he wanted to clear himself of any suspicion or whether he wanted my help.

It was as though Buzunov guessed what I was thinking. He said that at first he was suspicious of the 'Home Army', and merely watched the fighting from the background. Then gradually his doubts gave way to sympathy and admiration, and he'd helped build anti-tank traps, had given advice to men less experienced than himself in street fighting, he'd watched for saboteurs who shoot insurgents in the back. Then he'd seen Soviet soldiers serving with my men and wearing the red-and-white arm-bands of the Home Army. He'd talked to them.

At once the thought flashed through my mind that he'd insist on the Caucasians taking off their Home Army arm-bands and being placed under his command.

He rose to his feet, straightened his jacket and stood to attention, telling me that he was now under my command and ready for orders.

Monday, 4 September

We've been under artillery fire from dawn to dusk, and there can be no doubt that the Germans have decided systematically to wipe out our entire sector. Most damage is caused by a heavy cannon which has been brought into position on the circle railway line, in Wola. It fires twenty-two-inch shells, and they come over regularly, every five minutes. You can see them coming over, flying fast over the ruins from beyond Zelazna Street. Then, a fraction of a second later, they disappear from sight and only the terrifying shriek overhead shows that the danger has passed—the shell has gone over. Then, when you look in that direction, you can see the shell falling on to the roof-tops in Sliska or Sienna Streets.

Each explosion means the destruction of part of some as yet undamaged house, the ploughing-up of some dozen cubic yards of rubble or another great gap in one of the streets. Sometimes they mean dead and wounded. It is just as well that the shells only explode when the fuse is hit and so often fail to go off. Three such unexploded shells have just fallen near our billet, and a sapper patrol assisted by German prisoners-of-war has come to remove them. I recognised a couple of the engineers we took prisoner on 1 August in the Dering fuse-factory.

The Germans apparently don't place much faith in the aim of their 'Big Bertha', since the shells never fall in our lines, and this, we think, must mean that the Germans are afraid of the shells landing close to their own positions. Not one shell has fallen in Ceglana Street, nor to the west of Zelazna Street. The civilians have noticed this too, and whole families with their belongings are now moving closer and closer to the front-line positions. Some hundred families have found refuge in the big cellars of the Makowski factory, the entrance to which is at No. 16, Ceglana Street. These cellars continue underground as far as Grzybowska Street and are crammed with boxes and barrels, mostly empty, though some contain fruit-juice, syrup, preserved cabbage, dried fruit and vegetables.

Cadet Roman thinks the civilians should be evacuated from these cellars. If the Germans were to capture our position in Ceglana Street, then the civilians would be in danger, for they couldn't be evacuated during fighting. It was difficult to know what to do, but I didn't share his doubts about our ability to hold out in this sector. The men here haven't taken part in any serious offensive action, but they have shown themselves to be reliable in defence, and haven't surrendered a single barricade, even during the worst fighting. So I gave instructions that every-one was to stay in the cellars, so that they can at least have the benefit of the dry and extensive shelters and can also make use of the supplies there. But sentries will have to make sure that noth-ing is taken away without my permission.

Meanwhile, the German attack on our lines is building up. I

issued orders that our fortifications should be strengthened, trenches dug deeper along the barricades and firing positions made of paving-stones should be replaced by sandbags, which are more reliable and don't cause bullets to ricochet.

We must also dig trenches from the ruins of the 'Little Ghetto' to our billets in Panska Street, for it is dangerous to cross the open street. Clearly the Germans already know that we've moved our headquarters, for their machine-guns and grenades now fire from the bunkers in Towarowa Street as soon as anyone appears in the street.

A civilian was waiting for me in the gateway of the head-quarters.

'May I speak to you?' he began.

'What is it?'

'I've heard that you have no chaplain in your battalion.'

'No, I haven't. Still, what's that to do with you? Let the clergy worry about it.'

'As a matter of fact, they've sent me here. I'm Father Oracz.'

I looked at him more closely. He was perhaps a little over thirty, lean, not tall, wearing a threadbare grey suit and down-at-heel boots. He looked like an 'intellectual', one of the people you see in lawyers' offices or behind the counter in a book-shop. It was not until this moment that I noticed the small metal cross in his buttonhole.

'So you'd like to be our chaplain? Well, I ought to warn you that you won't find much to do here. My men are of all kinds of nationality and faith. The Poles here are mostly ordinary local working men, who don't much like "devil-dodgers", and besides, nearly everyone is out in the line all the time. There's plenty of work and no one has time for saying prayers.'

'All the same, I'd like to stay. If you've so much work to do, then you can surely find some for me too.'

This startled me. I'd expected him to ask for a room to use as his chapel, for the men to be marched in for confession and services, and yet here he was asking for work. Then I noticed his lively, sincere eyes, full of expression.

'In that case, all right. First of all, I'd like you to take over all the papers and other things left by people who've been killed—my aide, Lieutenant Wislanski, will let you have them. You may be able to unearth their real names or find their next-of-kin. It would be useful, too, if you could make a note of the names and graves of those who've been killed, for many of them have disappeared without trace—either killed by shells or buried in the ruins.'

I then told the runner on duty to ask Tabaczkiewicz to find a billet for the priest.

Alexander and I called in Maria and Alicia, as I must transfer them from No. 4 Company to the battalion first-aid post. Zofia is not badly wounded, but she won't be able to report back for duty for a time. It has now been confirmed that Kasia, whose illness a week or two ago was diagnosed by Dr. Leopold as a 'subconscious flight from reality into illness', has in fact got typhoid fever.

Wounded men from the Old Town now almost fill our battalion hospital in Zlota Street, so that we have nowhere to send our own wounded. Thus we must try to fix up a field hospital of our own on the spot, in Panska Street. The first cases of typhoid have presented us with another problem, as they should be kept in isolation and if possible out of the sight of the civilians, for fear of starting a panic.

But Maria and Alicia both begged me to keep them in Alexander's company, where they feel at home and know they are useful and necessary. Besides, they dread more misunderstandings with Dr. Leopold. I saw their point, and was grateful for their loyalty but could not alter my decision.

A few minutes later, a delegation from No. 4 Company appeared, consisting of Olgierd, Oscar and Jerzy, to protest against the transfer of Maria and Alicia to the battalion first-aid post. But a protest of this kind is most improper; it was almost a mutiny. All the same, I couldn't bring myself to enforce military disci-

pline, the more so as none of the youthful 'delegates' had ever
been in the Regular Army and consequently didn't realise how
improperly they were behaving. So I pointed this out to them,
and at the same time explained why I'd made this decision; then
asked them what they'd have done in my place.

'We'd have transferred them both to the battalion,' they replied, after only a momentary hesitation.

'Very well, now go back and tell your comrades that. And in
future I think it would be better for all of us if you came and
talked things over with me before you decide to make any more
collective protests.'

Now it is my turn to have dysentery. Even vodka mixed with
pepper doesn't help. My legs keep giving way under me, and
coloured specks float before my eyes.

Tuesday, 5 September

Five weeks have passed since we
began fighting. Now the sixth has begun—surely the last. The
newspapers today report the liberation of Brussels, Antwerp,
Metz and Nancy, while the Allied armies in Alsace and Belgium
have reached the pre-war frontiers of the Reich. The Red Army
has started an offensive to the north-east of Warsaw. Captain
Buzunov, who is still waiting for some decision to be made about
him, sits by the wireless set nearly all the time listening to news
bulletins from Moscow. He says that the Soviet Army have
occupied over 150 places in the basin of the Rivers Bug and
Narew in the last two days.

'And they'll be here the day after tomorrow!'

But the doorman prefers listening to the news from London.
This morning he brought us the news that the Allies have captured Breda, in Holland, and Saarbrucken. Soviet aircraft are
supposed to have been seen over Warsaw. Nobody actually saw
them over our sector, but German anti-aircraft guns were heard.

Captain Jerzewski has not forgotten us. He keeps sending over
a few men at a time as reinforcements and replacements, and to-

day he even sent me two officers, Lieutenants Adam and Starry. Both are over forty and say they were business-men in civilian life. But the likeness ends there, for Adam is short, with a grizzled beard and walks about like a fighting-cock. His restless eyes, with an irritable look, reveal a tendency to cruelty. Lieutenant Starry is a tall, carefully shaved, fair-haired man, lean and with the look of a sheep, who cannot conceal under a military attitude his eagerness to be liked.

I have sent Adam to No. 5 Company, but have kept Starry for the time being at my headquarters, as I am afraid that Alexander may break up at any time. He says nothing, but is clearly using up the last of his strength. All I hope is that it isn't typhoid.

Wislanski brought in a lad.

'This kid says he wants to talk to you, sir. I asked him what he wants, but he insists he'll only speak to you.'

The lad was perhaps twelve years old, not more. He stood in the doorway, fidgeting with a grubby cap.

'Come over here. What is it you want to tell me, sonny?'

The kid looked up anxiously at the window, then stubbornly stared at the wall, silent.

'Speak up, there's nothing to be afraid of.'

'I . . . I want to join the army, sir.'

'Join the army? How old are you?'

'Thirteen. I'll be fourteen next year. And your men told me there was another boy in your unit who was only eleven and was killed. I'm much older than him.'

'Haven't you any family? Where are they?'

'Father is in the army, only I don't know where. He never said. And mother is here, she's waiting outside.'

'Does she know why you've come here?'

'Of course she does!'

'Well, ask her to come in. I can't take you without her permission.'

'I'll go and get her.'

He ran out cheerfully, and a moment later brought back a still young, though tired-looking, woman.

'Are you this lad's mother? Please sit down. He wants to join the army.'

'That's what I'd like, sir. I can't look after him at home, he's always going off somewhere for hours at a time, and besides, I've no food for him. He'll be fed in the army and learn proper manners. Everyone says your lads are fair, so he won't be put upon. And I won't be so worried about him.'

'Don't you think he's a bit young?'

'He's not very big, I know—but he's a good boy, he's quick and bright. He can learn quick too.'

'All right, you can leave him with us. Do you live far away?'

'No, very close by, in Sienna Street.'

'Then I'll send him home every day. What's your name, sonny?'

'Pataszon—that's what they called me in the Underground.'

'Well, listen to me, Pataszon. You're going to be a runner for H.Q., and you mustn't go anywhere until I tell you. You'll get a uniform, arm-band and papers.'

'And a belt? I want a belt too.'

'All right, you shall have a belt.'

'Two belts—one for Miki.'

'Who's he?'

'My pal. He's waiting outside too. I'll bring him in.'

'Just a minute, Pataszon, now, tell me the truth. How many of you are there?'

'Only the two of us, honest! And he's brought his mum along too.'

Miki turned out to be even smaller than Pataszon, though they were both the same age. Then, armed with a note to Henio, they both ran off happily to the stores in Sliska Street, to get themselves uniforms and belts.

There was an air-raid after lunch. Three Stukas dived one after another on our billets in Panska Street, and a bomb hit No. 65— the very place Tabaczkiewicz had suggested to me as our headquarters. Other bombs have fallen in the ruins between the sawmill and Twarda Street, opening up a convenient way through from the mill to the end of Sliska Street. Fortunately there were no casualties, but the people living in the blocks of flats there are worried. They claim that the air-raid was the result of our moving in, and that the Germans will repeat the raids until all four of the hitherto undamaged blocks of flats are razed to the ground.

So the people living in these houses are moving all their belongings down into the basements, though Wislanski says that the soldiers, on the other hand, are still more firmly convinced that no one will get killed where I am. They have moved into more comfortable flats, now vacated by their tenants, on the first floor. It looks as though Alexander shares this belief too, for he has brought his wife and their baby over from Grzybowska Street. He thinks they'll be safer here.

Wednesday, 6 September

I have heard that a Frenchman is fighting in my sector. He does not belong to any particular unit as he doesn't like people giving him orders. So he just joins in when men are going out on patrol or turns up wherever the enemy is attacking most strongly, and at night he goes by himself into the ruins. He wears a red-and-white arm-band and a tricolour in his cap, and has his own rifle, with which he is a good shot. The lads think he is crazy and say he's looking for death, but they like his courage and his friendliness when they talk, mainly by means of gestures.

One day Tadeusz and I calculated how many religions and nationalities there are in our battalion. We have Catholics, Greek Orthodox, Lutherans, Calvinists, Hebrews, Moslems—Poles, Jews, Ukrainians, White Russians, Russians, Georgians, Armenians, Azerbaidjanis, Daghestanis, Spaniards—and now a Frenchman. In other sectors, on our side, there are Englishmen, Dutch, Czechs.

Dysentery is spreading fast. Nearly everyone has it at the same time, but in the main it is not serious. Yesterday I did not go up into the line for the first time since the beginning of the fighting.

Today I feel a little better, but Alexander has had to take to his bed. Krysia, the telephone girl, had to be taken from the headquarters office almost by force, as she refused to go sick. The number of people who are seriously ill and not fit for any duties is about fifty. The rest of us still on duty are weak and irritable, and it is increasingly difficult to find anyone to carry on with essential jobs. Digging has stopped altogether.

I realise very well that the prompt digging of a well and tunnel under Zelazna Street are just as important for the defence of our sector as the endurance of the men in the line. The only well in this area, in the ruins of the 'Little Ghetto', is running dry, and drawing water from it not only takes a long time but also means more casualties. I can't help wondering what will happen to us should a shell from the 'Big Bertha' bury the well.

The tunnel under Zelazna Street is essential, both as a link between the companies across this street and to everyone in the centre of Warsaw. I have now been instructed to occupy the mill in Prosta Street, which has been guarded up to now by a group of men from the first battalion, under Captain Zelazny. The Quartermaster is interested in this mill because of the flour stored there.

So I told off three men under Sergeant Premier to occupy this mill, and instructed them to see how much flour there was. However, this proved to be impossible, as it would have meant going over thousands of sacks which are scattered all over the place. It was clear at first glance that there were hundreds of tons of flour in the place. Surely someone in the starving city must have known this! Then they explained that it was kept a secret to avoid confusion in the immediate neighbourhood of our positions.

Now the Area Quartermaster wants this treasure looked after and issued only against special forms provided by him. This reminded me of similar orders issued during the first days of August.

'Let them fill in forms if they have to,' I told Jerzewski, 'but the main thing is to get the flour away and shared out before it catches fire. Besides, we can't be sure that the Germans won't occupy the place,' I added finally.

However, I myself was quite happy about all this, for despite the continually increasing enemy pressure, I have the utmost faith in my men and know that they will not yield a foot to the Germans.

However, I'm not so happy about the position in other sectors. News has come in that our rebel units are withdrawing along the banks of the Vistula, while refugees from that area have been telling everyone that further fighting is impossible. Fierce bombing in the City Centre has led to the risk of panic spreading, quite apart from the destruction and casualties it causes.

It has become increasingly difficult to distinguish between truth and lies, since all rumours seem to contain a grain of truth.

Someone has said that the Commander-in-Chief of the Home Army, General Bor, and his Chief of Staff, Colonel Grzegorz, were killed the day before yesterday in an air-raid on the Savings Bank building in Jasna Street. I checked on this and was able to deny it. Not, however, that many people believed me.

'Just as we said,' they whispered. 'They won't tell the truth. Besides, has anyone actually *seen* Bor?'

And in fact I still don't know, even today, who Bor is, and I haven't any idea what he looks like.

Thursday, 7 September

I don't know what has become of our young chaplain, as I haven't set eyes on him since he joined our battalion. Perhaps it was too hot for him here, or perhaps he's been saying his prayers in a cellar somewhere. Wislanski said that he doesn't think so, for no one has yet seen him at his prayers, and he only comes into the battalion office from time to time, when someone has been killed. He's never in his billet. At night he goes off somewhere and doesn't come back till morning. He's an odd man altogether.

Alexander is still sick. It is only now that I am beginning to realise what a lucky chance it was for me that he was here at the outbreak of the Insurrection. Now I'd feel almost lost without him, even though Tadeusz is very conscientious and Wislanski tries to protect me from dozens of minor problems—but Alexander used to cope with everything without bothering me. I'm only now finding out about all the squabbles which took place in the past and which seem to be more and more frequent just now.

So far today has been nothing but a chapter of accidents. It started with the petrol. We didn't bring the stores of petrol with us when we left Grzybowska Street, and they said at the time that we'd be able to collect more from the military police store when we wanted it. But the lads I sent over, with a chit, have been sent back with a note to the effect that petrol can only be had if it is paid for. Admittedly, Janusz used to pay for rifles with butter, but it is unthinkable to have to *pay* for the petrol for our home-made petrol-bottles. So I went over there myself, with an armed patrol, feeling very fierce, and the M.P.s tried to make out that it was all a joke, helped us to fill up barrels and hinted that they'd like a piece of meat from the horse we killed today.

Then there was a squabble over this horse, the last from the Fischer racing stable. Naturally this was about sharing it out. Then there was almost a pitched battle at the well, due to people not taking their turn to draw water. Adam has hit a civilian in Ceglana Street, and I can't make out what happened nor who is to blame. All we know is that both were tight. After an unpleasant interview I transferred Adam to No. 5 Company.

What I dislike most of all is interrogating any people my lads have arrested. Their mania for seeing a spy or saboteur or looter in any passer-by has fortunately decreased, but someone is always reporting someone else for something. It would be simpler to pass matters like this straight on to the Security authorities, but none of us have very much respect for the Security, and misunderstandings, which happen easily enough, might well lead to even my best friend being arrested. I gave instructions for anyone arrested to be taken first of all to the battalion headquarters, and I now find myself faced with them all.

For instance, there was a painted creature who swayed her hips coquettishly as she came through the door, and who sat down with one leg over the other so as to show her knees. According to her neighbours, Germans used to visit her night after night, and they even brought her a suite of furniture from the Jewish quarter. Then there was a spiv caught supplying the soldiers with spirits, and an elderly gentleman, who looks like a respectable shop-keeper, was accused of threatening people that he'll 'show them who's who when the Bolsheviks arrive'.

What was I to do with them all? To begin with, I dismissed their escorts, saying that we'd deal with them ourselves: then, after a brief sermon, I sent them all away, telling them not to let themselves be caught again by any of us. I have only sent one of them on to be dealt with by higher authority: someone recognised him as a German even though he spoke perfect Polish. The fact that he had a German surname meant nothing. All the same, the name was familiar to me.

'Please turn out your pockets. Put everything on the desk here.'

Starry helped go through his wallet. Then we found a photograph of a family group, with a young man in Luftwaffe uniform.

'Is he your son?'

'Yes.'

'A father isn't necessarily responsible for what his sons do. All the same, it looks bad. You're a Pole and yet your son is a German.'

Starry read a letter in German.

'It only deals with family matters,' he said. 'It's from his brother, in Ostrowiec.'

Then, all at once, I knew why his name was familiar. Barbara was born in Ostrowiec and has relations there. I'd stayed with them several times.

'This is rather bad luck for you,' I told him slowly. 'The trouble is that your brother was one of the Gestapo heads in Ostrowiec. Haven't you ever heard of the public executions that took place in the market-place in Ostrowiec, when the Germans hanged innocent people they'd taken as hostages?'

He was silent. I went on after a pause:

'You're not responsible for what your brother does either,
however. You may be a good Pole as you claim . . . but I'll have
to leave it to others to decide.'

The fighting in our sector is intensifying day by day, even
hour by hour. Yet it's difficult to call it 'fighting', since all it
amounts to is that the soldiers on both sides have taken cover in
heaps of rubble and remain there almost motionless, unable to
show even their tin hats. On our side, this is often nothing more
than hanging on in the face of increasingly heavy attacks, and
sometimes when the Germans see no signs of life at all on our side
they will throw a unit in to attack, only to withdraw immediately
in the face of the noise and dust raised by our infallible home-
made grenades.

But the men left out there must be assured that God and their
fellows have not forgotten them. I attach a good deal of importance to frequent visits by company commanders and N.C.O.s,
both when fighting is going on and also regularly, to the lads in
holes and bunkers. I myself try to inspect the entire sector twice
a day, usually in the company of an officer from Region or
District Headquarters, or one of the reporters who often visit my
sector for news. The reporters are cheerful and courageous and
act like well-trained soldiers when we're in the line and they
always find something to say to the lads.

The lads themselves grin whenever they report,

'Everything's under control, sir.'

Then they show me the little improvements and comforts
they've been able to make in their burrows, such as a new and
carefully concealed firing-post, or they tell me what happened to
a dead body that's still lying out a little farther away, as yet unburied, and point out the way for me to go on. In a good many
places we have to talk in a whisper, and the way to some of our
positions leads among tottering walls and arches, while others can
only be reached by crawling along shallow trenches and yet
others must be gained by getting across several yards of open

ground. But everything here is foreseeable, surprises just don't occur. There are no long minutes of waiting for the next bomb or shell to fall as there are in the rear positions, a few hundred yards farther back.

Nearly all the lads now have helmets, though some are very odd. You find German, Polish, Russian crash-helmets, even sun-helmets. They're not used for protection against shells or shrapnel, but against falling cinders and bricks and for protecting the head against low rafters, or in narrow tunnels and holes in walls.

We haven't seen a copy of the 'News Bulletin' today. Apparently the printing-press has been bombed. So the lack of any reliable news is causing some concern about the defeat of our comrades on the Vistula embankment. We know that the Germans have occupied three streets there.

And against the leaden sky over the entire City Centre great bursts of smoke continued to well up time and time again.

Friday, 8 September

                                I'd hoped that I'd be able to get five hours' sleep during the night. What a hope, though! Just after midnight Stefa, a girl reporter attached to Area Headquarters, woke me up. Heaven knows why she chose to visit our sector at this time of night, and to ask me the same tedious questions and get the same answers:

'What's going on?'

'Same as usual.'

'Have the Germans been attacking?'

'Yes.'

'Anyone killed or wounded?'

'Yes.'

'How many?'

'Have a look at my report.'

Tonight I'd have sworn at her for waking me up just after I'd dropped off if she hadn't looked so charmingly young and attractive. Instead, I took the opportunity of asking her for news

of other sectors. The Insurgents have now withdrawn entirely
from the Powisle district, and the spirits of the people of Warsaw,
without light, water, food or medical aid, are low. Representatives of some political parties and the civilian authorities have
demanded a parley with the Germans to save the rest of the town
and the townsfolk. But General Monter, commanding officer
of the area, has turned down the idea. In the end it has been
agreed that civilians are to evacuate Warsaw this afternoon, and
an agreement to this effect has been signed by delegates of the
Polish Red Cross and the Germans.

An order is to be issued by our military authorities for the
evacuation of women, children, old people and the sick—at their
own risk. Fit men are to stay behind.

I'd only just dropped off again after Stefa's departure, when the
telephone girl Kula shook my arm. Captain Zelazny had told her
to wake me.

'Can you come over here right away?' he asked.

'What is it?'

'Something very serious and urgent has arisen, which puts
both you and us in danger.'

'Do you want help?'

'In a way—well, yes, we do.'

'Shall I bring some of the lads with me?'

'They may be useful, but don't wait for them.'

I gave orders for a reserve platoon to be woken and prepare for
moving off. I took Olgierd, who as usual was ready, with me. It
was not far to Zelazny's headquarters, and his sentry showed me
the way upstairs. It was easy to find his room on account of the
noise from within. Inside, over a dozen officers broke off a noisy
conversation. Then I saw that Zelazny was very pale and his
hands were trembling.

'Some of these gentlemen think that we ought to take our
units across to the southern sector of the City Centre,' he told me
when we'd shaken hands. 'They say that if I don't give the order
for this to be done, they'll take their men across themselves before it's too late.'

'I don't understand. What's this all about?'

'Don't pretend you don't know,' one of the group of officers interrupted. 'The Germans have crossed Nowy Swiat Street from the east, and by this time they'll have reached Napoleon Square. There's no resistance any longer. Have we got to wait here like fools for them to attack us from the rear?'

'I suggested inviting you over here in order to have your opinion,' Zelazny explained to me. 'You won't withdraw, will you?'

'Do you want me to be honest? All right. As far as Nowy Swiat and Napoleon Square are concerned, someone else can worry about them. That's not my business. Nor does it concern any of us. But if anyone wants to quit the position he holds, then let him. That is what I think, personally. After all, you can't force anyone to stay. But if you haven't enough men left after the others have retreated, then my lads are at your service. I'm going to get some sleep. And I'd advise you all to do the same. Good night.'

On returning to my own headquarters I rang up Zelazny just in case.

'Will you want my relief platoon?'

'No, thanks. No one has quit. But it was very nearly mutiny; it's terrible how much trouble a few people with shaky nerves can stir up. I'm glad you came over. When you'd left, the rest of them went off too, one by one, saying good night!'

Yet another unpleasant matter awaited me in the morning. Igra has asked me to release him from duty. He didn't want to tell me why, but explained that he wanted to go for purely personal reasons. In order to gain a little time, I told him he ought to discuss the matter first with his company commander.

It wasn't too difficult to find out what was wrong. Igra is Jewish. I didn't know this and hadn't even guessed it. There's nothing in his looks, ways or speech to betray the fact, and no one knows how the lads recently transferred to his platoon found out his 'secret'. Finally they asked him point-blank. Probably it would have been left at that if Igra had simply said 'Yes'.

But for some reason he tried to get out of admitting the fact. Perhaps his feelings about the persecution of Jews were so strong that they prevented him from realising that there are several dozen Jews in our battalion, some even obviously Jewish in their looks, but all of whom are generally popular with their comrades. Or perhaps painful experiences with Polish anti-semites made him try to avoid any unpleasantness. So, when they asked him if he was a Jew, Igra denied it, or at least, according to other versions, gave an evasive reply.

And from that time on Igra hasn't had a moment's peace. The lads tell the most malicious jokes about Jews in his hearing, or they pretend not to notice him and carry on carefully planned conversations about him. Igra was wretched, and they've been playing with him like cats with a mouse.

I was able to discover which of the lads started and who organised this merciless 'joke', and had them brought to my office. There I told them that it was entirely their own affair whether they liked Jews or not, but that I would not under any circumstances tolerate anti-semitism or racial discrimination in my battalion. I told them that Jews have been fighting with us from the first day of the Insurrection, and that they shared with us the long Underground conspiracy that preceded it. Then I told them how Igra had been rescued by one of our patrols from a heap of dead people in the Mirowski market, and how he'd immediately joined us and had done much towards holding our street during the worst days of fighting.

The lads listened to me attentively, and admitted that I was right and that they respect other Jews, but . . .

'Why didn't he want to say he's a Jew when he is one?'

I brought out other reasons for explaining away Igra's reply and showing them the stupidity of their behaviour. Alexander joined in the conversation, as well as Barbara and Wislanski. The lads agreed to everything we said, but they also agreed when one of them, with almost insane persistence, insisted:

'I don't want a Jew as my N.C.O.!'

I'd already decided to transfer this man to the reserve company; but Igra was equally decided, and in spite of everything we said he repeated his request to be released altogether from the army. He thought it would be better both for himself and for the lads. Nor did he want a transfer. He wanted to go on working to help what was left of the Jewish population in Warsaw.

I was sorry to see him go. He was a good soldier and a fine N.C.O. But I had to release him in accordance with my decision to release any man who wants to quit.

Late at night, while I was taking off my boots to wash my feet, I saw I'd been wounded. A piece of shrapnel had hit the leg of my boot in front and cut through to the flesh. It was only a small wound, the blood had already dried, but the bone was bruised and sore. It's odd, though, that this is the second time I've been wounded and not noticed anything until several hours later. Now I've no idea when or how this happened. But it doesn't matter and is not even worth bandaging.

Saturday, 9 September

Quite by chance I've tracked down our chaplain. I'd just finished inspecting the new positions in Ceglana Street when I caught sight of a mysterious human form rooting about in the still-smoking ashes.

'Who's that?'

'It's the chaplain,' said the lads. 'He's all right.'

And they told me how he spends the nights with them, in the line, and relieves the tiredest on duty.

'Have a nap for half an hour,' he'll say. 'I'll keep my eyes open and wake you up at once if necessary.'

He's got a keen sense of smell, too, and can tell directly if any of the lads hasn't changed his underwear or socks lately. Then he clears off for a bit and comes back with what's wanted. Also he'll bring them water from the well in Twarda Street, and when the lads haven't any cigarettes, he can always manage to scrounge a few.

'Look, he's found something.'

As Father Oracz came up, I saw that he was carrying a heavy pack. My unexpected presence embarrassed him a little.

'What have you got there?' I asked him.

'Nothing much, some books. They'd have been burned otherwise. Just look. . . .'

And he brightened up as he pulled out some finely bound volumes.

'Here, for instance—a copy of *Casus conscientiæ in præcipuas questiones theologiæ moralis*. I took it on account of the motto . . . and this *Voyage dans le Mer du Sud*, published in Paris in 1774. I couldn't leave them there.'

I took the first of the books and read the motto, which said, '*Longum iter est per præcepta, breve et efficax per exempla—Seneca epist. VI*'.

'Why are there so many books out there?' I asked, looking round the ruins.

'Someone must have been trying to hide part of the University Library,' young Corporal Rys explained, showing me another book with a University Library book-plate. The title of this was *Course of Mathematics*.

'What do you want this for?' I asked him.

'I'm very keen on mathematics. I'm studying it when I have the time. It's a good book. Besides, Vera said I might have it.'

'How does Vera come into it?'

'I had to ask someone, and she's running the place here.'

Then the lads eagerly passed a copy of the 'News Bulletin' from hand to hand. I'd brought it up with me.

'It's about us! Look, on the front page! Mind, you'll tear it! Let the chaplain read what it says. . . .'

'I'll read it, but let's go into the shelter first.'

Then he started to read aloud.

'One sector of the front in Warsaw has particularly distinguished itself during the last six weeks' fighting. This sector starts at the post railway station, then, roughly, runs along Towarowa Street, Grzybowska Street and Krolewska Street. The sector has a magnificent fighting record and history will some day proudly

Wacław Zagórski ("Lech"). This portrait was drawn by Zb. Sadowski in a prisoner-of-war camp in Upper Bavaria

(*Above*) Underground news-sheet issued by the Home Army during the German Occupation. The issue for 2 August contained General Bor's 'Order' for the Insurrection to start

(*Right*) The symbol of Polish resistance, 'Poland Fights'

(*Above*) Insurgent patrol in the streets of Warsaw, 2 August 1944

(*Below*) Poster issued by the Home Army: 'Avenge the blood of thousands of Poles by fighting!' 7 August 1944

(*Above*) Tram-cars were used to form barricades, 3-4 August 1944

(*Below*) A Home Army patrol set out to contact the Red Army on the far side of the Vistula, 4 August 1944

August 1944. (*Above*) One of the barricades manned by Insurgents in the Warsaw City Centre, and (*below*) Insurgents on one of the barricades

ULTIMATUM

do ludności miasta Warszawy!

Niemieckie naczelne dowództwo pragnie uniknąć niepotrzebnego przelewu krwi, który szczególnie dotknie niewinne kobiety i dzieci, i wobec tego ogłasza następujące wezwanie:

1. Ludność zostaje wezwana do opuszczenia Warszawy w zachodnim kierunku z białymi chustkami w ręku.

2. Niemieckie naczelne dowództwo gwarantuje, że żaden mieszkaniec Warszawy, dobrowolnie opuszczający miasto, nie dozna żadnej krzywdy.

3. Wszyscy mężczyźni i kobiety zdolni do pracy, otrzymają pracę i chleb.

4. Niezdolna do pracy ludność zostanie ulokowana na zachodnich obszarach warszawskiej gubernii i otrzyma zaopatrzenie.

5. Wszyscy chorzy oraz starcy, kobiety i dzieci, potrzebujące opieki, otrzymają pomieszczenia i opiekę lekarską.

6. Ludność polska wie, że armia niemiecka walczy jedynie z bolszewizmem. Kto w dalszym ciągu daje się wykorzystać, jako narzędzie bolszewizmu, bez względu na to, pod jakiem hasłem, zostanie bez wszelkich skrupułów pociągnięty do odpowiedzialności.

7. Ultimatum to jest terminowe.

Głównodowodzący

(*Above*) 10 August 1944: the German issued an ultimatum in Polish to the inhabitants of Warsaw, calling on them to leave the city

(*Left*) Supplies were dropped by aircraft of the R.A.F. on 12 August central Warsaw

(*Above*) Insurgents armed with anti-tank guns dropped by the R.A.F.

(*Below*) On 15 August a German tank was captured by Insurgents

(*Above*) Home-made mortars were produced by the Home Army, August 1944

(*Below*) Identity cards of the Home Army were issued, signed by the author, 19 August 1944

ARMIA KRAJOWA
Okręg Warszawski

Nr 1565

Zaświadczam, że

„Zofia" – Zast. Kierowi. płtu sa
stopień wojsk. (pseudonim i imię)

Lucja Chobrzyńska jest
nazwisko

żołnierzem A. K.
Dnia 25.VII.1944 r.

Komendant Obwodu

(-) Radwan

Miejsce pieczęci

Sanitariuszka Zofia – z
sanitarnej Baonu II S
„Chrobry II". D-ra Ba
Lec

19.VIII.44r.

(*Left*) On 20 August, the Central Telephone Exchange was set on fire by Insurgents and the Germans finally driven from the building

(*Below*) German troops emerged from the Telephone Exchange after a siege of twenty days

(*Right*) On 23 August Insurgents captured the Police Headquarters and the Germans brought a wounded comrade out with them

(*Left*) A German mine-thrower in the ruins of the Warsaw Ghetto, August 1944

(*Above*) Warsaw's 'skyscraper'—the Prudential Assurance building—was captured and held by Insurgents

(*Below*) Insurgents at dinner, August 1944

(*Above*) The Warsaw Opera House arcade, where a German anti-tank gun was stationed, in August 1944

(*Below*) Defenders of the Old Town made their way to the City Centre through the sewers, 2 September 1944

(*Left*) 3 September 1944. The cit
water supply failed and wells had to b
dug

(*Right*) An unexploded shell from the
German 'Big Bertha', 4 September
1944

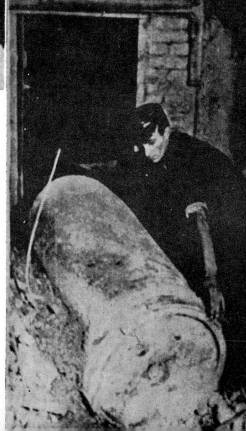

(*Left*) Rifleman Smial
September 1944

(*Right*) Insurgents were buried
where they fell

(*Left*) General BOR (Tadeusz Komorowski)—now in London

(*Right*) Colonel RADWAN (Edward Pfeiffer)—now in London

(*Left*) BARBARA (Mrs. E. B. Zagorska, the author's wife)—now in London

(*Right*) Major RUM (Kazimierz Bilski)—now in Croydon, Surrey

(*Left*) ZOFIA (Mrs. L. L. Kaczorkiewicz)—now in Alta Gracia, Argentine

(*Right*) Corporal RYS (Ryszard Syski)—now in South Harrow, Middlesex

(*Left*) Lieutenant PULI (Bronislaw Kotynski)—now in New York

(*Right*) MISIA (Mrs. Michalina Kopczewska)—now in Munich

(*Left*) Corporal DESKA (Stanislaw Wasik)—now in Cobridge, Stoke-on-Trent

(*Right*) Corporal ROLA (Kazimierz Szczepanczyk)—now in Hayes, Middlesex

(*Left*) JANKA (Miss J. Bogdanska)—now in London

(*Right*) Lieutenant DABROWA (Edward Krutol)—now in New York

(*Left*) Corporal DZIECIOL (Tadeusz Specht)—now in Vancouver

(*Right*) OLA (Miss Zofia Trenkner)—now in Oxford

(*Left*) Rifleman LECH—now in Poland

(*Right*) WANDA—(Mrs. Wanda Wlodarska)—now in London

relate how these soldiers, despite their meagre equipment, held
out against a six-weeks-long deluge of fire and shells. . . .'

'Hey, Kary! You're going to be in history.'

'Don't interrupt, there's more yet.'

'For the last five days the German attack on this line has
greatly intensified. At the same time, merciless bombing from the
air and heavy artillery fire has been going on along this line:
nevertheless, the Towarowa–Grzybowska–Krolewska line is
holding out, throwing back frequent attacks and themselves taking offensive action. The men of this sector are rendering an immense service to the fighting city by their heroic attitude. They
are withstanding the heaviest enemy attacks and providing a
shield for the remaining sectors of the city, including those which
are farthest away from their own positions.'

'Is that all?' someone asked.

'That's all—isn't it enough?'

'It'll do.'

The lads were radiant.

Then Turek spoiled everything.

'They're pulling our legs,' he said. 'Personally I'd sooner get
hold of a cannon and do without all that sort of thing.'

'A cannon?' Okularnik put in. 'Is that all? Why not ask for
two bombers and a submarine as well?'

Captain Jerzewski has just summoned all officers in command of
battalions in order to appeal to us (and he insisted that it was not
an order) to get together as soon as possible, preferably today,
the best men of our battalions and, with our best officers, to form
one full-strength assault platoon each. This platoon will then be
transferred to the City Centre Headquarters, under Colonel
Radwan. These men are to be used to hold back the Germans as
they try to move into the centre of Warsaw from the Vistula
district.

'For heaven's sake! Don't you realise we're using the last of
our strength as it is? Every man still able to fight is worth his
weight in gold. I only have a weak platoon in reserve, practically
unarmed, for they have to leave their weapons in the line when

they come in. And the men in the line haven't been relieved for days,' I protested.

'I know all about that, but you've got to realise that the position in the east sector of the City Centre affects you as well, and very directly,' said Jerzewski.

'Yet there are plenty of men there. There's Bartkiewicz and his group, the "Kilinski" battalion, the "Home Guard", "Security troops", the "People's Army" . . . and still others. I know what their strength is, as they've been coming to collect flour from the mill in Prosta Street. And what about the men from the Old Town? They must have recovered by this time. And some of the men from the Vistula district must have got out too.'

'It isn't merely a question of numbers. What they want are men like your lads.'

'What do they take my men for? I haven't a single Regular officer, my companies and platoons are commanded by cavalry officers, by sailors, doctors, workmen. . . . More than half of my men never fired a rifle before the Insurrection began. It seems to me that the best men are in the City Centre already.'

I had to bite my lip to prevent myself from adding, 'It's just that they want to save their own skins at our expense.'

'It isn't a question of which soldiers are the best. I assure you that the men there have been fighting very bravely during the last two days in the counter-attacks which saved the City Centre. But it will be some time yet before the men who went through the withdrawal can put up a strong enough defence. What they need now is someone to inspire them once again with belief in their own strength and power to resist. What they want are men who can dig their way into the ruins with bare hands and hold out. . . .'

I didn't listen to any more, but was trying mentally to form a platoon—there'd be Tadeusz in command, Zenek as his second-in-command and in charge of the first squad, with Ostoia in command of the second squad. . . .

'Where are the men to report?' I asked at length.

'Can you manage it tonight?'

'Yes.'

'Then tell them to report to me at seven o'clock and I'll send them on.'

Half an hour before the appointed time, Tadeusz reported to me that the platoon was ready to move off. There were thirty-five men, all well-armed, with one light machine-gun. Nobody made any fuss, everyone handed over to them what they needed. At the last moment, one of the lads who was staying behind tossed a few rounds of ammo over to a comrade as he went off with the platoon. I was puzzled by a feeling, which we all had, that we were saying good-bye to them for a long, long time.

Sunday, 10 September

I have never yet visited Lieutenant Czarnecki in his domain in Sliska Street. However, people are always coming over to me with complaints about him. The civilians say he treats them like sheep, and the girls in his unit have threatened to stop providing meals if people keep poking about in their kitchen and trying to 'help'. I ignored all these complaints.

'Don't bother me. Sort it out among yourselves. I have neither time nor inclination to decide on your squabbles.'

All the same, there is always someone or other who feels hard done by and insists that his affairs be looked into. Then, when they get no change from me, these people go and demand justice from higher authorities, who are in turn beginning to lose patience, as they don't like being bothered either.

'Go over there, Lech, and do something to stop all these complaints,' they told me.

So, willy-nilly, I had to go. Wislanski reminded me that Czarnecki has his office and stores at No. 52, Sliska Street, while the cook-house is at No. 56, almost immediately opposite the hospital. I decided to start at the cook-house.

Stukas were flying over Warsaw, and I stopped in the gateway to see where the bombs were falling. A young lad with his cap on crooked told me he was the runner on duty.

'Take cover!'

The bombs were falling immediately behind the hospital—one, two, three. . . .

Grzmot, a 'civilian lieutenant', rushed down the staircase within, and into a corner of the yard, protected by the wall.

'Is that your air-raid shelter?' I asked the sentry.

'No, it's the latrine and the "lieutenant" bolts down there whenever there's an air-raid.'

More bombs fell, but this time a little farther away. A loud bawling from the corner of the yard now made itself heard:

'Runner, come here!'

'What for?' the lad retorted.

'Come over here and reach me my ammunition pouch!'

The lad strolled across the yard and glanced over the wall.

'Yes, you've gone and dropped it,' he remarked. 'Now you'll have to root about for it yourself.'

'I'll put you on a charge for refusing to obey an order!' shouted Grzmot, doing up his trousers.

The runner showed me the way into the cook-house, where I found a well-scrubbed floor and gleaming pots and pans. Then I heard raised voices in the next room.

'Let him eat his bone himself, if he wants it.'

'You mustn't talk like that! Don't forget you're in the army!'

I recognised the voice of Czarnecki.

'What's up?' I asked, going in. 'More squabbling?'

'I'm glad you've come, Captain. You can settle it on the spot. Sergeant Shaw is making a fuss because we don't want to make soup with the thigh bone of a horse, and the lieutenant here is on Shaw's side. But whoever heard of bilberry soup made with horse bones?'

'It's a perfectly good bone, and it would be nourishing for the men too. These girls don't know what they're talking about,' Czarnecki complained.

'Calm down! I'd sooner you left the cooking to these ladies,

Czarnecki. I'm more concerned with what happened to the sanitary inspector, because the police have sent in a report about him to H.Q.'

'It was Janka who talked to him,' said Bogda. 'Janka, tell the captain what happened.'

'I'm ever so sorry,' Janka explained, gazing at me with big, innocent eyes. 'A gentleman came in, dressed like a civilian and wearing a smart mackintosh and gloves, with a dispatch-case. I'd just done washing the floor, and there he was walking all over it with huge muddy feet! That made me wild, but all I said was "Be off, you, before I lose my temper and clout you one with this rag." And he turned round and said I was stopping him from seeing whether the place was clean or not. He flew off the handle at me and said I'd have to go before a court-martial. But he didn't even tell me where the court-martial is. Do you know where it is, Captain?'

'You won't be court-martialled.'

'But maybe I'd better go, because if I don't turn up there might be trouble.'

'None of you can be court-martialled without my knowing and giving proper orders. Still, if anyone else comes on a tour of inspection in future, be nice to him. . . .'

Then I went on, to change the subject:

'Any other troubles? Do you need anything?'

They gazed at one another, giggling and nudging each other.

'Go on, say it!'

'No, you tell him. . . .'

'Come on, out with it,' I urged.

'We want some D.D.T.'

'Lice?'

'Not us, but Grzmot and Jerzyna have, and we don't like seeing them scratch. We ought to give them a bath and de-louse them.'

'And Janka wants a belt, because the trousers she's got are too big and they keep falling down, particularly when she's carrying the soup.'

'Why doesn't she tie them up with string, like everyone else?'

'We haven't got any! We've looked everywhere for a piece.'

When I got back to Panska Street, I learned that Miki, one of our runners, had been wounded in Sliska Street as he was coming back from delivering the daily report to Headquarters. He had been taken to our hospital in the cellar. The first-aid girls said he's plucky and hasn't cried, though his wounds must be painful.

Alarming reports were coming in from Lieutenant Iran in Lucka Street, where No. 5 Company was under unusually heavy fire, and they were expecting the Germans to attack at any time. Our lads are below strength now that we've had to transfer some of them and take away some of their weapons too.

I took Alexander with me. Beyond Zelazna Street we met Sergeant Hem, who had come out to meet us and lead the way, as we were obliged to get across Panska Street under heavy fire and without cover into the gateway of No. 88. Alexander went first, followed by Hem. A shell landed between them, and for a moment both disappeared in a cloud of smoke. I ran through this cloud, holding my breath. Both were standing on the far side of the street, stunned and pale, staring at each other, but not even a scrap of shrapnel had touched them.

We hurried on. There was still Lucka Street to cross. We made it just in time, for the girls were carrying away Cadet Olszyna, and his platoon, which was lost without their leader, was breaking up. We had to force the lads to return to their positions.

'The grenades, hurry up!'

A tin hat flew out of a gap in the ruins and we heard a German cursing.

Nurses summoned from the Headquarters first-aid post were examining Olszyna as he lay there motionless.

'He's lost a lot of blood. We've given him the last of the morphia. He can be carried now.'

'You'll have to stay here,' I told Alexander, 'at least until I can find someone to take over command of No. 5 Company. I'll take over your men till you come back.'

Towards evening they brought two more wounded men in

from Lucka Street. Then Tabaczkiewicz drew my attention to
an unusual thing: not a single plane has been over for four hours.
And the sky was clear, wonderfully blue.

Monday, 11 September

At last I've heard from Tadeusz.
When he and his men left us, they went straight into action in
Chmielna Street, where they captured No. 14 and then No. 12.
Apart from a few minor wounds, they suffered no casualties, and
are now holding out, getting to know their new sector and are
all in high spirits. One group of his men has already crossed over
to the other side of the street.

I didn't bother about the shrapnel wound in my leg and the
small cut has gone septic. It is oozing pus and the bone is sore. So
Maria has given me an injection of some sort and bandaged it. I
had some trouble getting my boot on and, despite my protests,
Maria decided that I must have an injection of glucose too. The
nurses have plenty of this from the lads in No. 5 Company, who
have managed to get hold of a store of medical supplies. The
most valuable part of their haul was cat-gut for stitching wounds.
Previously the surgeons in the Sliska Street hospital were using
ordinary thread.

Lieutenant Starry had the bright idea of asking for some German prisoners-of-war for digging. Captain Jerzewski backed this
proposal and was able to get permission for forty Germans to be
sent over from the main prisoner-of-war camp. I sent a party of
men over to act as escorts. They are to dig tunnels and a well. We
have to take advantage of this relatively quiet period, which has
lasted since yesterday. No German aircraft are to be seen, the
'Big Bertha' has ceased and the crackle of machine-gun fire from
the front-line positions is increasingly rare.

We wonder what the silence means. The rumours of a forthcoming attack by Red Army troops on the far side of the Vistula
seem more and more likely. But we are too far from the river
bank to see the fires which are said to be blazing on the far side or

to hear the artillery from over there. But this relaxation on the part of the Germans makes it only too clear that now at last something is going to happen.

Alexander and I went, without any trouble, over to Twarda Street and had a look round the ruins which lay quiet under the sun; we kicked a few scattered tin pots and pans lying about, then stopped to look at a tiny grave, on which two forget-me-nots lay, with a little board over it, saying, 'Here lies Anielka: born 28th August, 1944, passed on 10th September, 1944.'

The German prisoners-of-war worked till nightfall, digging deep under Zelazna Street from both sides, although they haven't yet finished the tunnel. I would not let them cut and remove the many water and gas pipes and electricity and telephone cables which they found under the pavements, even though these make work much more difficult and will impede the tunnel when it is finished. They tried to dig it deeper, but came on the vaulting of a sewer.

The officer in charge of the prisoners-of-war warned us, via Headquarters, to send back all the prisoners before darkness falls, and if they hadn't finished we were to send for them again to-morrow. But I don't see any point in driving them to and fro every day; they can stay in our sector, for there will always be work for them and I can provide them with rations. This last argument was the most convincing and induced the prisoner-of-war camp commandant to get round the rules and regulations. In the end, I sent him back twenty, and am to keep the other twenty for as long as they are likely to be required.

I went to give them their instructions, and took Wislanski with me as interpreter. After work, the prisoners-of-war were put into the left wing of our building, since this is the least safe place on account of artillery fire, and had been vacated by the inhabitants and cleared of furniture. They were being guarded by one lad with a dangerous-looking, though really useless, revolver, very intent on his job and keeping out the little crowd of inquisitive men who wanted to see what the conquerers of the world look like now that they've been disarmed.

'Make way for Captain Lech!' Wislanski shouted.

The young sentry told me that the prisoners had had their supper, as well as water for washing and cigarettes. They had asked for a razor to shave with. Might he let them have one?

'Let them shave if they want to. But who gave them cigarettes?'

'Our lads.'

'That's a fine state of affairs! Here am I with nothing to smoke and yet the Germans get cigarettes.'

Inside, the Germans were all standing to attention. One, apparently the senior officer, reported to me in German. I then told them we'd decided to keep twenty of them here, that they'd be exposed to the same risks as our own men. Our sentries have been told to fire without warning at any men trying to escape, and we shall consider that any man who crosses the demarcation line by as much as a single pace is trying to escape. Then I asked if any of them wanted to volunteer to stay.

They all wanted to stay. Not a single man wanted to go back to the prisoner-of-war camp. So I suggested they draw lots.

Tuesday, 12 September

A mysterious aircraft flew very low over Panska Street and the 'Little Ghetto' last night. It flew very slowly, its engines stuttering like an aged motor-bike. In the darkness our sentries could not make out any markings on it, but Buzunov declared that he recognised the sound of the engines of a Soviet reconnaissance plane, which is used to support infantry. He sees this as proof that the Soviet forces are very near and may storm Warsaw today or tomorrow.

Then they brought me a leaflet someone had found, in which in wretched Polish the Soviet Headquarters offered help to the inhabitants of Warsaw who are still fighting. The leaflet appealed to us to mark out the lines of our positions so that Russian aircraft and artillery can avoid bombing or firing at us. The leaflet also gave instructions how to signal what we most urgently want—food, arms, ammunition or surgical supplies. After making a

copy of this, I sent the leaflet to Area Headquarters. The officers
and men in my sector are only interested in two signals—those
indicating that we want anti-tank arms and ammo.

At midday we saw three Soviet fighters overhead, for the first
time since the end of July. They came over from the east, drew
fire from the German positions to the north and west of our lines,
then turned and came straight towards us. Suddenly, one of the
planes dived, the second shot upwards and the third came straight
on. Two Messerschmidts then flew up from beyond the central
railway station, almost as though they'd been hiding in the
ruins. The Soviet plane which had gone into a dive cut across
their line of approach, and the Germans separated, one going off
in the direction of the Vistula, while the other, just above the
roof-tops, was about to attack the Russian from below. Then the
plane which a few seconds before had gone into a climb turned
and came down again with a furious whining of engines. Its
guns crackled and echoed. Then we saw the planes diving down
towards the horizon, like iron birds of prey.

It didn't matter to us much whether or not one of the aircraft
was hit, for the very fact that we'd seen an air battle was an immense relief. The Germans can bomb us now, but they can no
longer do it with impunity. We no longer feel helpless in the face
of air-raids.

Then we saw another plane and recognised the sound of its
engines as it came in, low enough for us to see the bomb carriage
and the red star painted on its fuselage. Its shadow flew across the
ruins of the Little Ghetto. Then the bombs started falling, somewhere near Wronia Street and Towarowa Street. It really looked
as if they were co-operating with us! Fortunately we hadn't
waited for orders before indicating the line of our positions, as the
leaflet suggested.

Suddenly the telephone rang in my office.

'Captain Lech, please remove the signals indicating your position. The Reds are bombing our barricades. They've deliberately
bombed our clearly marked barricade in Lucka Street. There are
several wounded. . . .'

For several days past towards dusk I've heard a hymn being sung in the little yard of the block of flats where my billet is: *'Now our daily task is done. . . .'*

I hadn't paid much attention before, and I knew that no one had organised any meeting of the men for prayers. It's their own business. Today, however, I couldn't help being struck by the force behind the singing.

Although I was still running a high temperature, I went into the gateway and found the yard crammed with people, all facing a small altar on the wall opposite. Men of the platoon which was relieved today from the line were standing immediately before this little altar, while there was a group of wounded from the battalion hospital in the left-hand corner, some with ambulance girls supporting them. Then there were the Georgians, Azerbaidjanis, Armenians and Tartars from the 'Caucasian platoon', still in their grubby working clothes. Civilians from round about filled the rest of the yard, while I saw German prisoners standing at attention at the open windows of the second floor. They had finished digging the tunnel under Zelazna Street and had had their supper.

The hymn ended and there was a moment of silence. Then, all at once, everybody burst out singing.

> *O Lord, thou hast to Poland lent thy might*
> *And with a Father's strong, protecting hand,*
> *Hast given fame and all its glory bright*
> *And through ages saved our Fatherland,*
>
> *We chant at thy altars our humble strain,*
> *O Lord, make the land of our love free again.*

Even if a shell had fallen in the courtyard at this moment, I am sure no one would have paid any attention to it. Then someone touched my arm.

'Captain, be careful . . . the Germans are so near. They'll hear us and something terrible will happen. . . .'

'If you're afraid you'd better clear out of it. I'm not going to interfere.'

I looked round for Father Oracz, as I could not see him at the little altar. Then I caught sight of him in the darkest corner of the yard, standing behind all the people—lean, ill-looking and yet smiling.

Wednesday, 13 September

Maria and Alicia have taken charge of me. I'm in charge of the lads, and, willy-nilly, of everything that goes on in our sector, but they're in charge of *me*. They give me injections of glucose, and order me to take pills and tell me what to eat and drink. In the meantime they use all sorts of medical words and phrases, from which I've deduced that they're trying to stop the bone of my leg from festering and that —if I don't do exactly as I'm told—I'll find myself in the next world before I know where I am.

In return for these deeds of Christian charity they expect me to settle all their worries about the progress of the fighting in Warsaw, as well as the international situation, the tactics of the British, not to mention the attitude of Soviet Russia to us and to the Polish units fighting, under General Zymierski, with the Russians on the far side of the Vistula. And this is only part of it: I've told them to read what the newspapers say. It is worse when Maria, as she sees to my wound, asks me to decide on problems of ethics, of law, social problems and philosophical problems as well. To make matters worse, many of these problems turn out to be connected with people and episodes in which we are ourselves concerned. Maria is very forbearing and can overlook anything done by one of the lads who are fighting, but she is exceedingly sensitive to signs of human frailty when the administrative staff or 'important people' are concerned, and she is quite merciless towards the other 'ladies of the battalion' if they are not quite up to the standards of Joan of Arc.

I couldn't help listening rather sceptically to her latest complaints about Dr. Leopold because he doesn't visit the wounded and sick often enough and doesn't bother much about the convalescents, and because he doesn't go up into the line with ambulance patrols and doesn't try hard enough to obtain medicine and bandages. However, I didn't feel myself entirely without blame when I heard that Zofia had been sent off somewhere or other and no one knows what has become of her. Furthermore, it seems that no one has taken the trouble to make any inquiries about what happened to those of our wounded lads who were transferred to the Vistula district and that no one knows how Corporal Marian died, after he'd had his leg amputated and was taken to Okolnik Street.

It's true that things are not always done properly. There's been a good deal of carelessness, of unfairness, of failure. Work hasn't been distributed fairly—some people work like niggers while others idle. But what can one do when some people break down both physically and morally, while others make superhuman efforts to carry on? I know that Jadzia has been avoiding jobs lately, while Elzbieta, who is much older than Jadzia and has recently lost her husband, nevertheless does as much work as two people in our little hospital. It's the same with the lads: some no longer believe that we have any chances of holding out against the Germans—even though it was their faith which, earlier, made it possible for us to keep hold of our sector during the worst fighting. This attitude is perhaps more understandable among the men from the Old Town. And I couldn't help wondering how many of my lads would have done as Staszek Toporowski or young Nawrocki did, when they volunteered to join us as soon as they'd emerged from the sewers through which they escaped from the Old Town.

Nor is the sharing out of food always fair. But people are only human, after all. Some are sharper-witted than others. The officers in command of a platoon are primarily concerned with their own men, while the men in turn are concerned only with those nearest to them. People who have something aren't always prepared to renounce their rights of ownership in accordance with the fairest and most just of principles. So what am I supposed to do about it? I can't fine them or put them under arrest, while the only punishment to which I can have recourse is execution. When I can't or don't want to use this one, all that's left is persuasion or public opinion.

'Never mind,' said Wislanski. 'Every day we're getting closer and closer to the levelling out of any unfairness—when we're all starving.'

But the sorest point of all is the relations between the lads and girls in the units. One of the youngest of the lads came to Maria for help, confidentially: Maria's tact and the way she looked after him resulted in three other boys from the same platoon also coming to her. We learned from what they told us in confidence that the source of infection was the same in all four cases—a seventeen-year-old girl from Grzybowska Street who worked with us as a runner during August. When No. 4 Company was transferred to Ceglana Street, she left the platoon to remain in the earlier sector, and as she was living with her family, Alexander gave her permission to stay and didn't even take back her identity papers. Now the lads decided that something must be done about this girl, and they went off to Grzybowska Street, found the girl and, only mentioning her desertion, took away her papers and arm-band, then made her take off her overalls and left her standing there in her underwear.

I didn't know what to say or do about this. Someone ought to see about curing the girl. But I don't wish to lay down the law. Besides, I haven't the right to do so.

But playing cards is another matter altogether. I don't confiscate the cards, nor have I forbidden the lads to play cards when they're off duty, even when they play for a grenade or some rounds of ammo. All the same, I can't permit Sergeant Wit to 'win' the lads' watches and cigarette-cases at cards. If he wants to play cards, he'll have to play with Lieutenant Starry, who was wounded in the leg yesterday and now must spend a few days in his billet. Wit will have to give back what he won to the lads.

I've now been able to transfer Lieutenant Adam from No. 5

Company, as Lieutenant Wir, who was sent to our sector a few days ago, and was temporarily put in charge of an anti-tank platoon, has shown himself a good company leader. I have sent him Lieutenant Silkiewicz, a sensible and level-headed officer, as his second-in-command.

I took Silkiewicz with me out to Lucka Street so that he could start his duties there. As usual, No. 3 Platoon were under heavy fire in Wronia and Grzybowska Streets, and we could hear the rumbling of tanks.

The lads showed me a burnt-out shed where the Germans had previously had a machine-gun post from which they would fire at our positions all day long and at night as well. Then, last night, a couple of the lads managed to creep up to this shed and set fire to it. Now the Germans have moved another forty yards back, and things have improved.

The second episode of the day concerned Rola.

'It's all very well to laugh now,' he said, 'but it was different at the time. Did you notice that wooden lavatory in the yard in Lucka Street? We all used to use it until today. When the tanks were coming up we had to get ready for them, so I nipped over there for a couple of minutes. I opened the door and realised there was no wall at the back of it. I didn't much like the look of things, but it couldn't be helped, so I squatted down. Then it felt kind of odd to be sitting with no wall there behind me, and I got up again to look for a better spot. And at that very minute they fired at me with a heavy machine-gun. One of the bullets got me in the behind and I thought I'd had it, till I saw it was only a scratch. But they ripped my trousers up altogether. Look at them!

'What happened was that the Germans had got up to the floor above in those ruins over in Wronia Street and had blown up the wall with a machine-gun and were waiting for someone to chance his luck.'

'There you are, Rola,' I said. 'Don't you remember you were worried about shooting down that German behind the police barracks, even though *his* trousers weren't down and he hadn't got *his* behind turned towards you!'

Thursday, 14 September

More Soviet reconnaissance planes came over our sector last night, and later the lads found a sack in the ruins, containing dry black bread. The bread was as hard as iron, and the sack was marked with Russian characters, dirty and split, probably as it fell. It looks as if these are the first supplies dropped by parachute that we've had. Help for Warsaw after six weeks' fighting!

The find caused something of a sensation and all kinds of comments were made.

'They couldn't afford to drop fresh bread! If I'd got a plane I'd send the sack back again to the beggars, with white flour—even if I died of starvation myself afterwards.'

One of the lads wanted to try the bread, but his more cautious comrades wouldn't let him. It may be poisoned. We've seen in the papers how the Germans dropped poisoned food in Zulinski Street, causing the death of three people.

So the lads decided to try the bread on a dog, though looking for a dog in our sector is worse than looking for a needle in a haystack. A sausage factory has been started beyond Zelazna Street, where they make sausages which aren't half bad from dogs and cats. You can get a couple of sausages or some cigarettes for every dog or cat you take in.

A few volunteers went off and came back a little later with a skinny mongrel. He sniffed the bread but wouldn't eat it, even though the bones were showing through his skin.

In the end we got him to eat some of the bread mashed up in water and flavoured with suet, and he trotted round the yard with his belly puffed out and without any symptoms of poisoning.

The bread was then shared about among the greediest of the lads, while the girls took what was left for making soup.

A very much more valuable discovery which the lads of No. 5 Company have made is—a real, live horse. We feel certain that it must be the last horse in Warsaw, though no one knows how it survived.

The lads said that from time to time they've been hearing

what sounded like stifled neighing at night, out in the forward positions. The sounds seemed to come from overhead, and though they'd searched and listened, it was clear that there was nothing overhead but burnt-out walls all battered with shells and inaccessible from below. They'd thought it was a ghost horse.

Then, at dawn today, they saw an old chap dragging a bundle of hay up a ladder to one of the first-floor landings, then he pulled the ladder up after him and went on again, still higher. The lads followed and there they found the horse, up on the fifth floor of a bombed house. It was a struggle to get him down to the ground, particularly as the Germans were there and had them under fire all the time. Still, as the lads said, they couldn't throw him down. When they'd brought him down, however, the horse had to be shot.

As the sector was comparatively quiet, I went with Okularnik to have a look at the horse and to supervise distribution of the meat.

Sergeant Kolba was already there, and had quartered the horse very fairly. The owner of the horse, an old cabby, was helping, but when he saw me he started to complain, and asked me to let him have at least some sort of a requisition order. But Kolba took responsibility for the whole business upon himself.

'What requisition order? You'll get no requisition order, and this is all going to be done without any forms or orders. To begin with, you haven't got forms to prove you're still alive.'

The cabby talked about regulations, that he'd a right to have a requisition order issued by the civilian and military authorities.

'That was all a long time ago,' Kolba told him.

'But he was my horse, he was my bread-and-butter, as you might say.'

'Well, what if he was?' Kolba asked, without pausing. 'You see that mattress over there? Someone used to sleep on it every night, it was *his* mattress. Then I came along and lay down on it, and now it's mine. If they bring up a wounded man or a woman in childbirth, well then, they'll pull me off the mattress and use it for someone else and it won't be mine any more. I'll have to find myself another one.'

'But a horse isn't a mattress,' the cabby persisted. 'How am I going to find myself another horse?'

'Anyhow, we can't find anything else to eat and we've got to eat something. You've got to eat too. Here, catch hold of some of his guts and f—— off. When you've got nothing to look after any longer, you'll realise what it means to be a free man. Then maybe you'll fancy joining us to fight the Germans.'

I supervised the distribution of the horse meat: the best pieces were sent to the hospitals in Sliska and Żlota Streets, the liver was put aside for our own wounded in Panska Street, some pieces went over to Group Headquarters, and the rest was divided out according to strength of companies and for the girls in the battalion cook-house. Families with children would get a share from the cook-house.

I took the opportunity of going over to the mill in Prosta Street, where Corporal Premier told me he still hadn't been able to count all the store of flour. He estimated, however, that there was enough for three to four weeks if we kept issuing it at the present rate, and providing, of course, that the mill isn't burned down. He'd been having most bother with transport columns which forgather in the narrow courtyard and, when several columns come in at the same time, he finds it difficult to cope with them all. Already there have been casualties from grenades, though fortunately not serious ones. He's made a new entry into the storehouse from the east side where there is a fairly wide-open space which is well covered from artillery fire. All the same, there's the danger that a factory chimney near by may collapse over this entrance, for it is already badly damaged.

I also saw that good old Premier was hardly able to get about, and I learned from the sentries stationed with him that for the last three days and nights he has only had a couple of hours' sleep. I promised to send him a few more men, unarmed of course; they'll have to hand on their revolvers to the next men when it is their turn to sleep, as the men in the line do.

I gave instructions for organising one-way traffic for the transport columns in order to avoid any more jams, and also forbade the issue of more than forty pounds of flour to any one man. This is not an economy measure, but simply because people are worn out and move slowly when heavily loaded. Furthermore, Premier will in future only issue flour on a written order from me, and even indents from the Area Quartermaster will have to bear my signature as well.

This will help control traffic when necessary and according to enemy fire in the sector. If necessary, the columns can be halted along the far side of Zelazna Street in the big cellars of the Makowski factory.

No change has been reported from No. 5 Company's sector.

The Germans have been putting up more bunkers beyond Wronia Street, and on their side of Grzybowska Street in order to install their heavy machine-gun posts on the first floor in the houses, thus obtaining a wider range of fire along the positions of No. 3 Platoon.

So the lads there have been building up the western barricade and digging deeper trenches.

Friday, 15 September

My instructions about the issue of flour from the mill in Prosta Street were made only just in time, for today the number of transport columns has almost doubled; they have been coming in from the most distant sectors of Warsaw. I have found out from them that the damage on the far side of the Jerusalem Way is very much less than in our sector, but that, on the other hand, over-crowding is far worse there and they are having great difficulties with food supply. They've been obtaining food supplies mainly from some warehouses some distance away and very awkward to get at, along a narrow road which was often under fire. Now, too, even this source of food has been stopped, for the warehouses have been cut off and heavy fighting is going on in their neighbourhood.

It is also very difficult for the columns of porters to get across the Jerusalem Way into our sector, since a crossing is held at only one point, protected to a certain extent by a barricade which is under constant attack by the Germans. Long queues form on both sides of the street and people often have to wait for hours. Still, nothing can be done, particularly as this state of affairs is not likely to last long, now that Soviet troops have occupied the suburb of Praga and the Vistula bank opposite the Saska Kepa suburb is in our hands. Thus there is nothing to prevent the Red Army crossing the river and entering Warsaw itself.

This long-awaited news, which has at last been confirmed in radio and newspaper bulletins, did not, however, cause any excitement or relief among the lads. If anything, they were more thoughtful and looked more tired than usual.

'Well, it won't be long now,' I remarked to a few lads on one of the barricades, trying to look cheerful even though I, too, felt oddly depressed.

'And what then, sir?' one of them asked.

'Cheer up, mate,' put in Slawek mockingly. 'Our "allies" are on the way. If you haven't got a "Cross of Valour", now's your chance to get an "Order of Stalin".'

But nobody found his joke particularly funny just then.

'Anyhow, why should we worry?' said Pekinczyk impatiently. 'As long as we're here and as long as we've got our weapons, no outsider will take over in Warsaw.'

Soviet aircraft have been appearing overhead more and more frequently. We've laid strips of cloth in the ruins of the Ghetto, to indicate to them that we need ammo. You couldn't wish for a better place for dropping supplies by parachute, but they haven't sent anything apart from the sack of dry bread yesterday. We have to withstand constant attacks with nothing but our home-made grenades. The Germans stroll up and down along Chlodna Street as though they're taking the air. This irritated Czes.

'Give me a fag, Lech,' he pleaded.

For some time now all the 'private' sources where we used to be able to buy cigarettes for the lads have dried up, and we can't get them in exchange for vodka or sugar or even for horse-meat. Yesterday I still had a few dog-ends left, but today I haven't had a smoke since early morning.

'We can't have that,' said Czes. 'Hold on a bit. I remember seeing two "spivs" who trade in cigarettes. I'll go and talk to them.'

An hour later, Czes came into the Headquarters office, very down at the mouth.

'They're up to something,' he said. 'They told me they haven't any cigarettes, but they can get hold of as many as we want. They know where there's a warehouse full!'

'Couldn't they take us there?'

'They don't want to. Besides, they say we'll have to pay for them either in gold or in dollars.'

'That's out of the question.'

'That "warehouse" of theirs is only a yarn, though. These two blokes are nothing but crooks, they've got the cigarettes hidden somewhere in the ruins in Ceglana Street.'

'Bring them both in here.'

It was some time before they appeared, and while waiting I signed an indent for flour, talked to Maria, dictated a list of names of lads to be put forward for the 'Cross of Valour', glanced at the newspapers: Le Havre has surrendered, in Paris Poles have hung out our red-and-white flag on the Polish embassy, Premier Mikolajczyk has seen Mr. Eden, a total of 4,500 Allied aircraft took part in raids over Germany yesterday. . . .

Then they brought in a cross-eyed, fair-haired youth in his mid-twenties: he wore a brown jacket and had a big signet ring and some smaller ones on his well-kept white hands

'This is the fag-merchant.'

'Where's the other one?'

'They're waiting for him to come back from somewhere or other, and they'll bring him in too.'

'What's up, Cap'n?' the fair-haired youth asked, shifting away from the sentry who'd brought him in as if to make it clear that he could manage all right on his own. 'What's all the row about?

If they'd told us before that you haven't any fags, I'd have brought you some myself, free. Here you are! Here's a hundred of the best, Cap'n.'

And he placed some unopened packets on the table in front of me.

'And here's more for your Missus,' he went on without a break, fumbling in another pocket. 'You're married, I'll bet? And your wife smokes too, don't she?'

'Well, thanks . . . but there's more to it than that,' I said, looking stern as I inhaled deeply and passed the packets over to Wislanski, telling him to hand them round to everyone and send the rest to the hospital.

Turning back to the 'fag-merchant', I went on:

'There are four hundred men in my battalion, and about three hundred of them smoke. So I want at least three hundred packets.'

'On my word of honour, those were the last. I had to stop myself from smoking them. . . .'

'Come off it or I'll clout you one,' I interrupted, rising to my feet.

He withdrew a pace or two and eyed me as though to find out whether I meant what I'd said. I went on:

'I'm no "Joe Soap" and I'm not going to argue. Four armed men are coming with you, you're to show them where your "warehouse" is. Either we get the cigarettes or else . . .'

He eyed me a moment or two longer, cautiously. I watched him. Then he grinned.

'You should have said that at the beginning, Cap'n. I knew we'd understand one another and that you'd see me right!'

'You'll take the lads there?'

'Sure I will. But they'll have to look sharp, because it's right under the Germans' noses.'

'Where?'

'In the cellar of a tobacco shop in Grzybowska Street. The bloke who owned the place had it bricked up. We've gone and dug a way in from underneath.'

Saturday, 16 September

Now we have plenty of cigarettes, for we have stored away two big wooden cases in a handy little depot near the Battalion Headquarters, and can safely issue several cigarettes a day to every man. They should last us several weeks. Some have also been sent to the hospital, and Tadeusz and his lads in Chmielna Street have not been forgotten. They are fighting there continuously, gradually regaining lost ground in the direction of Nowy Swiat.

Rumours that Soviet aircraft have dropped arms and ammunition continue to circulate, even though we have not had anything so far. I commented on this at Group Headquarters, and said that if in fact Soviet aircraft have dropped as much material as the news bulletins claim, then we ought to get some of it. I had a look at a Russian machine-pistol: they have greater firing power than our home-made machine-pistols, Sten-guns and even than the German type, as they take fifty rounds of cartridges. Their grenade-throwers and anti-tank guns are also supposed to be excellent.

Captain Jerzewski promised to try to obtain an issue for us, even if only as compensation for the arms we had to hand over to Tadeusz and his platoon for the defence of the other sector. But the difficulty is that the weapons are dropped without parachutes, so that many are smashed or damaged as they fall. So I asked him to get me some damaged weapons, as we have a good armoury which can cope with almost any kind of damage.

The fire from the enemy's lines is increasing. Heavy shells are coming over from the 'Big Bertha' and drop regularly every five minutes. Artillery shells of lesser calibre come over too. There are some wounded men near our well, and fighting is increasing along our positions.

The two 'spivs' who kindly provided us with cigarettes were lurking round our gateway and in the courtyard.

'How's it going?' I asked them. 'You put up a good show, so I hear. You ought to get a reward for it.'

'That's up to you, Captain.'

'Come in, I'll give you some vodka and a few hundred cigarettes each. And it'll be honestly come by.'

'We're not bothered about that any more. We don't fancy going on with it.'

'What do you want, then?'

'We'd like to join your army.'

'My "army"?'

'We've taken a fancy to it. You've got a good crowd there. You're all right yourself; you know how to treat a bloke right. Besides, no one asks questions. What's past is over and done with. We're Poles too. . . .'

And they stood there in front of me, just the same as yesterday—and yet how different! It struck me that perhaps this was the only chance they'd ever had in their lives.

'All right, I'll try. Alexander, you take charge of them.'

I read through the reports that had just come in. Corporal Rola was shot in the groin yesterday in Lucka Street, and has been taken to hospital in Sliska Street. Cadet Smigly is wounded. The number of casualties from the Soviet bombing as shown in the previous report was inaccurate and the list now includes a fourth name.

Our telephone connection with the Ceglana Street position has been cut. The officer in command there has sent a runner asking for the first-aid squad, for Slawek has been hit. Turek has just been brought in on a stretcher and placed gently in the courtyard. There is no morphia left. . . .

'Try caffeine. . . .'

Turek threw his head back and stared at the sky. Then Cadet Jasio, who had been leaning over him, straightened his back and took a deep breath.

'It doesn't matter. He's dead.'

The last report which I read said that Father Oracz has been killed by an artillery shell in Sliska Street, on his way to visit a dying woman. He was dead before the first-aid squad could reach him.

Just before his death some of the girls had been talking to him.

He'd visited the battalion cook-house and they'd given him a bowl of soup. Then, as he was leaving, he told them that he disliked hearing confession, but that if any of them wanted to attend, then he'd take confession next day after mass. Nearly all the girls had decided to go.

Finally I noted down the daily situation report:

'All positions still held in 2 Battalion sector of the "Chrobry II" group.'

Sunday, 17 September

While graves were being dug for Father Oracz and Rifleman Turek in the little space of ground behind our headquarters, an artillery shell killed our Moslem Mullah, leader of our little group of 'Caucasians', and seriously wounded one of his Armenians. Four more men from the Caucasian platoon immediately volunteered to carry on, and by midday the job was finished.

But I didn't attend the burials. The Germans have been attacking from two sides, from Towarowa Street and also from Grzybowska Street. So I gave instructions that the burials were to take place quickly and that as few men as possible should be present. I heard afterwards that a priest had been in attendance, but that he'd cleared off again after saying a short prayer, without waiting for the bodies to be lowered into the graves. At the last moment, someone revealed that Oracz's real name was Father Jozef Kowalczyk. A scrap of paper bearing his name was placed in a corked bottle at the dead man's feet in his grave.

Some hours later I crossed the little space where they'd been buried, and saw that the little cross which had been placed on Oracz's grave was already damaged. He'd only been with us twelve days, but we all knew we'd seen the last of a good friend. In him, I bade farewell to one of the finest soldiers in the whole battalion.

Immediately afterwards, I was told of the death of yet another of my friends—Lieutenant Tadeusz. He has been killed in

Chmielna Street, as he was leading his men in to a counter-attack. A grenade ripped open his abdomen, and he died in very great pain. Marta has been wounded in the head. Zenek took over command of the platoon and carried on, and they drove the Germans out of No. 8.

Thus Tadeusz is dead. I'd worked with him two years in the secret printing-press, and yet I knew very little about him—where he came from, whether he had any relatives or even what his real name was. Sometimes he called himself Tadeusz Mycke, at other times he used identity papers in the name of Marian Tarski. All I know is that if a 'hero' is a man who always does his best no matter what happens, then Tadeusz was a 'hero' right up to his death.

At dusk his men brought his body. They placed the stretcher bearing his body wrapped in a blanket in the gateway. I saluted and told them to leave him for the night on the landing by my billet. As they were about to obey, one of the men took hold of the blanket in both hands and drew it off.

'Look, sir,' he said.

I looked at him. I had to.

I went back to my reports: as usual 'All positions held'. It was already quite dark when Wislanski handed a note to the runner, Pataszon.

'Take it to Group H.Q. and bring a receipt back.'

A few minutes later Wanda came into the office.

'What's the matter with Pataszon?' she asked.

'He's gone over to Group H.Q. with a message.'

'He must have come back then, or something must have happened, for he's sitting on the stairs and crying.'

I went out and saw him there, sobbing.

'What is it, Pataszon? Why haven't you taken the message?'

'I'm . . . afraid.'

'You've never been afraid before, so why are you now? What is it? Listen, they're not firing any longer.'

'It isn't the firing that I'm afraid of. Only it's so dark out there,

and quiet. And the chaplain, and Turek, and Lieutenant
Tadeusz. . . .'

'Yes, I see,' I said, trying to sound kind and putting my arm
round him. 'All the same, that's no reason for crying, is it?
You're a big boy now. Still, don't worry, I'll get someone else
to go.'

'No!' Pataszon exclaimed. 'I'm not crying because I'm afraid,
but because I haven't taken the message! I've *got* to take it.'

'Good for you, Pataszon. But hold on a minute. Wanda has to
go in that direction; you can go together, and you'll both feel
better. And you take this revolver. I've got a Mauser, and can
manage without it.'

He stood speechless for an instant. His eyes gleamed as he took
hold of the revolver tightly.

Monday, 18 September
                              Today started off badly. Ever
since dawn, heavy artillery shells from 'Big Bertha' have been
coming over regularly every five minutes, but today the shells
have been going over us and falling nearer to Twarda Street and
in the eastern part of the ruins of the 'Little Ghetto'. There is
no one in that sector, but we fear for the bake-house and also
our access to the nearest well is being rendered difficult. Now
and again the field artillery from the goods station goes into
action.

I have forbidden the men to gather for the burial of the
'Mullah' on account of this troublesome fire. His fellow Moslems
have performed all the proper rites and they have asked for permission to bury him next to Father Oracz.

Then came the burial of Tadeusz. His men wanted to bury him
in Grzybowska Street, near the ruins of the printing-press, and
have somehow managed to get hold of a coffin. They have
already taken his body from my headquarters over to Grzybowska Street, as it is nearer the German positions and therefore
quieter.

Tadeusz's platoon has been relieved from Chmielna Street for a few hours, in order to attend his burial. I telephoned to Jerzewski, to find out whether the order has yet come through awarding Tadeusz the Virtuti Militari Cross. It hadn't, but Jerzewski knew that the order had been signed, so was able to authorise me to fasten the blue-black ribbon to his body in the coffin.

Two coffins and two graves were waiting in Grzybowska Street. After six weeks they had at last been able to extricate the body of Stas-the-Sailor from the ruins of No. 17, and they told me they'd found his head lying several yards away from the rest of his body. He died swiftly, not by suffocation. His coffin had been nailed down, for his body was already in a state of decomposition.

No chaplain has yet been posted to our sector, and the men asked me to say something. I tried to explain how hard it would be. For the first time since the beginning of the Insurrection—perhaps even since the beginning of the war—I felt like breaking down. I was ashamed, and went off into a gateway and lit a cigarette without waiting for them to scatter earth over the coffin.

And it was at this moment that a couple of civilians started bothering me. To begin with, they talked about the shortage of food, of water, of light. Then about diseases, wounds uncared for, men killed. Then about politics, that there's no sense in the Insurrection, that we ought to surrender. They became more and more excited and stubborn, and took offence, and held me responsible for what they are going through, because I insist on holding Grzybowska Street.

I listened without a word until one of them came at me with his fists clenched, shouting:

'You want to be a hero, but who is going to look after *us*?'
Then something took hold of me.

'Are you talking to me?' I burst out. 'Why talk to me about it? Look there! All those men buried out there died carrying out orders I gave them. None of them asked who'd look after him.

All I could give them was death. If you want to be looked after, go and ask the Germans. . . .'

I felt bad even before I'd finished letting myself lose control in this way. Just then some of the girls came up, turned the civilians away, then drew me into the shadows.

'Lech, calm down! They're nothing but cowards. Great strong men like them ought to be fighting with the rest of us, but instead they hang about in the cellars. They don't even want to help in digging. Don't bother about them. But we're with you, you know that. . . .'

This was said by Stasiowa Toporowska, whose husband had just been buried. Then Corporal Miecz's widow, Genia Iwanska and Mrs. Nawrocka, the tailor's wife, all took me by the arm and led me into a ground-floor flat.

'Come on, Lech,' they said. 'We've made some porridge for you, and there's a glass of vodka too. That'll put some heart into you again.'

But what really did put new heart into me arrived all at once from—literally—heaven.

I'd just got back to my billet in Panska Street and was listening to Wislanski's report, when the sentry at the gateway gave warning of aircraft approaching.

I went out to look. There, straight ahead to the north and very high up, I saw aircraft coming over. They looked like silver birds in a blue sky lightly scattered with little clouds. I counted twelve of them, then more and more, until I lost count. The roar of their engines grew, for they were coming straight towards us.

Someone was counting them aloud,

'102, 105, 108. . . .'

I looked through my binoculars. They weren't German or Soviet. Then someone shouted:

'They're Liberators! And they're ours!'

Everyone ran out into the street, and scrambled up on the rubble to try to get a better look. I didn't know where they'd all sprung from. It was as though the dead had arisen from their graves.

Then dozens of little clouds opened out round the aircraft as the German A.A. opened fire. But they were out of range, and the shells burst too low. Shrapnel began falling around us, and I shouted to everyone to take cover, but no one heeded. Then three black dots fell away from the leading planes, to be followed at once by more and more, while little coloured circles appeared over the dots—parachutes opening out.

'Parachutists!'

Everyone went mad. They jumped up and down waving, hugging one another. . . .

'No, not parachutists—it's arms! They're dropping arms.'

Now we could see the long metal containers more clearly, and the first fell directly into our sector. Then the wind carried the rest farther and farther away.

Suddenly, as the lads were hurrying to and fro and even before the first container had landed, there was a roar from the German positions—rifles, machine-guns, grenades, mortars, artillery—the lot. They were firing at us along the whole length of their line.

With Rys and Genek I ran out to the first container, which had fallen near Walicow Street in the ghetto ruins, fortunately in a deep hollow. The metal fasteners opened easily and inside we found boxes fitted with straps, ready to be slung over the shoulders. They contained British machine-guns with ammo, and a few minutes later the first were ready for firing.

I went back to our headquarters, where two still-unopened containers were lying in the gateway, brought in from farther away. The lads brought in more containers, and company commanders started to report to me by telephone how many they'd obtained. At the same time they all told me that they were going out in full force against fierce German attack. I asked if they needed any reinforcements, but no one did. Each officer said that today their lads would go out against the devil himself.

We then opened the other containers: the first held Sten guns and ammo; the next contained equipment for sappers—mines, percussion caps, revolvers; the third had anti-tank weapons; the fourth food, including corned beef from the Argentine, chocolate and biscuits; the fifth held medical supplies.

The hands of the ambulance girls trembled a little as we handed over phials of blood for transfusions. They bore labels in Polish, for the blood had been donated by Poles at the Polish hospital in Edinburgh.

Tuesday, 19 September

Oddly enough, despite the heavy enemy fire yesterday as we were collecting the supplies dropped from the planes, and despite the heavy German attack, we have had very few casualties. Only Zola, a runner in my headquarters platoon, was wounded, and Wisla in Kos' company. Some civilians were slightly hurt, but they have all been seen to by the ambulance girls.

And today there's a festive feeling everywhere as we count up the wealth we've acquired and show them to the people crowding round. Everyone wanted to have a good look and to handle things or at least touch them. We've barricaded up the door from Panska Street with sand-bags, and have laid everything out on the floor and shelves inside the shop front.

Nobody grumbled because most of the supplies fell beyond our lines and have thus got into the hands of the Germans. Even if nine-tenths of the supplies had been carried away by the wind, it wouldn't have mattered very much, for they have plenty of arms and ammunition anyway, as well as medical stores, while every single container to reach us has meant salvation.

What impressed us was that everything is just what we want, and we could see how much thought must have gone into every little detail and the care with which everything was packed. We found thick woollen socks packed tight in the spaces between the boxes of ammo; there were oil-cans with the machine-guns, even little keys for opening the tins of corned beef, not to mention toilet soap and towels used as protection for the medical supplies. And not a single item was damaged in the drop. The girls have been laying aside the fine silk parachutes, which are of various pastel shades.

We couldn't help laughing at the sight of some tins of corned beef which had been riddled by bullets so that they looked like sieves. These were from a container which fell in the no-man's-land between our positions and the Germans, and for which a desperate battle waged for several hours. Neither we nor the Germans could get at it. At last our lads managed to lassoo it, but before they could haul it in the Germans sprayed it with machine-gun bullets. Had it contained arms there'd have been hell to pay; as it was, however, the episode turned into a joke. Corned beef still tastes good even when it's been sprayed with lead.

Fortunately, food was the least part of the supplies. Only the wounded and ill will get the chocolate and biscuits, and this made me wonder whether I counted as one of them. Anyhow, as we were unpacking the containers, no one could resist trying the sweets, so I satisfied my greed by finishing off one of the biscuits and a bit of chocolate.

A more serious temptation confronting me was that of concealing from the higher-ups the amount of arms we'd acquired, for I knew that if I told them the exact number they'd order me to hand over the lion's share to other units. Yet they've never once shared their weapons with us! Every rifle, every revolver, has been 'won' by my lads from the Germans.

I told Captain Jerzewski this frankly, and in the end gave him a complete list of the containers and what was in them.

'Of course, you're in the right,' he had to admit, 'the more so as you're probably the only commanding officer of the lot who hasn't tried to hide something. We'll strike a bargain somehow, and I'll see you're not hard done by.'

So we got six machine-guns, fourteen Stens, six anti-tank guns and some revolvers with ammo to match, as well as a set of sapper's equipment. This is less than half of what we got altogether, but we're to have some Soviet arms in part exchange. What I want most of all are anti-tank guns and grenade-throwers. In any case, even though some of our 'booty' has gone, we have been left with a feeling of strength. Besides, we now have more ammo than the total quantity used since fighting started.

Just before dusk I went to a conference at Group Headquarters. I deliberately went rather too early, as I wanted to sort out the complicated question of daily strength returns, which are a constant source of misunderstanding between Captain Twardy and myself. As I crossed Twarda Street I met Bogda.

'If you're going in our direction, perhaps you could call in and see us,' she said. 'The chaplain would be pleased to see you.'

'A new chaplain?'

'Yes, he joined us yesterday, and today he held mass in the cellar at No. 56, Sliska Street. He looks very ill and could hardly manage to get over to Panska Street. But he said he'd like to meet the C.O. of the battalion. You'll find him in our billet.'

So I went into the little room behind the cook-house. A thick-set priest in a long black cassock rose to his feet with some difficulty. He had a dark-skinned face and his features were almost Eastern.

'Evidently I'm interrupting,' I said, after greeting him; then, in order not to involve myself in a long conversation, I added: 'I didn't want to disturb you.'

'The chaplain was just telling us about what it was like in the Old Town,' Maruta told me. 'He was there up to the last day and came away with the men through the sewers. You ought to listen.'

'Well then, you see . . . what was I saying?'

'You were telling us about the air-raid, when they dropped bombs weighing a ton!'

'Yes. . . . Well, just then I happened to be in the ruins of the Dominican Church. Do you know it? I'm sure you all remember the wonderful golden altars . . . but you'll never see them again now, they've been destroyed. Someone pulled me down into the crypt. Down there, deep under the earth, was the H.Q. and the hospital. Runners kept coming and going, ambulance girls were bringing in wounded. There were a few candles, flickering in the draught. The wounded men lay packed close together, and I went from one to the next to ask if there was anything I could do for them. One man was lying very still and I leaned over him. "My son, can I help you?" I asked him. But he didn't answer, and I took hold of his hand to see whether he was still alive. . . .'

He fell silent, staring in front of him, and shivered.

'Shall I get you some coffee? You're tired. . . .'

'No, my child. It's just that I can't help remembering. . . . For there, lying among the wounded men, I'd come on the miraculous wax figure of Christ from the Cathedral. I knelt down. The bombing started again, and then the roof of the crypt began to collapse. . . . I still don't know how I got out of the ruins. . . . I was the only one who survived of all those people down there.'

Wednesday, 20 September

Captain Jerzewski has just told me that I am to get another company in my battalion—Kos' company, which has hitherto been included in Captain Zelazny's battalion. This is as compensation for Jeremy's company, which was posted to the Jarnuszkiewicz factory some time ago and was finally taken over by Captain Rum's battalion.

This means that my sector has been lengthened to the south from Lucka Street as far as Panska Street, and will include, for tactical purposes, the position in the Hartwig warehouse between Panska and Sienna Streets.

I asked Jerzewski why this decision had been made, for I don't want Captain Zelazny to bear a grudge against me now that his battalion and sector have been decreased to my advantage. But I only got an evasive reply.

Not long afterwards, Marta came across from Chmielna Street, and said that the men formerly under Tadeusz's command have now ejected the Germans from No. 9, Chmielna Street. This action was led by Corporal Zenek, who carried it out without any casualties.

Three officers had just reported to me from Group Headquarters.

One of them, Captain Zet, who is a Regular Army officer, has thirty years' service behind him, and this bothers me a little. We both have the same rank, though I've held mine for only three weeks, while my experience and knowledge can't be compared with his and it is he who really ought to be in command of the battalion. On the other hand, it was immediately plain that he hasn't much energy or physical strength.

'You're a godsend,' I told him and meant it. 'Now that another company has been posted to me and the sector as a whole has been enlarged, I'll have to spend a good deal more time out in the line. Meanwhile, all sorts of things will have to be dealt with here at H.Q., so I'd be grateful if you'd take over as my deputy for tactics, organisation and training.'

The second of the officers, Lieutenant Wit, explained he'd come to us simply as a matter of form.

'All I want is for you, as C.O. of a unit in the line, to sign the necessary recommendation for me to be promoted to Captain,' he explained. 'That's all and there's no point in you giving me a job here because as soon as the promotion comes through I'll have to get back to Group H.Q., as they can't do without me.'

'In that case, you can spend those few days out in Lucka Street. You'll get plenty of opportunity there to earn your promotion. Might I ask when you were promoted Lieutenant?'

'In 1940, in France.'

'And Second-Lieutenant?'

'I don't have to answer that question. . . .'

Second-Lieutenant Kos reported for instructions during the afternoon. His head was bandaged as a result of severe bruises he'd sustained a few days before in Towarowa Street. He was accompanied by Sergeant Kuba who, as I soon realised, is Kos' right-hand man. They reported on their strength and arms. Kos' company numbers 196 people, of whom about 150 are actually in the line. They have three light machine-guns, each of a different make—one British, the others Belgian and German—as well as 20 rifles, 14 machine-pistols, 2 home-made machine-pistols, 13 revolvers and a heavy machine-gun (a Russian 'Maxim') which

they'd 'won' during the second week in August but which they'd
had to hand over to No. 1 Battalion. They had to obey the order
to hand this machine-gun over, but they still think that I ought
to ask for it back, particularly as the Belgian gun is useless, as
there is no ammo for it.

Kos' company, which was formerly No. 2 Company, has
been re-christened No. 6 Company.

I suggested to Kos that he should at once take me on a tour of
inspection of his sector, and Captain Zet agreed to come with us.
Sergeant Kuba had a wooden leg, but nevertheless could get
about on the uneven ground without assistance. I asked him
about himself, and learned that he was a car-mechanic and driver
and has a wife and four children. He served in anti-aircraft and
lost his leg at Kutno in September 1939. Then he took part in the
Underground, and served in a Home Army partisan group in the
forests.

From what he and Kos told me, I realised that our battalion
was not, as I'd thought, the only one to be formed out of nothing
when the fighting started in Warsaw. Apparently, a number of
units were formed out of various almost unarmed platoons and
sections of all kinds of Underground organisations, with single
volunteers who joined in during the fighting.

When we reached Kos' sector, I found that the area is divided
into two parts, and that the positions, situated in ruined houses, are
linked up by long trenches across an open space. The Germans are
sitting tight in bunkers along the western side of Wronia Street.

All the buildings in the sector are burned out, but as some of the
ruins are still standing, our positions in some places are not more
than twenty yards from those of the Germans.

All the men made an excellent impression on me. They're
well disciplined, though hardly anyone bothers about saluting or
the use of ranks; the lads (and the girls too) all swagger a bit, but
they don't show off. They're observant and vigilant and have
plenty of self-control when under fire. In fact, they're no different from the men of No. 4 and No. 5 Companies.

We climbed to the fourth floor of the Hartwig warehouse,

from which there is a good view to the west, over the chaos of dead railway lines and sidings. From this position our observers today watched Soviet planes bombing German artillery positions. Not one enemy aircraft had shown itself all day. Almost immediately below where we stood, we could see the Germans in their concrete hide-aways.

Thursday, 21 September

An Order of the Day issued this morning by the 'Chrobry II' Group Headquarters contains Alexander's well-deserved promotion to the rank of lieutenant. Wislanski was somewhat impatient because we haven't yet had any official confirmation of my promotion to captain, and without asking me he telephoned to Captain Twardy about it. There he was told that a number of recommendations had been burned during the bombing of Area Headquarters, and that probably the one referring to me was among them. Captain Twardy said he'd again put forward all the recommendations which have not yet been dealt with, and hoped that they'd be signed within a couple of days.

Soon after this, I was brought special Orders issued by General Bor, C.-in-C. of the Home Army, and by Monter, who is C.O. of the Warsaw area and who has also been promoted to general. These orders were to be passed on to all ranks, and they confirm something that each one of us already felt—that the worst and most difficult days are already past.

'Today we stand on the threshold of victory,' says Monter's Order. 'As a result of our heroic self-sacrifice and stubborn endurance, Warsaw has been able to hold out until help and succour are now at hand.'

General Bor writes:

'The battle with the Germans in Warsaw is drawing to a close. That which seemed impossible is in fact coming true.'

Both Orders anticipate the entry of Soviet troops into Warsaw very soon, and at the same time they dispel the doubts which every one of us has been feeling as to what is to happen next. . . .

'Our task will not end with the cessation of hostilities in Warsaw. We must recreate the Polish armed forces as soon as possible, and take our revenge on German territory for all the injuries, humiliation and losses inflicted on us by the German criminals. To achieve this, you will have to overcome your weariness, and maintain strong, inspired military units which will constitute the basis of the Polish Army.'

It was nearly time to report to Group Headquarters for further orders. I asked Olgierd if he'd like to come with me to the hospital in Sliska Street, as we ought to visit the wounded, and today we'd be able to take them some good news.

When we reached the hospital, they directed us down into the cellars. Most of the wounded were down here, for the upper floors were all wrecked. We were hit by the stench of festering wounds in the gloomy corridors, and had to get past corpses ready to be taken away for burial. Dirty, blood-stained mattresses lay on the stone floor and there were usually two wounded men to one mattress. It was difficult to get by on account of the ambulance girls hurrying about. Then someone called to me in Russian, and I had to lean over to make out his face. It was the Azerbaidjani who was wounded in the lungs a few days ago. He was muttering something, but I couldn't make out what. A nurse going by stopped for a moment.

'He's delirious and hasn't long to live.'

'When did they operate on him?'

'The men here are all still waiting to be operated on. The doctors are working twenty hours a day and can't keep up. In any case, I'm afraid it's already too late to do anything for him. . . .'

'All the same, perhaps we could save him if . . .'

A lean figure lifted itself on the next mattress and I saw a man's face distorted with pain, his eyes smouldering.

'What's that?' he demanded. 'There isn't room for our own men, and yet they bring in a Kalmuk and want to give him preferential treatment. That's a Polish officer for you! Shame on you!'

Farther along the wards, which were closely packed with beds, it was cleaner and lighter. I saw Rola.

'Everything's all right, sir,' he said, just as he always used to. 'How are they doing in Lucka Street? Holding out, I'll bet!'

'Don't worry about that. We've got hold of plenty of arms and ammo.'

'I heard about it. You've only got to look at those Huns over there on the other side of the ward and you can see our lads are coming out on top. They haven't said a word for two days. Yet whenever the Huns get the better of our lads somewhere, they know all about it better than we do, and they never stop jabbering. That makes us mad.'

'Where are the rest of our lads?' I asked him.

'I only know that White Russian who was in our platoon—he's in the next ward. He got gangrene in his leg but wouldn't let them take it off, and it wasn't until the gangrene spread above his knee that they decided to take no notice and cut it off. And you could hear the saw jarring against the bone from in here!'

When we got to Group Headquarters, I was shown an Order for the reorganisation of the Home Army units fighting in Warsaw into regular units of the Polish Forces, so that all the Home Army units in Warsaw and districts round the city will now become the Warsaw Corps of the Home Army, under General Monter, and which is to be composed of three divisions.

They'd summoned me in connection with a paragraph in the Order which concerns organising the 15th Infantry Regiment, as I am to be O.C. of a battalion in this regiment. However, as the formation of this battalion would involve the withdrawal of all our units from the line for at least twelve hours, it is out of the question for the time being.

So we decided to draw up the battalion on paper, i.e. work out in detail a plan for mobilisation which can then be put into effect within a few hours as soon as the Soviet troops enter Warsaw or the Germans pull out. Meanwhile, as long as fighting continues, we shall have to stick to our organisation as it is at present.

We have been issued with Russian weapons, and I asked Captain Buzunov to draw up instructions on how to use them, which Lieutenant Mazur will then translate into Polish. Then a squad of men from each platoon is to be trained in handling the weapons.

There is no shortage now of weapons, but we lack men able to handle them. We've been fighting for eight weeks, and sheer physical exhaustion due to shortage of food, illness and wounds means we can no longer keep the lads out in the line for several days at a time as we used to. Reinforcements are less than casualties. I didn't know what to do.

In the end, I gave instructions for a rifle platoon to be made up of women and girls. After some training, they will be able to relieve the men from sentry duty. There were plenty of volunteers for this platoon, and command was taken over by Barbara with the rank of corporal, and Olga as her deputy.

In the evening, we all drank to the decoration of Deska, Tadeusz and Ostoja. The celebration was held in the lads' billet on the first floor of our headquarters, and the whole thing horrified Captain Zet, who didn't at all approve of this undermining of discipline and proper respect for rank.

Friday, 22 September

The formation of a battalion to be part of the 15th Infantry Regiment is proving much more difficult than I'd foreseen when the Order was first issued. Moreover, the only advice I've been able to get on how to tackle the job is 'use my common sense'. So I've started from the top by appointing officers to the three rifle companies and the one machine-gun company. But it's almost as bad as trying to square a circle, for it involves finding suitable officers, which means I can only appoint infantry officers while officers in other branches will have to be transferred elsewhere and sorted out there. Besides, I have to consider age, medical category and training, so that hardly any of my soldiers fit in with what is required.

Lieutenant Alexander, for instance, is a cavalry officer—so he'll have to go: Wislanski is too old, Henio has bad eyesight, Czes was once trained in the artillery, Pataszon is too young . . . they'll all have to be transferred.

In the end, I sent Captain Zet to talk it over with Jerzewski.

'Ask him to make clear what it is they want,' I told him. 'Ask whether what they have in mind is a real fighting battalion which will be able to follow up on the German defeat, in accordance with General Bor's Order of the Day, or whether they want a good old peace-time formation to take over barracks somewhere as laid down in Regulations.'

'I don't think these requirements are necessarily contradictory,' Captain Zet replied. 'After all, an army has got to be an *army*—you can't run an army for any length of time purely by improvisation. Partisans can never replace a regular army, nor can personal initiative replace training and professional qualifications.'

'I quite agree that they should, for instance, transfer any Air Force men from my sector—as long as they've got planes for them. But what about men like Alexander? You must admit, after all, that he's an ideal company commander. But what will they give him to do? Put him on a horse, with a lance in one hand? . . .'

Buzonov has learned from today's papers that two Soviet officers have reached Warsaw by air in order to initiate 'tactical co-operation' with us, and he thought it was his duty to report to them. Thus he asked me to send him over to see them. As, however, I didn't know where General Bor has his headquarters, nor where these Soviet officers actually are, all I could do was to promise to try to find out. I soon learned that the officers, who are from General Rokossowski's staff, have no authority and are in fact nothing more than telegraph operators, whose job is to establish communications with the Soviet Headquarters by means of a short-wave transmitter and codes which they've brought in with them. After thinking this over for a long time,

Buzunov decided that, after all, he wouldn't report to them personally, but instead he's written a report which is to be transmitted to the Red Army staff 'by the proper channels via the Home Army H.Q.'. In this report, he gives details of himself and states that he is on duty in the No. 2 Battalion of the 'Chrobry II' group under Captain Lech Grzybowski, i.e. me. I passed this on to Group Headquarters and asked them to forward it to the right quarters.

Halina and Ostoja, from Chmielna Street, have put in an application asking for permission to see me in order to make a request. I was amazed by all this formality in approaching me.

'They don't have to go through all that just to see me,' I said. 'Why don't they simply come in and get it over?'

'They're particularly anxious for it to be done properly, according to Army Regulations.'

'Well, in that case . . .'

So I saw them both and learned that what they wanted was permission to get married.

'What has this to do with me? It's your own private affair.'

'We want you to stand for Halina's father, sir.'

'And for Ostoja's father, sir.'

They both called me 'sir', though as a rule we call each other simply by our Christian names.

'When do you want to get married?'

'Tomorrow. The chaplain says he'll marry us straight away, providing we get written permission from you, sir. We'd also like to have you as a witness.'

'Well, if all this isn't just about the last word. . . . All right, get married and I wish you lots of luck. I'll be glad to come, of course!'

Saturday, 23 September

The German artillery fire, instead of dying down, seems to be increasing from day to day, and I try not to issue passes to the lads even for them to go and see their families, since rather too many of them don't come back again. It isn't until later that we're informed by hospitals in other districts of the city, either that the man in question has been wounded or that he's dead. Instead, I encourage them to bring their families into our sector, where we've really settled down. All the gateways have been strengthened, the cellar windows blocked with sand-bags of earth and cement, the tunnels widened so that you can run through them if necessary; while all the entrances are accessible and well protected. The firm cellar vaultings in the big factory and warehouse buildings all stand up well to the artillery shells, and the higher the rubble overhead the stronger they are.

The lads continue to improve their methods of defensive fighting every day, and to gain experience and self-assurance. They now know which positions are out of range of particular enemy fire, and listen coolly to the shriek of shells going overhead or nip into a trench as soon as they recognise a shell from 'Big Bertha'. It is only shells from mortars which fall unexpectedly, reaching into holes and the narrow courtyards of houses.

Lieutenant Pszczolka has 'won' for us the equipment necessary for laying telephone wires, and now our battalion telephone exchange is connected with Group Headquarters and with the officers in command of near-by battalions and with all our own positions. All the telephone cables are double, and even when a shell rips them, Cadet Kario and four of his lads are always quickly on the spot to repair any damage.

Despite continued efforts, we haven't been able to dig a well anywhere, as we lack the necessary tools, and it's very difficult to dig deep enough with ordinary spades. The Caucasians help the ambulance girls by bringing water in, but their numbers are decreasing. Matros, for instance, was wounded in the legs while bringing water from the ghetto sector, and can't walk. His friend, the tall school-teacher, has broken down, and Ali hides in the latrine whenever someone has to go for water. Janka drives him out of it mercilessly. The three who are carrying on best are Volodya, 'The Engineer' and Ivan. They've paid a visit to the

Azerbaidjani in the Sliska Street hospital, and found that he
hasn't died yet, after all. Unexpectedly his temperature went
down and his wound, though not treated, has healed of its own
accord. Now they've brought him back from the hospital to their
billet, where he is recovering. The only trouble is that he won't
let anyone take off his turban, though it's infested with lice.

Wislanski continues to amaze me. He claims he was born in
1885, but we all suspect that he's hiding his real age. Of course he
has every right to do so. Yet he's on duty all the time and gets
hardly any sleep. Though he was wounded in the leg with shrapnel, he refused to have it seen to in hospital or even stay in his
billet, and simply came back to the battalion office and got on
with his work as if nothing had happened. And in addition he
fusses over me, brings me coffee, makes sure my revolver is
loaded, and makes me go and have a nap when he thinks I need
one.

I took Maria to the wedding of Halina and Ostoja, as she was
to be their second witness. We cut across Marszalkowska Street
to Szpitalna Street.

Bombing is still heavy in this sector and the streets were deserted, the blocks of flats were dead. Only now and then a stoop-
ing figure would hurry along under the walls, and as we were
about to go over a crossing, someone shouted to us from a
hidden sentry-post:

'Look out! It's under fire. . . .'

So we crouched down and quickened our steps. Nearly all the
paving-stones have been torn up and built into long barricades
across any point that is under enemy fire. In Chmielna Street we
could feel that the Germans were near, and we made our way
along from one gateway to the next into No. 10. We were among
friends here, and I was led down narrow stone steps into a low
cellar, where the priest and happy couple were waiting for us,
surrounded by soldiers all armed to the teeth. Ostoja handed his
home-made machine-pistol over to a comrade to look after.

'Chaplain, we can begin now!'

A small table served as altar, covered by a clean embroidered cloth, with a black crucifix standing on it, and from behind the Cross the Holy Virgin of Czestochowa looked gently down at us.

'There are Germans on the other side of that wall,' one of the lads whispered to me, indicating the wall behind the altar.

The soldiers knelt here and there on the floor, amidst scattered packing-cases, holding their helmets in their left hands and slowly crossing themselves with the right. The smell of wax tapers mingled with the smell of dampness and human sweat: it reminded me of catacombs.

When the ceremony was over and the documents signed, we all kissed the newly-married couple and made ready to be off.

'You can't go yet! We're going on to the reception now. The whole platoon has been relieved for the night in honour of the occasion. The chaplain is coming too.'

'Where to?'

'To the Palladium picture-house. That's our billet.'

Czes was in charge at the Palladium, and on the first floor a long table had been laid with plates and glasses. Sandwiches made of herrings and pickled cucumbers looked delicious, and three one-litre bottles of vodka stood among them.

The guests came in twos and threes, as the whole crowd from Chmielna Street weren't all able to come at once. Ostoja in a dark-blue uniform and Halina in a German overall sat at the head of the table, with the young chaplain next to them. There was also 'The Admiral', who represented Monter—though no one knew whether Monter had given his permission for him to do this. Then came Maria and I. We began to drink their health, and someone made a speech interrupted from time to time by singing. . . .

Then a shell burst somewhere very near.

'Quiet, Hans!' Czes shouted. 'Don't interrupt!'

Things were beginning to liven up and the lads were crowding round the bride, and I thought it was about time for Maria and me to get back to our home.

Sunday, 24 September

The Germans must have gone mad. The Bolsheviks have crossed the Vistula to the south and north of Warsaw and are attacking them from the rear, and patrols from the Praga suburb have landed on our side of the river, and yet the Germans are gathering all their strength in order to smash what are left of our positions in the city.

I haven't been able to keep my promise to Father Czeslaw to attend at least one of his Sunday services. Today I've been uneasily awaiting the arrival of some lieutenant-colonel or other who is to carry out an inspection of the battalion. I didn't know how we'd be able to undertake a tour of inspection under this heavy fire. Artillery was firing, the walls shook at every explosion and shrapnel was falling all round.

Two men have been killed in Ceglana Street: one was Cadet Bladolicy, killed while repairing a telephone line. The other has not yet been identified.

The ruins of the 'Little Ghetto' are under very heavy fire, and I've had to hold up the transport columns crossing them to the mill. Then we posted sentries to direct people by roundabout ways through the tunnels. One of the No. 1 Battalion squads has mutinied, led by Second-Lieutenant Danek.

Jerzewski told me he was sending them over to see me.

'They're fine men who'd go anywhere . . . if they want to. You'll be able to deal with them.'

Danek then turned up, a big chap, accompanied by his girl-runner and eight big Guardsmen. I hadn't time to talk to them, for the colonel we'd been expecting arrived at that moment. He wasn't interested in paper work, nor was he bothered by the firing, as he wanted to see the whole sector and inspect all our positions. We went out together.

Second-Lieutenant Mars' billets were empty, as all the lads were out in the line. Then we visited the sick-bay of No. 6 Company at No. 41, Zelazna Street, and after that we went on down Sienna Street to Kazimierz Square, where we found Sergeant Ursus and his platoon. He reported the strength of the platoon—43 people, of whom 32 are armed and 5 are girls.

The headquarters of No. 6 Company was at Miedziana Street. Here Lieutenant Kos, who is in charge of the company, came with us himself to the Hartwig warehouse. We went up to the positions on the second floor, and were shown a German bunker on the opposite side of Towarowa Street which had been destroyed during the night.

'Lieutenant Kos tried out a Soviet anti-tank gun.'

'How did it go?'

'It looked as though it had been put together by a blacksmith, but it worked all right and didn't jam like an English one does at the least bit of grit.'

We continued along the most outlying of our positions towards Panska Street. On the way the colonel stopped to talk to nearly everyone we met and to look out at the enemy fortifications. In a courtyard divided from Prosta Street by a high, strong wall we were told to crouch down.

'Why?'

The lads showed us a small round hole in the wall, about the size of a half-crown.

'We made this hole ourselves, as there's a strong German bunker opposite and we wanted to be able to fire at it. But now the German inside the bunker is getting fed-up and keeps on firing at this hole. He's a good shot, though—never misses. Look!'

Corporal Katyniak pushed an empty match-box into the hole. Bang! There was a bullet through it.

At No. 15, Lucka Street they showed us where a Russian bomb had fallen.

'This is where we'd put out strips of cloth as signals to them. It can't have been a mistake. The swine was flying low too.'

Things were getting hotter beyond Lucka Street, and as we went into the headquarters of No. 5 Company we saw the body of a youth, covered with a blanket, lying in the entry.

'Who's that?'

'It's young Plater, who was seventeen not long ago. He was hit a few hours ago in the trenches towards Zelazna Street.'

The colonel, deep in thought, saluted the boy.

'Captain, I want you to put his name forward for a posthumous award of the Cross of Valour.'

Lieutenant Silkiewicz told me that two ambulance girls have been wounded today, one in the stomach, the other in the neck.

Okularnik's comrades were making fun of him in the position in Ceglana Street. Two German officers, who clearly didn't know the terrain, had missed their way and gone past the ground-floor window at which Okularnik was stationed with a Sten-gun. He let them go past towards our barricade, and not until they wanted to get back again did he open fire at them at some twelve paces range. He'd missed.

'I was too sure of myself and my hands were shaking like a jelly,' Okularnik protested. 'But I'll make up for it.'

At last we reached Walicow Street.

'This is the weakest spot in our defence system, Colonel,' said Alexander, who had joined us. 'The street is where our sector links up with the next battalion, and we don't seem able to co-operate. Sometimes we simply can't make out why they open fire too soon, while at other times we have to withstand German attacks on our own, as though there wasn't anyone in their sector at all. I'd sooner hold the whole street ourselves.'

'But there'd still be that point of contact, except that it would be farther away. You'll have to find some way of reaching an understanding with them.'

Then we had to go back to Panska Street. The artillery and mortar fire had lessened somewhat. As my order about not crossing the Ghetto didn't apply to us, we decided to take a short-cut that way. Telephone cables showed the safest route across the maze of hollows and mounds, and in places the path was well trodden by telephone operators, ambulance girls and platoons moving up into the line. Before reaching Panska Street, the path turned a little to the east to go round the highest of the

piles of rubble which bars the entry to our headquarters, but at
the same time provides it with some cover.

Alexander went first, followed by the colonel, while I brought
up the rear.

'Come back!' I suddenly shouted to Alexander. 'Follow me—
we'll go over the top.'

'Why risk it? Don't try to show off,' Alexander shouted back.

'Follow me,' I insisted. 'Didn't you hear what I said?'

I clambered up the steep slope and the other two scrambled
after me. We'd reached the top when a mortar went off in the
hollow we'd just left. The colonel crouched down, biting his lip.

'My heel. . . .'

The sentry at headquarters had seen us, and two ambulance
girls came running out of the gateway. The colonel's wound was
superficial—a fairly big fragment of shrapnel had cut into the
tough leather of his boot at the heel. When he took his boot off,
the fragment fell out and he picked it up to keep as a souvenir.

'Look,' he said to Alexander, 'the shell exploded exactly in the
place where we'd have been if we hadn't obeyed Captain Lech
and gone the other way.'

After a moment's thought he asked me why I'd told them to
go the other way.

I didn't know, and still don't. There had been no reason at all.

Monday, 25 September

We've been installed very com-
fortably indeed for the last three weeks in the building I chose as
headquarters. In fact, we've got everything we need—including
an office, a telephone exchange, an arsenal, billets for No. 4
Company, for the Headquarters staff, for the platoon of girl
sharp-shooters, the runners and prisoners-of-war, the battalion
sick-bay and surgery, the company first-aid post, not to mention
a crowd of civilians, mothers and children and old people.

During the past few weeks all the houses in the neighbourhood
have been reduced to piles of rubble and twisted iron, and are

ploughed up every day by more shells. There are still a few 'cave dwellers' living in Nos. 65 and 67; No. 71 is empty. And yet this building of ours seems to be challenging Fate itself, with its four storeys reaching up into the sky. Of course, it may be that we are out of range of the tanks, anti-tank guns and artillery situated far down Zelazna Street and Walicow Street, which continue ceaselessly to batter the neighbouring houses; or that if the Germans aimed their artillery from the west low so as not to go over our heads, they'd only crash into the remains of the walls of buildings on the other side of Zelazna Street, which provide us with a kind of high pallisade.

This may be so, but how is one to explain away the fact that not a single bomb has been dropped on this house, even though many aircraft have dived straight at us? People have all sorts of different theories: some think it is a miracle and a sign that God has us under his particular care and protection, while the unbelievers claim that I was able to 'smell' the site out, and that we're having the 'devil's own luck'. The cynics, however, merely say with a shrug:

'Our turn will come.'

And now at last they've caught up with us.

First a shell dropped in the yard and exploded as it caught in a first-floor window-frame. There was a terrible shriek as fragments of shrapnel wounded Ela, the telephone girl, who happened to be crossing the yard at the time. I watched from my window as they took her away, still screaming.

Our paper work is mounting up, heaps of lists of personnel from all units of the 'Chrobry II' group lie on the tables. Captain Zet was just estimating the distribution as of today of the German forces in Grzybowska, Wronia and Towarowa Streets, while Wislanski was complaining about the daily reinforcements, for the strength of the battalion is decreasing while the number of sick and wounded continues to increase. Barbara and Zola at a table near the window were copying names of N.C.O.s recommended for promotion.

Then, all at once, the whole building shook violently and the room became quite dark. Tiles fell on the pavement outside, while flames burst up just outside the window, making a red curtain which veiled everything. I leaped for the door, thinking that the frame would perhaps serve as protection against falling walls, and in the light of the flames I caught a glimpse of Captain Zet and of Barbara farther away, as she pulled down the curtains, then gathered the papers that were scattered over the table. Seconds passed, but the walls held firm. The flames gradually died down to reveal the yard full of clouds of smoke, from which Alexander emerged.

'Keep calm,' he shouted. 'Everything is all right.'

A shell from 'Big Bertha' had hit the top of the left wing and smashed a part of the roof and the top floor. The shrapnel had burst the bottles of petrol which someone had placed just under the office windows. These were soon extinguished and we had no casualties.

Captain Zet went across to Barbara and took both her hands in his.

'I've never seen anything like your calmness—it was worthy of a fine soldier. If I were your C.O., I'd recommend you for the Cross of Valour.'

'If the Cross of Valour were given for that,' Wislanski put in, 'then half our girls and women would have been wearing one long ago.'

'All the same, I've never seen anything like it. Each one of us, I'm sure, thought first of all of himself, and yet you were concerned for the curtains and documents. It would be hard to imagine more appropriate action.'

'Hard for you, maybe, for you've never seen our girls covering their saucepans up when shells come over—instead of taking cover themselves—to prevent plaster falling into the soup.'

This comparatively trifling incident and Zet's words echoed in my mind as I went out on my daily tour of inspection. What worried me was the contrast between my reaction and Barbara's. Nor is this the first time I've had these none-too-pleasant thoughts about myself.

Sometimes, as I watch ambulance girls running along under machine-gun fire to a wounded man lying out in front of one of the barricades, or the lads as they dart through fire from tanks to place a home-made grenade beneath the very caterpillars of the tanks—then I ask myself whether they aren't afraid, whether they don't feel that terrible emptiness of mind and pressure on the heart which comes as shells fly or a bomb shrieks down? And I wonder how much truth there is in a phrase I once heard that 'courage is primarily a lack of imagination'.

I asked Olgierd about this as he accompanied me through the Ghetto. He'd just scrambled to his feet with that careless grin of his on his face, as always, following the explosion of a twenty-two-inch shell.

'Tell me, Olgierd—aren't you ever afraid?'

'What of?'

'Well, death. . . .'

He gazed at me with his bright eyes full of rather baffled interest.

'No—no, I'm not afraid,' he replied, as if to himself.

'Honestly?'

'Yes, honestly. I'm not afraid of death. I was once, but now I've got used to the idea. Sometimes, though, I'm afraid of something else—of being sent from one hospital to another, or of lying in a cellar unable to move, stinking. Or that they'll amputate my leg, like they did to that White Russian. I'm afraid of that.'

'What about the others?'

'How should I know? It depends . . . if a man's afraid he won't say so. All the same, I believe that the others are afraid least of all when the Germans are attacking and there's no time to think.'

We went on for a little while in silence. Then Olgierd said:

'It's funny, but the lads feel worst when they're on sentry-go during a quiet night. They don't mind talking about that, and I know what they mean. The sky is quiet, and so is the earth. Your mate is lying near by, asleep, but you can't call to him. You can hear every sound, and you look into the darkness, at shapes like ghosts and monsters. Then you feel a creepy sensation down your spine, and no amount of thinking helps. It helps a bit to know that there's a German out there somewhere with his teeth chattering with fear. But the nightmares come back. Some of the lads have told me that they'd be glad to hear a bomber coming over or a gun going off on one of those nights. They'd like to throw a grenade or to fire a shot, so as to shake off their own thoughts.'

'What sort of thoughts?'

'Everyone has something that bothers him. One lad's mother has died, or he's a child ill somewhere in a cellar, or doesn't know what's become of his wife. Everyone has something on his mind. But we've all got to keep up appearances and not show what we're feeling. You do the same yourself.'

I glanced at him. We'd often talked, of course, but it dawned on me that I'd never realised he could talk like this. . . .

Tuesday, 26 September

Lieutenant Maszyna, who took over command of Tadeusz's platoon, has just sent a message to say that his platoon in Chmielna Street has forced the Germans to quit No. 7. He didn't have to report this to me, as it isn't in my sector, but all the same it was pleasant of him to share his good news, and to know that they want to keep in daily contact with us.

No. 6 Company have confirmed that more units of German infantry are massing in front of their position, though the purpose of this isn't yet clear. We wonder whether they mean to try to break through our defences here. If they do, it will be so much the worse for them.

Meanwhile, our barricades in Zelazna Street and Walicow Street are under very heavy fire. The strong barricade on the corner of Ceglana and Zelazna Streets will hold out for a long time yet against tanks and anti-tank guns, but the barricade which seals off the Walicow and Ceglana crossing is weaker and may give way. We don't know whether it will be for Hal or us to rebuild it under fire. But we can squabble about that later, the point now is to try to prevent the barricade from being razed to the ground completely.

On the other hand, I had no one to send to undertake this job—until I remembered the prisoners-of-war.

'What about international law?' someone asked.

'They needn't erect the barricades, but they can dig a trench across the street. The most urgent problem is to maintain communication along Ceglana Street.'

'Are you worried about keeping up appearances or is it your own conscience you're trying to cheat?'

'What I'm most concerned about is preventing people being killed as they cross Walicow Street. Don't let's try to kid ourselves that there's any basic difference between digging a tunnel under Zelazna Street and a trench across Ceglana Street.'

'They didn't have to dig the tunnel under fire.'

'There are casualties during the digging of wells and graves too. And everywhere is under fire. Besides, I warned them they'd be exposed to the same risks as all of us.'

'When they see their own men a few dozen paces away they'll try to escape.'

'That's what the escort is for.'

In the end I had my way and gave instructions for ten of the prisoners-of-war to be taken over to Ceglana Street, all armed with good strong spades.

The first-aid squad, summoned to the flour-mill, got there too late to help Premier, who had been shot by an officer and was dead by the time they arrived. The officer was brought in to me, and I was told, indignantly, that he'd taken some men to the mill to get flour and had handed over a requisition form. Premier then told them to wait. A few minutes later the officer began fiddling with his machine-pistol. A shot was fired and Premier fell. The officer tried to get away and had been caught in Panska Street.

When he heard that Premier was dead, the officer was very shocked. He didn't know how it had happened, he hadn't meant to shoot. He was only making sure that his gun was loaded, and he couldn't explain why he'd run away. Then he produced identity papers of the Communist 'People's Army' and explained that he'd been made an officer only a few weeks earlier. He'd never been in the army before August this year, and had never had any training. He'd been made an officer because he'd attended a secondary school before the war and had a 'Certificate of Education'. His English Sten had been given to him only today and no one had shown him how to use it. His company belonged to the 'Bogumil' group.

Lieutenant Starry continued the interrogation. There were no reasons for suspecting the man of deliberate murder. It was a fatal accident, and if anyone is to blame it is those who made him an officer and gave him a gun. We kept the Sten, but let the man go, with orders to return to his unit and await further decision there. Meanwhile we sent a report in to divisional headquarters.

Then they telephoned from Ceglana Street that one of the prisoners-of-war had been killed while digging the trench. They'd all stopped work to await orders. I went there quickly, and found a German soldier lying on the pavement under a wall, in a pool of blood, while two others were digging a grave. The others were standing round smoking. I had to salute the dead man.

'Which of you speaks German best?' I asked the escort. 'Tell them I'm very sorry this happened and ask if any of them knows how it came about.'

A grey-haired N.C.O. came forward and started to explain. I understood about half of what he said, and the interpreter explained:

'He says you can tell by looking at the man. Where they were working, his head or at the most his shoulders might have been exposed, but he was hit by a bullet in his stomach, below his belt. So he must have got out of the trench on purpose. He must have thought they wouldn't fire at one of their own men.'

'Send the N.C.O. to the H.Q. office and tell him to make a written statement. How is the trench getting on? Is it deep enough?'

'Only half.'

'Tell them to hurry up with the burial and get back to work.'

A violent explosion threw us all to the ground as a black and foaming cloud of smoke rose between us and Grzybowska Street. We could hear walls crashing down.

'It's one of their "Big Bertha" shells!'

'They must have gone mad—it hit one of their own positions.'

'Surely not—it was too near.'

I thought I knew all our positions, but as I looked round I could scarcely recognise the courtyard, so changed was it.

'There was a one-storeyed block here and a high wall there. Yesterday we installed a rifle position on the landing of the staircase.'

A patrol ran in from Ceglana Street.

'This is where those two brothers were stationed. . . .'

We tried to find a way to get at the heap of still-smoking rubble, but the wall to the right was on the verge of collapsing and we had to make our way in from the north.

'It's under fire there. . . .'

'Don't worry. That shell must have fallen right under their very noses, and they'll have withdrawn.'

One of the two brothers had already managed to extricate himself, and he pointed out the place where the other man probably was. As we dragged away the bricks, our hands grew raw until they bled. After a minute or two, we uncovered his head, facing downwards. He was still alive. After a sip of vodka he recovered consciousness, and we tried to lift the rafter which lay across his shoulders.

'Never mind that,' he said. 'Under my head . . . my Sten.'

We uncovered his hands which were still clutching his gun, and took it from his powerless grasp. He watched as I tried to shift the magazine and unload it.

'Is it all right?' he asked anxiously. 'Will it still fire?'

Wednesday, 27 September

The second platoon of No. 4 Company spent last night in their billet, and as they hadn't been able to attend mass on Sunday, the girls arranged to give them an early call and take them over to the service held every day at seven o'clock in the morning by Father Czeslaw. The girls told me this yesterday, and have just reported that the platoon has returned to duty.

They got back just in time, as we heard heavy firing start in the ruins of the eastern sector of the Ghetto somewhere near Twarda Street.

'Where's that coming from?' I asked the sentry at the gateway.

'It sounds as though it's near the well.'

Burst followed burst of machine-pistol fire.

'What the devil is going on? Are all Hal's men asleep or have they let the Germans get at them from behind, through the sewers?'

'Alarm! Alarm!'

The lads came running out into the yard, putting on their helmets and with their rifles at the ready. The firing had already died down. I hurried with the first of the lads across to the ruins beyond Panska Street, shouting to Alexander as I went:

'Get the others together and keep them on the alert. Come in after us if we start firing.'

We spread out and moved quickly from one heap of rubble to the next towards Twarda Street. Everywhere was silent and deserted. We reached the end of the Ghetto, from where we could see the remains of sentry-posts standing at the shattered main entrance. I heard a stifled laugh. A moment later I found myself in a narrow passage leading downwards, at the bottom of which was a botched-up doorway of planks indicating the entry into an underground shelter. An old woman was standing by this door, laughing to herself.

'Granny, did you hear the firing?'

'I did, I heard it!'

'Where was it?'

'In there,' she said, pointing to the entrance to the shelter. I
made a signal with my fist. Sokol, who was looking down from
above, repeated it and helmets and rifle-barrels appeared round
the edge of the hole. I beckoned to two of the lads to come with
me, and we went down a few more broken steps into the dark
interior. A young woman with both arms outstretched was lying
on some blankets, there were great dark splashes of blood on her
light dress. Immediately beyond her was an older woman,
huddled in a corner, with blood pouring from wounds in her
head. A door to the right led into another room, dimly illuminated from a narrow hole in the wall. It was difficult to make out
how many bodies there were lying huddled against the opposite
wall. They were all women. Some suit-cases, broken open, lay
scattered about the floor, their contents in disorder.

'Sir, I can't. . . . Let me get out. . . .' whispered one of the lads
behind me.

I myself could hardly endure the sickeningly sweet odour of
blood in the air. I knew I was going to vomit.

All the same, I had to see whether any of them were still alive.

No, all were dead. We went out.

The old woman was still standing where we'd left her, with
an angelic smile on her wrinkled little face.

'Did you see who it was that shot them!' I asked her.

'I did! I saw them! 'Twas soldiers. . . .'

'Whose soldiers?'

'Ours, ours! Good soldiers . . . they gave me some golden
roubles.'

She opened her tightly clenched fist and showed me golden
coins in her palm.

'Golden roubles!'

Suddenly she closed her fist and hid her hand under her shawl.
Then she looked round anxiously and scuttled away. One of the
lads made as if to seize her.

'Leave her alone,' Sokol said. 'Can't you see she's out of her
mind?'

He was right. Further questioning of the old woman would

have been pointless. From where she was standing down there she could not have seen which way they went. It would also have been pointless to take her round the whole city in the hope that she'd be able to recognise her 'benefactors'. Even if she were to recognise them, no one could depend on a crazy old woman at an identity parade. Besides, how many men would be required to hunt down those responsible for the crime? And what cause would there be for suspecting anyone, since nearly every soldier has a gun that has recently been fired and nearly everyone has been touched by human blood?

We were only a few dozen paces from Captain Hal's billet. A sentry was always on duty at the big iron gates that lead into the Haberbusch warehouse. He must have heard the firing and perhaps saw the men running away.

Hal was standing near the sentry, wearing his long officer's great coat.

'Nice to see you, neighbour!' he said.

But the civil phrase contained a note of almost imperceptible irony.

'To what do I owe this unexpected pleasure? Is it sugar you're after? Or maybe something a little stronger, for a birthday party? We'd be delighted to share anything we have with you.'

'I'm not concerned with anything like that now. Did you hear the shooting in the Ghetto?'

'I did. What were you up to?'

'Us? We came over to see what was happening. Didn't it occur to you to send a few men out to check?'

'You're jumpy, Captain. If I sent men out every time we heard firing, they'd be running about all the time. I thought you were having a bit of fun or giving your harem some exercise.'

'This is your sector, not mine,' I said, checking my anger.

'Everyone has the right to come into my sector, and we're always glad to see them—apart from Germans, of course.'

'Not all of you, though. There are the bodies of seven Jewish women who've been robbed and murdered in that shelter.'

'If they're corpses they won't run away. What's it to us? Why

don't you come in and have something to eat? It's just the right
time. Jewish women, were they? Well, the burial squad can deal
with them.'

'That's not the point. The affair will have to be gone into, the
murderers caught.'

'That's the job of the police or Security people. Come on in,
I'm hungry. . . .'

'No, thanks. I haven't time and I'm not hungry either. So long.'
'So long!'

We went back along Ceglana Street. Czes came up to me on
the way, pondering about something.

'Listen, Lech,' he said at last in an undertone. 'I'll bet my life
that it was that notorious gang over there. They've already
shot more than one man for nothing at all, and buried him there
in the courtyard. Everyone knows what is going on, but they're
afraid to say anything. They say it's military law. . . . So why
shouldn't we deal with them in the same way? Plenty of the lads
would volunteer and they'd keep quiet about it afterwards. . . .'

'No, we can't, Czes. If we'd got there in time today it would
have been different. As it is, all you can do is to tell a few of your
comrades whom you trust about it and keep an eye open in
future. If anything occurs, let me know immediately. But promise you won't start anything on your own.'

'All right.'

I told Captain Jerzewski what had happened, and he asked me
to submit a written report.

'Tell the men who were with you to keep quiet about this,' he
added, 'and I give you my word I'll do all I can to find out who
was responsible and have them punished.'

But I didn't need his word. He was so worried and angry that
he'd have called the devil himself to task.

Thursday, 28 September

A bright, clear day. The sun
reaches down into the depths of our courtyard and the whole
sector is quiet. The heavy guns are silent, so are the mortars.

But there's a terrible crush in the battalion office—lads and girls are crowding round to wish me a Happy Birthday, as well as the usual crowds applying for issues of flour and rations. Runners keep coming in from neighbouring sectors, and even some quite distant ones, bringing me good wishes and presents and promises of personal calls. Captain Zelazny has sent me a piece of horse-meat, Hal has sent wine and tinned sardines, Romanski a bottle of best vodka; cakes and sweets have appeared, and there's clearly a big celebration in the offing. I signed requisition forms for flour outside in the yard, as I was ashamed for strangers to see all the good things.

Some very welcome visitors had just arrived—tenants of our own No. 17, Grzybowska Street—when Lieutenant Silkiewicz telephoned.

'Sir, I have to report that the Germans have put out a white flag on their position in Wronia Street. They shouted across that they want to hand over a letter to the Polish H.Q. in Warsaw.'

'What letter? Who's the letter from?'

'From some S.S. Obergruppenführer. They want us to appoint an officer to meet an officer from their side half-way between our positions. Lieutenant Wir doesn't want to decide for himself and he told me to ask you what to do.'

'Don't take any letters.'

'But. . . .'

'I forbid you to take any letter from the S.S.'

'Very good, sir. What am I to say to them?'

'That we're not postmen but soldiers.'

Wislanski told me that he'd invited some forty people to supper—we couldn't get any more into the office, which is to be converted for the occasion into a dining-room. Major Zagonczyk is coming, as well as Jerzewski, Rum and others, and all company commanders are bringing with them one N.C.O., one rifleman and one ambulance girl or runner each.

Then Lieutenant Wit spoiled things. He brought me a thick

envelope, addressed to the Polish Headquarters in Warsaw. The envelope was unsealed, and on opening it I found a bundle of typed pages and photographs. Pinned to them was a letter, in German, signed by:

'S.S. Obergruppenführer Gen. Leut der Polizei von dem Bach.'

I lost my temper.

'Who gave you this?'

'A German officer.'

'What do you mean? Where?'

'Between Zelazna Street and Wronia Street.'

'What were you doing there?'

'He came over to us and delivered it. . . .'

'Why didn't you fire at him?'

'He was unarmed and there was a man with a white flag with him.'

The silence in the room was broken by Wislanski saying, in an elaborately cool voice:

'Nobody told us to fire.'

The tension relaxed at once, and we laughed. Then we looked through the letters and photographs. Some were in Polish. The Germans were proposing a cessation in the fighting, and referred to their 'humanitarian principles', which have made them spare us up to now as they did not want to cause suffering to innocent civilians. Then they pointed out that further resistance is useless, now that the Old Town and suburbs of Mokotow and Czernia-kow have fallen.

'Mokotow?' someone repeated. 'They're still fighting in Mokotow.'

'But this says that the units in Mokotow surrendered yesterday.'

Some of the photographs showed our men from Mokotow after they'd been disarmed by the Germans, and are clearly meant to provide proof of the way in which the Germans observe the Geneva Convention with regard to the Insurgents. Other photographs were intended to show how the Germans have provided Polish civilians with medical attention and assistance. Altogether the collection was an indigestible mix-up of flattery, tempting

promises and vulgar threats, all meant to persuade us to surrender.

'If they were strong enough to get us out of our positions here,
they wouldn't promise anything or suggest a parley.'

'It can't be helped. You shouldn't have taken the letter,
Lieutenant, but since you did, then we'll have to send it on to
H.Q.'

All the party guests had gone and Krysia and Zola were clearing up. Zygmunt and Pataszon took away the tables we'd borrowed. Wislanski got a pile of papers out of the cupboard, and
Barbara sat down at the typewriter to take a delayed report. For
the first time in a good many days we were able to leave a blank
space after the words 'our casualties'. However, I had to add a
P.S. saying: 'One girl newspaper correspondent was killed at No.
16, Ceglana Street.'

Olga, in her dark-blue uniform, was on sentry duty in the
open doorway, with a candle burning on the table near her. She
had just relieved Czarna. Second-Lieutenant Miecz stood opposite
her, for he always keeps her company when his platoon spends a
night in billets. It looks as if another wedding is coming.

Miecz's presence here meant that another platoon had gone out
into the line. Then we heard the voice of Second-Lieutenant
Danek angrily shouting at him:

'Clear off! Let me catch you here again, and I'll shoot you like
a dog.'

'Lieutenant,' Olga protested, 'what are you doing? Let him
alone!'

Olga tried to shield Miecz and pushed aside the muzzle of
Danek's Sten-gun.

I saw that it was time to interfere, and told Danek to come over
to me.

He obeyed and sprang to attention.

'What is it?' I asked him.

'He's a Communist,' Danek said, pointing at Miecz. 'I have to
send him away.'

'Lieutenant Miecz is an officer of our battalion. I'm the only man who can "send him away".'

'Then do it at once, sir.'

'Just a minute . . . Lieutenant Miecz has been with us longer than you have; he's a good officer.'

'I've got proof he's a Communist. He gives the men copies of "Voice of Warsaw" to read.'

'He has the right to do so. They're just as legal as the newspapers of the Polish Nationalists which you distribute. We all have the right to our own beliefs, and you know that there's no censorship of any kind over newspapers and propaganda on our side. And that's something we ought to be proud of.'

'But the Communists abuse this freedom, and they appeal to the men to quit the Home Army and go over to the Communist "People's Army". Do you expect us just to sit and wait for them to replace our White Eagles with portraits of Stalin?'

'Nobody has left our battalion for the "People's Army". As long as we're free, I'm not afraid of any foreign propaganda. Anyhow, if a man wants to leave—let him.'

'So you stand up for the Communists? That means you must be one yourself.'

'I'm your O.C., and I'm ordering you to get out.'

His runner drew him aside, into the gateway.

'Let him be, sir,' she said. 'I'll look after him. He's been drinking. Calm down, Danek, for goodness' sake.'

But Danek broke away from her and came up to me again.

'F—— you,' he said. 'A fine O.C. you are, standing up for Communists.'

Although it was late at night, the noise attracted quite a number of soldiers and civilians into the yard.

'Lieutenant, I'm putting you under arrest. Hand over your pistol!'

'I'll shoot the pair of you first, you f——,' Danek shouted, shoving the barrel of his Sten-gun into my chest.

I punched him hard in the teeth. As he lay stretched out on the asphalt, his girl-friend lifted his head and shook him.

'Danek . . . Danek . . . it's me! Don't you know me?'

Alexander came up.

'Take his gun from him and get an escort ready. When he comes to, they're to take him over to Group H.Q.,' I said.

The bystanders drifted away in sullen silence, not looking at each other. I went into the battalion office.

'Put me through to Major Jerzewski,' I said to the telephone girl.

Friday, 29 September

Judging by the amount of talk, yesterday's episode with Second-Lieutenant Danek has impressed the people in our little community even more than the letter from General von dem Bach. Zet and Starry, Wislanski, Tabaczkiewicz, Wanda, the ambulance girls and the telephone operators have all been talking about it. They have not said anything about it to me yet, but I feel that I'm being talked about.

So I joined in the conversation:

'A wretched business, I know . . . but what else could I do? There was no alternative!'

'We think there was, and that's what all the talk is about.'

'What was it?'

'You might have shot him.'

'Shot him?' I echoed. 'If I'd started to draw my revolver, Danek would have shot me there and then.'

'You shouldn't have given him a chance to point his gun at you. Instead you ought to have shot him as soon as he started swearing at you. You'd have been in the right.'

'Not in my conscience, though. I'd have felt like a murderer. It's bad enough having to kill people when it's necessary.'

'You'd have been defending your honour as an officer.'

'All right—but I don't see any difference between my honour or that of Antoni or Olgierd here, even though I'm an officer and they're not.'

'You don't pay enough attention to keeping a proper distance

between officers and men,' Captain Zet remarked with a hopeless gesture.

'You might as well talk about keeping the proper distance between the men and civilians. I don't see the connection. . . .'

'You don't, but other people do. What has made the worst
impression about that scene with Danek is that the man you hit is
an officer and that it happened in the presence of civilians and
other ranks.'

'That's terrible. . . .'

'There's no cause to worry too much about it,' Wislanski inter-
posed cheerfully, trying as he always does to dispel any storm-
clouds. 'Most of the lads are mainly interested in the technique
of that blow you gave Danek. And what's more important is that
not one of Danek's tough lads has gone after him or tried to stand
up for him. They're saying they had an O.C. who turned out to
be good for nothing but talk.'

The Germans today increased their fire on the city, though they
concentrated it on more distant districts of the City Centre. Transport columns keep bringing in news of still more serious damage
and still greater casualties among the civilians who are crowding
together on the other side of the Jerusalem Way. But the calm in
our sector seems to make people come out with all sorts of
troubles.

Although it was supposed to have been kept a secret, news of
the murders in the Ghetto area has spread among the men of No.
4 Company. The men who are in on the secret keep asking
whether those responsible have been traced, and are impatient
because there haven't been any results yet. They want to take the
matter into their own hands.

'Unless we do something about it, people will say that the
Home Army kills Jews,' they argue.

'Nobody will have the right to say any such thing,' I countered,
'or at any rate nobody who's honest about it. In any case, this is an
isolated episode.'

'That makes no difference. Are we expected to wait until
killings like this become everyday happenings? Have we been

fighting so that Polish brigands can take over where the German S.S. left off?'

'Don't worry too much about that. The same fate awaits them too. And this doesn't mean that we can take justice into our own hands. If we did, there'd be little difference between us and the way the Germans behave.'

'That depends. Certainly there's no difference now, as far as the murdered women are concerned.'

'But there is for those of us who are still alive, and for the murderers too, even though they haven't yet been caught. Men were able to murder openly during the Occupation, for they had the law and the authorities to back them up. Now they have to hide themselves, they're afraid. We must expect them to hide by putting on red-and-white arm-bands like the rest of us.'

'It's our duty to see that they don't get away with it,' Staszek insisted. He is one of the more serious-minded of the lads.

'Staszek,' I went on patiently, 'my father was a lawyer and an old-fashioned democrat, and he always told me that it was better for ten guilty men to escape punishment than for one innocent man to be punished unjustly. Can you be certain who the murderers are in this case?'

'No.'

'No more can I.'

'But if we're going to be so soft about it . . .'

'I don't think there is anything more to be said.'

I broke off, realising that I couldn't persuade him. Besides, bitterness can't be assuaged by raising one's voice.

Barbara, who had been listening, felt that too and she went over to Staszek.

'You know, deep down, that Lech is right,' she told him gently. 'You're worked up about this because it's shocked you—isn't that so?—and it's made you afraid of what the future may hold?'

He said nothing.

'Listen—we all appreciate your taking the matter so much to heart, and we feel the same about it as you. I understand you're impatient because you want everything to be fair and just and right at once. Then suddenly something like those murders happens. . . .'

An aeroplane flew low over our heads as Barbara went on,

'But just think, Staszek. For five years the Germans have been trying to destroy everything that was good in us, they hunted down every human instinct and encouraged everything that was inhuman, they fostered cruelty and injustice. And now there's all this chaos of the Insurrection, with nothing left of our normal way of life, including laws or indeed any kind of order. You'd expect this state of things to be a paradise for all kinds of scoundrels and rats and yet you've got to admit there are very few of them.'

I glanced at Staszek, who was still silent. But the look of stubborn resistance on his face had gone.

'It isn't that you should repress your own feelings, but you ought to try to see things in the right perspective. Don't ever forget these tens of thousands of ordinary people who're fighting and working on our side, putting out fires, building barricades, carrying food and water, digging out people in bombed houses, looking after the wounded, helping one another, sharing everything they have. No, I don't think we've any need to be afraid for the future, Staszek.'

The argument gradually changed to different though equally urgent matters. Why have the Russians again stopped the offensive which began so well? What attitude will the Polish troops now fighting alongside the Red Army adopt towards us? After all, they're Poles too. They're fighting under Russian generals because they had no choice in the matter. Will they come over to our side? And what about the units of the Home Army now fighting in Central Poland? What is the Polish Parachute Brigade waiting for? And why haven't any Allied Missions from the West come to Warsaw yet?

The questions and the doubts increased. All we could do was to guess. We have freedom of the Press, we're linked with the free world by radio, we have our own government, ministers and staff in London—and yet how little we know. There are two

Polish corps, armoured divisions, a navy and an air force, and ⟳
yet for two whole months we've been fighting on our own in the
city we've liberated with our own hands. And here we are, on
our own, seeking in vain for answers to the simplest of questions.

Saturday, 30 September

If I were able to arrange for
flour to be taken from the mill in Prosta Street over to the other
side of the Jerusalem Way, I wouldn't let a single column come
over into our sector. The mere sight of these starving people,
often dropping on their feet, is having a depressing effect on my
men. I haven't yet met anyone who's actually seen people starving to death—a sight common enough a couple of years ago in
the Warsaw Ghetto—but there are signs of real and widespread
hunger.

A lean, haggard little girl with skin the colour of earth, her
eyes sunken and her lips dry, came in to ask me to sign an indent
for some unit or other. She spoke without looking at me, for she
could not stop staring at a loaf of bread that was on the table.

'You're hungry, aren't you . . . would you like that bread?'

Either she didn't understand or she couldn't believe her ears.

'Here,' I said. 'Take it. We've got enough.'

She took it, but I had to turn away quickly. She was staring at
me, and there were tears in her feverish eyes. But at least she
didn't say anything. There are others who will talk without being
asked, and more and more often we hear the words 'truce' and
'surrender'. They ask the men whether it's true and whether
they'll know when it happens. And the men reply:

'It isn't going to happen'; or, 'You'll have to wait until May,
when the Carnival comes. . . .'

All the same, they keep telephoning to Headquarters or coming up to me and asking:

'What's going on? Is it true?'

It is difficult to keep order among the starving columns, even
though each column is now accompanied by an armed escort.

Yet the stronger push the weaker aside and shove their way up to the front, as if afraid there won't be enough flour for everyone. This kind of attitude soon had effect. One of the columns came under fire from a German tank in Zelazna Street near the barricade, and several people were badly wounded.

An officer came in this morning, and asked for a permit for flour for men in a workshop producing hand-grenades in Mokotowska Street.

'How many grenades have you brought us?' I asked him jokingly.

'Do you still need some?' he replied, clearly surprised by my question.

'Of course we do!'

'Then take as many as you want. We've stopped making them, as we hadn't any storage space, and nobody comes to collect them any longer.'

'How's that? Have they got too many?'

'I shouldn't think so. But there's a feeling in the air as if the fighting were over. . . .'

'Do people expect the Germans to withdraw?'

'Everyone has his own ideas of what's going to happen. And in the meantime the grenades are just lying about.'

'I'll let you have some of my men to help you carry the flour, and you can give them as many of your grenades as they can carry. All right?'

'Certainly. . . .'

He went out, only to return a moment later.

'There's one other thing,' he said. 'Suppose . . . if the rest of them surrender, would you let me join your men?'

'Yes—you and anyone else who wants to.'

He had just left when another officer came in, a big tough man carrying a machine-pistol and looking very military.

'I'm Captain Piorun . . .' he began.

'I've heard a good deal about you—your unit is somewhere in Hoza Street, isn't it? How many men have you brought for flour?'

'You guessed it. We're at the stage where a sack of flour means more to us than arms or ammo.'

'Well, we're not, and I still begrudge you that Sten-gun that rifleman Czarny took with him when he went over to join you. Wouldn't you like to give it back?'

'Czarny said it was his own property.'

'Arms were never private property in our sector. We haven't nationalised them—yet; but they're regarded as belonging to all of us. . . .'

'In that case, I'll have it sent back to you . . . if you still want it.'

His last words disturbed me, for a man like Piorun must, I thought, have some reason for saying a thing like that.

I told Lila to put me through to Major Jerzewski.

'I'm glad you rang,' he said. 'Have you read the Order yet? You ought to have had a copy by now, as I sent it over specially. The truce starts tomorrow, at 5 a.m.'

'The truce . . . sir, please tell me the truth. Does this mean we're surrendering?'

'No, certainly not. The truce is purely temporary, and will be in force tomorrow and the day after from five in the morning to seven in the evening. Its purpose is the evacuation of civilians and nothing else. But it will affect you particularly, as the Germans have proposed that the exit points for civilians to leave Warsaw to the west are to be in Grzybowska Street and Panska Street.'

'Why should we be honoured like this? Nobody from here wants to leave Warsaw. I should think there will be more volunteers in the southern part of the town, where people are hungrier. What's the idea of making them come across the Jerusalem Way right over into my sector? Surely nobody expects us to take down our barricades for them? Besides, they'll be able to see our positions as they go.'

'You'll have to discuss the technical details with the German C.O. in your sector. Only please don't make difficulties, Captain! I think that as things are at present we ought to encourage the civilians to leave Warsaw. The more people who go the better, as we'll then have a better opportunity to continue our resistance.'

A runner brought me the Order, and from it I saw that the 'agreement concerning the evacuation of civilians from Warsaw' was in fact reached the day before yesterday, on 28 September. This explains why so many rumours have been going round.

When the men in the line heard the Order, there was great excitement.

'We'll have to let them get in more shooting today,' Alexander suggested, 'otherwise they'll make fools of themselves tomorrow.'

'All right, let them, only watch out that they don't overdo it. We've got just about enough ammo, but we can't afford to waste any.'

Soon the line livened up. We could hear single shots from a Soviet anti-tank gun from the direction of Towarowa Street, and we knew it was either Kos or Sek smashing German bunkers —a job they both specialise in. Short bursts from the British machine-guns dropped to us by the planes could be heard from beyond the ruins of the 'Little Ghetto'. These, we guessed, were some of our lads 'controlling the traffic' along Chlodna Street, and the Germans replied by long bursts from their machine-guns and heavier grenade fire. We're now able to distinguish any kind of firing even in the greatest din, just as an old gamekeeper can distinguish the voices of birds and animals.

The officer in command of the position in Ceglana Street kept telephoning for the ambulance squad. He had a number of badly wounded men. The ambulance girls brought in sixteen-year-old Smialek, who had been hit in the stomach. They gave him a morphia injection. He was unable to speak.

I wanted to find out what had happened, and telephoned to the 'Miecz' post, where Adam told me that Olgierd, Rys and Smialek had taken a machine-gun up to an attic from which they were able to fire at Germans passing along Chlodna Street. Olgierd fired, and as usual never missed: they'd shot up two or three motor vehicles and a motor-cycle, when the Germans caught sight of them and opened up with a heavy machine-gun. One of the bullets severed Olgierd's wind-pipe. He is dead. Rys managed to escape, but the British machine-gun has been wrecked. The Germans used anti-tank ammo.

When the girls who'd brought in Smialek heard that Olgierd had been killed, they hurried to Ceglana Street again, ignoring the order not to cross the Ghetto. They refused to let Olgierd be buried there, but are to bury him in Grzybowska Street, near Tadeusz. At dusk they brought in his body so that we could all bid farewell to him.

I'm worried by the rumours about surrendering. I haven't seen any newspapers for three days, and nobody has brought us a paper today either. The 'News Bulletin' appears now in the form of a small leaflet and in yesterday's issue I read an article called 'The mystery of victory and of defeat'.

'. . . When victory and defeat are in the balance, then the decisive factor is more often than not the state of mind of the leader and of his men. . . .'

I recalled what happened in Grzybowska Street on 15 August and decided to take advantage of tomorrow's truce and call a conference of all officers and senior N.C.O.s in my battalion.

Sunday, 1 October

A total silence descended on the entire line at 5 a.m. precisely. It was the truce. All the men stayed in their positions, fully prepared to start fighting again should even a single shot be fired by the Germans, for no one believes that the Germans have proposed the evacuation of civilians purely out of the goodness of their hearts. They will rob the people who leave Warsaw, and drive them away somewhere to concentration camps where they will be left to die. There's clearly some other purpose in it.

The men stationed in our observation posts watched through field-glasses all the time. As the Germans did not trouble to keep under cover, it was easy enough to make out their camouflaged positions, bunkers and communication lines, and we'd be able to hit them even in the dark.

Nobody has yet appeared at the points which have been set up
for the civilians to get out of Warsaw. But there is still plenty of
time. Little groups of people are gathering in the courtyard,
earnestly discussing whether to leave or not. They are waiting
for news and instructions, but spend their time repeating absurd
rumours.

A few German officers came towards our barricade in Zelazna
Street and asked for one of our officers to be delegated to talk to
them. I sent out Lieutenant Starry. He was in America for some
years and knows English. They can talk to him in English, if they
have anything to say. Not one of us has the slightest intention of
speaking German.

So Starry went limping out beyond the barricade with his leg
still bandaged, leaning on an elegant cane with a silver knob. The
best of our marksmen covered him all the time from concealed
positions behind the near-by walls.

But he didn't have the chance to show off his English, for the
Germans started talking straight away in Polish. The conversation
didn't last long. We would not have to take down the barricades.
But we were to let through anyone who wanted to go, together
with what luggage they could carry. How many were ready to
leave? That, Starry said, would depend on how they were received
on the other side. If the Gestapo were waiting for them, then no
one would leave, for we'd warn them in advance. The German
officers then declared that the civilians would be evacuated to a
camp at Pruszkow, some ten miles west of Warsaw, and that the
evacuation would be carried out by the Wehrmacht but under
their personal supervision. They were trying to arranged wheeled
transport for the sick and wounded, and would not separate
families. But we decided to wait and see what happened in
practice. Meanwhile the Germans were unusually civil and talked
to Lieutenant Starry as though he were a general.

The word 'surrender' has been heard again among the civilians
waiting. Some people know 'for sure' that terms have already
been agreed on, and that the International Red Cross is to take
charge of the whole city and food supply. Many people who had

previously made up their minds to leave have instead gone back to their holes in the ruins.

I tried to check on this news at Group Headquarters.

'Don't you believe in these rumours, Lech,' said Jerzewski. 'I know that talks have been going on about surrender, but they referred only to the Zoliborz suburb and nowhere else. Zoliborz surrendered yesterday. They'd been driven back into a couple of streets or so, and were entirely cut off and in a quite impossible position.'

'But there are people who say that *we're* in a quite impossible situation. Can you give me some definite assurance that the central and southern parts of the City Centre aren't going to surrender today or tomorrow?'

'There's no question of that happening. The City Centre is regarded as a whole, and if surrender is discussed at all, then it will concern the City Centre as a whole.'

'So there's a likelihood of it?'

'I can't say. You know very well that it doesn't depend on me, and that neither you nor I have been asked for an opinion yet.'

'Thank you, sir. That has made the situation clearer. All the same, I'm going to ask my men what they think of it all.'

'I'd like to know what they say.'

Today the front page of the 'News Bulletin' gives details of the truce, the decision to evacuate civilians and the lay-out of exit-points. Posters have been put up also, signed by the District Representative of the Polish Government in London. More and more people with bundles were gathering near the exit-points, but nobody wanted to be the first to go.

Our officers and N.C.O.s were coming back to Headquarters quite openly, walking along the middle of the streets. They were thoughtful and said nothing. Some came into my office and got in the way, but showed no signs of wanting to talk, not even to Wislanski. Others hung about the gateway, or in the street or courtyard, frequently looking at their watches.

Then the time came. I asked the men to fall in. There were thirty-five officers, cadets and N.C.O.s, both men and women.

Then I said a few words about the situation and how I see it, and asked them to say whether they think surrender is unavoidable or whether they see any point in fighting on.

Nobody spoke. In the silence I could hear the heavy, rapid breathing of big Lieutenant Kos, who was leaning forward, with his head bandaged, as though wearing a turban.

At last he said:

'Surrender now, when we have so many weapons and plenty of ammo? When we're all hardened veterans? We held out when we only had a few old rifles to each company, no ammo for our revolvers, and nothing but bottles to fight tanks with, stones to use against machine-guns and our bare hands against bayonets. . . . Two months of it! And now—surrender?'

It was as though everyone had been waiting for these words. Kos had lit the spark, and now everyone wanted to say something.

'Hunger? I've seen worse,' Kuba kept saying. 'It was no better in the concentration camp. . . .'

'What if the Reds don't come over the Vistula as long as we're fighting?' Ursus exclaimed. 'We can manage without them. I'm in no hurry to be locked up or sent to Siberia. . . .'

'What if they destroy what's left of our art treasures?' Wislanski said angrily. 'We had their Deutsch Kulturhaus in the Warsaw Art Gallery, and Feldgendarmerie barracks in the University Library. Anyhow, if we laid down our arms, Stalin's mob would start on Warsaw.'

'What if there are thousands more casualties?' said Silkiewicz, calmly and yet clearly weighing his words. 'The surrender of Warsaw in 1939 didn't prevent us from having casualties. We've lost six million people in the last five years. They could kill a thousand people in five public executions or by half a day's work in the gas-chambers. Now at least the Germans are having to pay dearly for the life of each one of us.'

'But suppose other units lay down their arms? Suppose the southern sector of the City Centre surrenders as Mokotow and Zoliborz did? What then?'

'We'll fight on alone.'

'Alone? One battalion of us?'

'What of it? Everyone who still wants to fight would join us. There's Jeremy's company, for instance, and very likely Rum and all his battalion would join us. The lads would come back here from Zlota Street. This would let us man new defence lines along the south and east.'

'We'd be shut up in a very little area, not much bigger than half a mile square. The Germans would use everything they've got to destroy us.'

'There wouldn't be anything for them to burn or blow down. We'd move out of these few wrecks and old blocks of flats into shelters underneath the ruins.'

'How long for?'

'The Ghetto held out for five weeks and didn't get any supplies by parachute. They hadn't any anti-tank guns either. If we can show the same determination that the Jews showed, the Germans wouldn't be able to destroy us for quite some time. And at least we've a chance of pulling through, which the Jews didn't have.'

'What sort of a chance?'

'Well, the Germans themselves haven't a chance any more. They'll have to surrender; if not in a few days, then in a few weeks. We might be able to get by.'

'There's still one question. How long will our food last out? What do you think, Quartermaster?'

'That depends. . . . If only the army stays behind, then it should last for some time. There's flour, some bran and oats, dried vegetables, sugar. . . . And nobody knows how much Hal has stored away in his cellars.'

'We can only count what we have ourselves. Let's reckon on two battalions, or about a thousand people.'

'It should last from four to six weeks.'

Wislanski discreetly handed me a note marked 'Secret'. I opened it and read four words: 'There's still one horse'.

I went on.

'So I take it that we've decided to fight on, even if the other sectors of the City Centre fall. Even if the City Centre as a whole

were to surrender, we'd go on fighting. But this is clearly a decision that each of us must make for himself, nor can anyone be
forced to decide one way or the other. If anyone feels he isn't
up to it, now's the time to say so. I'll release him or transfer him to
another sector. We'll respect frankness and won't hold it against
anyone. Now I'm going to put it to you one by one. Captain
Silkiewicz?'

'I'll stay.'

'Lieutenant Alexander?'

'I'm staying.'

'What about your wife and the child?'

'They can go without me.'

'Lieutenant Puli?'

'I'll stay.'

Every man said the same: 'I'm staying.'

Finally I asked Captain Zet:

'How about you? I'm sorry to ask you last, but I never manage
to treat you as my subordinate. I'd be glad to know what you
think. You haven't said anything so far.'

'I was listening and I . . . I'd just like to thank you all. I'm an
old soldier, you see—with thirty years in the army, and I've seen
so much fighting in my time. Now I haven't much time left. But
I'm thankful that God has let me live to see this day. And if you
don't think I'll let you down, then I'd like to stay.'

I then gave orders for a parade to be held for all companies and
that each man was to speak his mind freely. I barred any sort of
pressure being brought to bear on any man. What was decided
at these parades was then to be reported to me by telephone. I appointed officers to talk it over with the commanders of other
units. Company commanders were then told to undertake building new defences where necessary, for although we were not
allowed to build up any of the barricades or positions in the front
line during the truce, we thought we might as well seize the
opportunity of strengthening the positions farther back and also
preparing new defence positions in the rear.

The parade over, the room quickly emptied. Every man

hastened off to his unit. I reported what had happened by telephone to Major Jerzewski, who listened patiently, and gravely he asked me to repeat some sentences, as he was taking notes.

'Thank you,' he said finally. 'You know I couldn't very well say so, but I was counting on your men all along.'

I then went out with the company commanders to decide what was the most urgent task for the sappers to tackle.

When the sector isn't under fire and we can walk about freely in the streets and climb over the hillocks, the whole lay-out looks quite different from the view we have of it from tunnels and trenches. For over a month we haven't been able to go over the crossing of Zelazna and Prosta Streets, so we now dug in a heavy Soviet anti-tank gun at this crossing. Near by, underneath some walls piled high with rubble, we found the remains of a strongly-vaulted cellar, and decided to transfer our headquarters, the telephone exchange and battalion ammo store here. There is a great deal of work to be done digging tunnels in order to obtain an entrance from the rear and a short-cut through to No. 5 Company, but even so, once the work is done we'll be able to hold out here as though in a strong fortress.

A melancholy procession of civilians was moving along Panska and Ceglana Streets. They were mostly old people, women with children in arms and cripples. Some were stumbling under the weight of bundles carried on their shoulders, others were trundling prams loaded with bags and boxes, while others were trudging along empty-handed. Two women were carrying a man along in a chair: he had both legs encased in plaster.

Some of them greeted us cheerily:

'God bless you!'

'Hold out, lads!'

Others, who seemed ashamed, avoided our gaze.

Captain Zet was waiting at Headquarters to report that everyone in No. 4 Company is staying, as well as everyone in No. 5 Company. Two men are 'thinking it over' in No. 6 Company. All the girls are staying, and the armourers too. The ambulance squad hasn't yet reported. A report had come in from Jeremy, giving his strength as 15 officers, 1 officer of the 'Women's Army', 8 cadets, 12 N.C.O.s and 25 riflemen. Their armament is 3 fifty-mm. mortars, 1 light machine-gun, 4 hand machine-guns, 12 machine-pistols, 25 rifles, 30 revolvers, 80 hand-grenades, 300 anti-tank shells and 2,790 rounds of other ammo.

'We'll have to make a deal with them, and give them more hand-grenades and shells for their mortars, and in exchange we'll have half their anti-tank shells.'

The load of grenades from Mokotowska Street had just been brought in—over 500 of them.

Captain Zet was in the best of spirits. He straightened his back and his eyes were sparkling.

'Sir, you must have seen that I didn't approve of a good many things that went on in the battalion. What I saw here was often entirely against my own ideas of what an army should be like. But if my comments have ever offended you, then please forgive me. I see that I was in the wrong all the time.'

Monday, 2 October

The night passed quietly, and although the truce was suspended from yesterday evening until five o'clock this morning, there was silence along the whole line, except for infrequent and single shots from rifles and revolvers. The Germans showed no signs of wanting to risk night fighting, and our lads didn't waste any ammo in view of the long, difficult period of fighting that lies ahead. Only the German artillery was firing unceasingly at the less-damaged and more crowded area of the City Centre, as though to try to encourage people to leave it. We could hear this 'concerto' away to the flank as we dug ditches and trenches. Occasionally a mortar shell fell somewhere nearer, as though to remind us that renewal of hostilities will involve us too.

When it was light again, another procession of refugees started to move along Grzybowska and Panska Streets towards the west. We didn't actually encourage anyone to leave, but we didn't prevent them either. Soldiers of the Wehrmacht were standing at the exit-points. Tabaczkiewicz has been finding out who of our immediate neighbours has left, but the number could be counted on the fingers of two hands. Before leaving, they bricked up their valuables in the cellars, but the neighbours are now insisting that the freshly plastered walls should be pulled down and the hoards searched.

'They've hidden all their things and cleared off. The rotters think they'll come back and find it all there waiting for them, and they'll be able to lord it over the rest of us.'

'One family had any amount of ham and sacks full of grain. They can't have taken it all with them. How could they go off without leaving anything for the children? If they couldn't fix the children up, then it's our duty to do it for them.'

There was no difference of opinion about this at all. I decided not to protect the hoards from 'justice', and thought it was better to have it done in a regular way than to leave it all to chaotic looting. So I gave orders for the first cellar to be searched in No. 65, Panska Street, and we found that the neighbours were right. The first wooden packing-case we discovered was full of flour, bacon, grain and tinned food. Then we found some dozen new blankets and towels, and a locked pig-skin suitcase. When the lads forced this open they triumphantly pulled out a German officers' uniform, two new pairs of boots, field-glasses, pullovers and underwear.

So I appointed 'commissions' to undertake more searches and requisition what they find. Each 'commission' consisted of the block air-raid warden, two representatives of the tenants and two soldiers appointed by me. I gave instructions that only essential materials for the men or the civilians should be requisitioned, while the food is to be shared between the tenants of the respective blocks of flats, and the cellars should then be sealed up again.

An hour later, one of the 'commissions' brought several dozen outfits of ladies' underwear to our headquarters which they considered 'essential for the army'.

Olgierd's funeral was to take place early in the morning in

Grzybowska Street, but we decided to wait for what had been Tadeusz's platoon. Olgierd fought with them all through August, and his comrades must of course attend his burial. As they'd been in Zlota Street for a few days on relief, and fighting is temporarily suspended, Lieutenant Maszyna was able to get leave of absence from the officer commanding the sector without any difficulty. The platoon arrived two hours late, but fully equipped and with a good stock of grenades and ammo. Maszyna then announced that the platoon had come back 'for good'.

'What do you mean?'

'They told me we needn't go back, as they won't want us any more.'

Olgierd was lying in his coffin with his name inscribed on a piece of tin: 'Corporal Olgierd Paderewski'. There was a little bunch of fresh flowers on the coffin, and although we wondered where they'd come from, this remained Maria and Alicia's secret.

One more grave has now been added to the couple of dozen in the courtyard from which, two months ago, we set out into the streets to fight. Two platoons of men stood facing these graves, and a fair-sized group of women and children had gathered too.

'Who is it this time, Lech?' one of them asked me. 'Not that tall, fair-haired boy who was always smiling? He was so young, so nice to everyone. . . . Oh dear, why is it always the finest who have to die?'

'Attention! Eyes right!'

His comrades slowly and carefully lowered the coffin into the grave, as though they feared to awaken him from his quiet slumber. Someone was crying.

'At ease!'

The commanding officers took their platoons back along Panska Street. Little Kazik, Czes' five-year-old son, trotted after his father.

'Daddy! Give me a grenade. . . .'

'Be off with you, son. Go back to auntie.'

I lifted him up.

'What do you want with a grenade? What would you do with
it?'

'I'd kill all the Germans. . . .'

Captain Zet has now got all the reports on the decisions we
reached yesterday. All the men of the neighbouring units say
that when surrender comes they'll join us, either singly or in
whole squads. Nobody speaks of the surrender as 'likely' any
more: but as 'certain'.

Only one report grated. Lieutenant Narocz, of No. 6 Company,
and one N.C.O. have gone over to the German lines, taking
with them a Soviet machine-pistol. They didn't even pretend to
be civilians, but went still wearing their red-and-white arm-
bands. We couldn't have prevented this, since they weren't seen
until they'd reached the German lines, and it would have been
against the rules of the truce to fire at them then. Narocz was in
command of a platoon in Kos' company for a time. Two weeks
ago he was removed from his command and Sergeant Ursus took
over. Since then Narocz had been unattached, and he was not
present at yesterday's meeting. Still, he knew what took place
and could tell the Germans what we intend to do. In fact,
he may have already done so, and his departure may well
be connected with the appearance, which we noted this morning, of new German units along the other side of Towarowa
Street.

I had to discuss the manning of a new defence line along the
east with Jerzewski. It has occurred to us to prepare defensive
positions along Marszalkowska Street, supported on one flank by
Gurt's battalion which is holding Chmielna Street, and on
the other by the strong 'fortress' which is No. 16, Krolewska
Street, and Jeremy's well-constructed defensive positions
between Zielna and Wielka Streets. As a final line of defence,
we'd have an irregular sector made up of Twarda, Marianska,
Komitetowa and Sosnowa Streets. The short sectors which
make up these streets would enable us to be at close quarters
with the enemy, and thus prevent them from using heavy
artillery.

But Major Jerzewski didn't keep the conversation going.

'Don't let's talk about that.'

'You think it's premature?'

'Either that—or too late.'

'I don't get you.'

He went on:

'This hasn't yet been confirmed, but I know that official talks were started this morning on the subject of our surrendering. General Monter held out for a long time against the proposals, but the pressure on him was very strong. If an agreement is reached, we shall all have to lay down our arms. Everyone—without exception.'

'Surely each man has the right and duty to fight on to his last bullet? That's what they used to teach us.'

'They also used to teach us that it is a soldier's duty to obey and carry out orders.'

'I know they did, and it was that kind of discipline which made us renounce even the most elementary human rights to self-defence for five long years. There were very few men who didn't obey the order which said "Don't fire, don't resist, because your resistance will be paid for by the lives of others". Now at least we have the right to die freely and fighting. And we like this freedom.'

'You're exaggerating. Nobody is asking us to die without fighting. And the first condition of any parley with the Germans is that they recognise to the full our rights as combatants and the Geneva Convention.'

'Do you believe that, Major? I had the impression that you said something rather different when we talked yesterday. You're backing out. . . .'

'Not at all. The position taken by your battalion—and not yours alone—was and still is very important in estimating our chances of fighting on. But we can't go on fighting just for the sake of fighting. The army is and must be only a tool for carrying out the decisions of statesmen. And this decision is being made at a level where our chances of fighting on, our man-power and ammunition, the spirit of the men, are but one element that has to be considered. We cannot let our will to fight interfere with the carrying out of such decisions, however difficult or incomprehensible they are.'

'In that case, Major, would you please answer one final question. Will the parley with the Germans refer only to Warsaw or to the whole of the Home Army?'

'As far as I know, it will refer only to Warsaw.'

I called in the company commanders, and repeated what Jerzewski and I had just said. At once there was an outburst.

'The rights of combatants? The Convention? They'll apply on paper just as long as we still have arms. They'll find out our names, and even if they don't shoot us for taking part in the Insurrection, they'll find some other reason—some of us were in the Underground, others are not of Aryan descent—and the rest will end up in concentration camps.'

'What are we waiting for? Let's get the battalion out of Warsaw before the surrender comes into effect!'

The truce was to last until 8 p.m., and we decided to start with an attack on the railway-sidings beyond Towarowa Street at 10 p.m. The order of companies in this attack was to be: No. 5 Company, then No. 4 and finally No. 6 Company. We would have to reckon with heavy losses, though the greater the element of surprise and the farther we can fight our way out of Warsaw by dawn the better. Once they've fought their way across the railway lines, the platoons are to make their way to a meeting-place about a mile to the north of Izabelin. This is about ten miles away as the crow flies.

Then at 6 p.m., I got a telephone message from Group Headquarters, sent by Major Zygmunt.

The truce was to continue after 8 p.m. until further notice.

Tuesday, 3 October

So this is the end.

An official communiqué was published in today's issue of the 'News Bulletin' stating that talks on the cessation of fighting started at ten o'clock this morning, and that until they end the truce will go on. We have also been informed, through official channels, that an agreement on the cessation of hostilities in Warsaw has already been signed.

Alexander told me that there was a meeting of all those whom he'd been able to get together, and that they'd have to be told something, though neither of us knew precisely what. They all knew already that the fighting was over and that we were to be sent into captivity. I wondered whether to say something to the effect that we 'were never defeated in fighting', or that 'the Germans didn't defeat us by force of arms', or whether to say something about politics—that the 'mighty and victorious Red Army' is stationed on the far side of the Vistula, ready to enter the capital of Poland? Or should I mention the storm of freedom that even now is blowing across Europe, unfurling the tricolour above the Arc de Triomphe in Paris?

The men were standing at attention, looking at me, and tears were streaming down their faces, as when, two months ago, we all sang 'Poland is not lost yet' there in the yard of the Dering factory, and unfurled the red-and-white flag. But this time they were not tears of joy.

I saw the tear-stained face of young Pataszon. Wislanski, with his head turned away, his shoulders bent, suddenly looked very old. Captain Zet was dabbing his eyes with an enormous handkerchief. Lech too, who could whistle cheerfully enough when Dr. Mieczyslaw was extracting fragments of shrapnel from his body without an anæsthetic, was crying. Adam as well as Zenek, and Deska—all of us.

I could only say what had to be said—that a soldier's job is hard and cruel, often merciless. We've carried out all the orders given us, and now we must carry out the hardest of all—that to lay down our arms.

Then someone tried to start singing in a strange, choking voice: 'Poland . . . is not lost. . . .'

The rest of us tried to join in, but it didn't sound right. Even the old Polish tune itself was crying.

Fortunately there was plenty to do, so we hadn't time to brood.

Various orders started to come in, following up the news of the surrender. We had to send back the German prisoners-of-war to a transit point in Zelazna Street, near the viaduct. We also had to set about dismantling the barricades; then draw up a detailed report giving the strength of the battalion and all the auxiliary services and a nominal roll for pay. An additional list of recommendations for promotion and awards for both officers and other ranks had to be prepared. A copy of the agreement on the cease-fire and other detailed orders were to be sent to us later. I gave instructions for all unit commanders to attend a parade in the evening.

The German prisoners asked me to see some of their number before they left. They had come to say good-bye and thank us for treating them well. I asked if they had any complaints; but they had none, nor had they lost any of their own belongings. They refused our offer of food. Then there was a difficult pause. The senior German officer stood tense as we looked at each other. When they still didn't go, it dawned on me that they expected me to shake hands with them. I was tempted to say that we'd probably meet again very soon, when they start work on clearing Warsaw of the rubble. But it wasn't worth it. In the end they saluted, made a smart about-turn and went out. I drew a deep sigh of relief.

Then Czes burst into the office like a bomb. 'Lech, guess what I've seen?'

'What?'

'Hal is drinking with the Germans.'

'What are you talking about? Where?'

'They've brought out tables into Grzybowska Street from the Haberbusch warehouse, with tablecloths and bottles of wine, and now they're sitting there drinking together. When I saw what was going on, I felt like opening up at them and their bottles with my machine-pistol. If the lads hadn't held me back, I'd have done it.'

'The lads were right. Don't you realise what a mess you'd have got us all into?'

'Me? What about Hal? How can he do such a thing in our street, in broad daylight too? And you're not stopping him? . . .'

I've given the men of the 'Caucasian battalion' three choices: first, they can go into captivity with us as soldiers of the Home Army. But they dared not do this, for they believed that the Germans would know by their looks and speech that they're from the Soviet Army and would then either send them to a camp for Soviet prisoners-of-war or simply shoot them on the spot. The same peril faces them if they choose the second method —that of trying to get away with the civilians. Finally they gratefully accepted our third proposal—that they should be sent away under escort as men of the 'Soviet Liberation Army' (formed by the Germans) whom we'd taken prisoner. There were only twelve of them: three have been killed, two disappeared, while the wounded will have to stay in hospital. Ali proudly told me that he'd stay on as a soldier of the Home Army.

The Spaniards chose to be handed over to a representative of the German armed forces along with other German civilians, as nationals of states friendly to the Germans who'd been interned during the Insurrection. After thinking it over for a long time, Captain Buzunov decided to join the Caucasian group with the aim of breaking away at the first opportunity and then getting through the lines to join his own people.

Then there were the wounded. They didn't want to stay in the hospital, but to leave with the rest of the battalion. Even young Smialek, wounded three days ago in the stomach, tried to raise himself from his mattress in an attempt to show that he had sufficient strength to undertake the march along with the rest of his comrades. So their comrades agreed to carry the wounded on stretchers, although it looks as if the Germans won't allow this.

Dr. Leopold has already cleared off, so someone will have to take charge of the hospital. Maria and Alicia said they couldn't stay with the wounded, as they are both exhausted and have no proper qualifications. Finally our ever-reliable Zofia sorted the matter out, even though she's been wounded twice, and only came back to the unit five days ago, as a convalescent.

'I've just come from the Malta hospital,' she said. 'I arranged with them that I'd be back and would stay in Poland with them. It's my duty to look after my old aunt. She brought me up and I can't leave her now. Please try to understand. . . . All the same, if you order me to stay with your men, I'll obey.'

'It's an order. . . .'

Even though the firing has stopped, these three words may mean life or death to the wounded.

The rest of the food had to be shared out, and I gave instructions for the flour and bran in the mill in Prosta Street to be given to anyone who asked for it. Then I said that as many people as were needed should be sent to the bake-house, and that as much bread as possible should be baked during the next twenty-four hours.

Then I had a surprise. It turned out that we have a cow in the sector, and that she is the property of the battalion. They'd kept her hidden somewhere in Sliska Street.

'How was it that I never knew about her?' I asked.

'It was a special secret. We were afraid that if the battalion didn't have enough to eat, then you'd order her to be slaughtered. She was giving milk for the babies, and they wouldn't have survived without it. But now the mothers and babies have nearly all left, so if you don't mind we'll milk her once more and then slaughter her. She'll provide one good last dinner, and there'll be some meat for the hospital stores too.'

I gave instructions for the best uniforms in the stores to be left for the wounded and what was left distributed to anyone who wanted them, while the girls were issued with the underwear we acquired yesterday and the silk from the American parachutes. They'll be able to make what they need from it. Two hundred cigarettes from the cigarette store were issued to every man in the hospital, and the remainder were divided among the rest of us.

I still hadn't had a copy of the surrender agreement, even

though they promised me one from Group Headquarters. The parade of unit commanders took place, but we only talked about unimportant technical details and I was unable to answer any of the more fundamental questions asked. Afterwards I signed the full-strength return of the battalion. The battalion numbers 559 people, of whom 98 are women; this includes the wounded at present in various hospitals and men on special duties.

Wednesday, 4 October

I have finally obtained a copy of a shortened version of the agreement on the cessation of fighting, which has also been published in the 'News Bulletin'. I also received the printed Orders issued by the C.O. of the Warsaw area.

At last I was able to answer the men's questions. They learned with some amazement that according to the agreement they will not be held responsible for taking part in the Insurrection or for any activities whether military or political against the Germans during the Occupation.

'Does that mean I can tell them I took part in the assassination of General Kutschera and they won't hold it against me?' someone asked.

'That's what they say in this agreement. All the same, you'd better not say anything about it. You don't have to.'

During the Occupation, any officer, whether of the Regular Army or of the Reserve, who didn't report to the occupation authorities was liable to the death penalty. Yesterday some of my officers wanted to remove their badges of rank and also asked to have their identity papers altered to those of N.C.O.s. The agreement guaranteed them safety. The Germans have undertaken to ensure that, as prisoners-of-war, we shall be dealt with by the Wehrmacht—not by the Gestapo or S.S. or 'Cossacks'. It is up to us to decide who is a soldier or a civilian.

'Isn't that good of them! It just shows what a state they must have been in. . . .'

The men's spirits improved hourly. Everyone had plenty to do.

We are to march out along with the 15th Infantry Regiment along Grzybowska, Chlodna and Wolska Streets early tomorrow morning. We are to be armed but without ammunition. So the men got busy cleaning their rifles, mending their uniforms, washing and shaving. There were even some barbers, who cut the lads' hair whether they liked it or not.

'What the devil do I want my hair cut for? Is it a prisoner-of-war camp I'm going to—or a dance?'

'Wake up, man! Don't you remember what the Reds looked like when the Germans marched them through Warsaw—and the Germans themselves when we'd got them out of the Telephone Exchange? They were a shower. . . . *We're* not going to look like that!'

Our ammunition and explosive material is to be sent to Grzybowski Square, and each unit commander was made responsible for seeing that no man kept even so much as a single bullet. This was a hard job, for the lads always used to pretend to have less ammunition than they really had, so as to get more issued to them; and now they're ashamed to own up to these 'private supplies', and instead go off somewhere and bury it in the ruins. In addition, it was difficult to keep an eye on the riflemen told off to take the boxes over to the collecting-point. I caught four of them in the act of burying a heavy box full of mines in the ruins of the 'Little Ghetto'.

'What's the point of us dragging it all that way?' they protested, in an attempt to justify themselves. 'They've got plenty of stuff over there, anyway.'

Admittedly they were taking all the proper precautions while burying the box; each side had the words 'CAUTION—MINES!' painted on it, and extra boards had been added so that the inscriptions wouldn't rub off. So in the end I let them get on with it.

The ambulance girls have most work to do. No decision or instructions about the evacuation of the hospitals have yet reached us. The badly wounded men are still lying down in the cellars, while those less seriously injured and who are to join us tomorrow when we leave must be provided with bandages and so on. Medicine must be issued to the sick.

A number of the men have asked me to release them, as they do not want to leave their families. I know that General Monter's Orders say that no man is to leave the ranks, but, all the same, I couldn't bring myself to stick too rigorously to this. Even when the fighting was on, I never refused to release a man, if he asked to go. In any case, other men take the places of those who leave.

The truce agreement and orders give the women who took part in the Insurrection the right to make their own choice: either they can go into captivity like the soldiers or they can be treated like the rest of the civilians. Our anxiety about the fate of the girls, particularly the youngest of them and those with no families, made us advise them not to take advantage of the latter alternative, but to go with the rest of the battalion.

As the time drew nearer for us to march out, the confusion increased. Stas-the-Tailor was measuring me for a new uniform. Rys brought in Puchacz's identity papers—he and his wife have already left Warsaw as civilians. This angered me.

'Why didn't he tell us what he was going to do? And then to clear off without even saying good-bye, like a deserter! Surely he wasn't afraid we wouldn't let him go?'

One of the barbers started to give me a hair-cut, while Maria came to change the dressing on my leg. Krysia and Olga came to say good-bye to me, as they'd decided to stay in Warsaw.

'What shall we do with the personal belongings of those who were killed?'

'Bury them.'

'There's still a box of grenades in the stores. . . .'

'Bury it!'

'Janka hasn't any shoes. . . .'

'Issue a pair to her.'

'But there are only men's—size eleven.'

'She'll have to take what there is. . . .'

The Germans have started to complain that the barricade in

Zelazna Street hasn't been dismantled properly, and that the ambulance squad wouldn't be able to get past.

'Tell them to blow it up themselves!'

'Will Ziuta be able to take her cat with her?'

'I don't know—there's nothing about cats in the truce. Don't bother me!'

Then they brought the money for the men's pay. Each soldier was to get 1,250 zlotys and ten dollars in American currency, no matter what his rank or how long he'd served.

Pataszon was the first to sign the pay-roll.

'Hear that, Pataszon? You're getting the same as the Commander-in-Chief himself. Never forget that as long as you live! That's what kind of an army ours is!'

Thursday, 5 October

All night long the billets were a hive of industry. Alexander gave instructions for the men to parade at 3 a.m. and although I pulled his leg for this excess of caution, it turned out that he'd been right after all. There was still a great deal to be done.

The men's pay has been a nuisance, for part of the money is in banknotes of 20, 50 and even 100 dollars. It's easy enough to find a couple of friends who take their pay in common in the form of a single note, and even a few groups of five men, who take one of the 50-dollar notes between them. But we had to try to change the 100-dollar notes somewhere and Lieutenant Wit, of No. 5 Company, offered to get it done by a money-changer he knew. So he took 200 dollars—and that was the last we saw of him.

Fortunately, we were able to make good this loss, since nearly a dozen women and as many men whose names appear in the nominal roll had, in fact, left the battalion before the pay was issued. In some cases, too, men were listed twice, both in the unit to which they belonged according to the records and also in the unit where they last served. In fact, there was enough money to pay everyone, and we also had a few dollars over. We split this money up between the hospital and the women, as a kind of social fund.

There was still the last job to do, and we set about burying all our papers in a metal box—all the orders, reports, sets of publications, records, photographs and maps, plans, drawings, identity papers and documents. Only four people apart from me know where these archives are buried, and afterwards the ground was well smoothed over and all traces removed and concealed.

The companies were late in turning up on parade. The chaplain wanted to say something to the men before the march-out, so I drew the battalion up in fours in Zelazna Street. This was the first time the whole battalion had been on parade together, and many of the men were seeing each other for the first time in their lives. They looked well, all wearing similar dark-blue uniforms.

The priest spoke of suffering, sacrifice and of the dead, and told us we must make our peace with God, for none of us know what is in store. The men listened attentively. Then the priest said a prayer for the dead, the men knelt and repeated the words after him. He gave them his blessing and gave general absolution. The men rose. There were no tears. Each man stared in front of him, his face set and hard.

The priest intoned the words of a hymn:

'*Land of our fathers. . . .*'

Four hundred voices caught up the words and continued. The singing was like a challenge. Defeated men could not have sung like this.

We went to Grzybowska Street, feeling we had to say goodbye to 'our' street, and as we stood in front of No. 17 a little crowd of people gathered on the pavements, their faces well known to all of us. I dismissed the men for a quarter of an hour, as nearly everyone has someone near to them here, either alive or buried in the ruins. Now and then someone would crouch over a grave and collect a little of the earth in a tin box or little bottle. Soon it was half-past ten, and we should have marched out at nine. The companies fell in again in fours.

'Battalion! Forward march!'

The orders rang out, the companies moved forward one by one, keeping step and marching firmly. People on both sides of the street stumbled along the shattered pavements, keeping up with us as far as the corner of Ciepla Street.

'Felek, take these gloves with you!'

'I don't need them! You keep them!'

'Take care of Mietek!'

'Don't worry, Mother. We'll be back by Christmas!'

'Come back to us! Come back soon!'

Beyond Ciepla Street we were in no-man's-land. The houses on both sides had been burned out down to the ground.

'Look, that's where Proboszcz was killed. . . .'

'And Miecz there. . . . That's the window we fired at the gendarmes from.'

From the crossing of Grzybowska and Zelazna Streets, we could see in the distance a group of German officers and among them was Colonel Pawel, the C.O. of our regiment, a tall erect man wearing a long officer's great-coat. I'd only seen him once before, but recognised him at once by his thick moustache. I halted the battalion and went up to him, pretending not to notice the Germans.

'The 2nd Battalion of the "Chrobry II" group on parade, sir! Our strength is 42 officers, 335 other ranks and 79 women.'

'You're almost two hours late, Captain. You're the last and we've been waiting just for you for an hour. The Germans were very worried, as they suspected that your battalion wasn't coming out at all. Why are you so late?'

'There's no reason—just that we weren't in a hurry to go into captivity, sir.'

I seemed to catch a glimpse of something like a smile in his eyes. Then it disappeared in a stern frown as he translated my reply for the benefit of the Germans and read aloud our strength return which I handed him on a scrap of paper.

'You will now march your battalion along Zelazna Street to Chlodna Street.'

We moved forward into an alley full of German positions. Lieutenant Czarnecki was marching a pace behind me, to the left. As he had a Polish uniform and great-coat, Wislanski had told him to act as my adjutant today, for appearances' sake. We were followed by the rest of the officers, formed up in fours. Then came Alexander at the head of No. 4 Company, followed by the women's unit; behind them was No. 5 Company, and No. 6 Company brought up the rear. Although heavily burdened, all the units looked fine. They marched in step, their heads up, keeping level. Nobody would have believed that at least half of these men were sick or wounded, and that many of them were marching in a column for the first time. What amazed me most was the number of weapons. I'd no idea that we had so many.

Germans in uniform hastily set up cameras, and got in our way as they took pictures of us from the rear, from above and all round, and filmed the scene. Some of the German officers saluted as I passed; later on they'd be able to show the world how 'cultured' they are. I passed them as though they weren't there. Each of us wanted to make it clear to them that as far as we were concerned they simply didn't exist.

All the time we were marching among total ruins and burned-out buildings, in which there was no sign at all of life, not even a blade of grass. Just before Kerceli Square we caught up with the unit which had marched out an hour before us, and there was a hold-up; they were handing over their arms. We formed a single file. Tables had been placed in the centre of the square, and as we passed we had to hand over our arms to German soldiers. I handed over two revolvers, and went on, still wearing my sabre. The Germans saw it but did not stop me. Then we crossed to the far side of the square and went back into Wolska Street.

From here I could see No. 4 Company moving along in the other direction. They still had their weapons. They were looking across at me, pointing out something to each other, and it was easy enough to guess that they were all looking at my sabre. Some of the lads raised their clenched fists in my direction, as a signal of satisfaction.

My useless, out-dated sabre had become a symbol now that we'd laid down our arms. But what was it a symbol of? Merely that the enemy would keep to their agreement? Or that all is not lost and that we are, after all, taking away something with us from Warsaw in addition to the bundles of belongings slung over our shoulders?

But I didn't try to define it. If indeed it meant anything to the men, then they should all see it. When I reached Wolska Street, two companies were still in Chlodna Street, and, before turning to the right, I went out into the middle of the road, and stood facing these companies, and the city, and drew the sabre from its scabbard and with it saluted the Warsaw we had left behind us.

Clouds of brown smoke were rising above the ruins, and we could hear artillery thundering across the Vistula. A half-hearted artillery duel between the two armies of oppression was still going on.

We went farther along a track that had been cleared of rubble and which used to be one of the main streets of Warsaw, with its million inhabitants. Here there were no more positions manned by Germans armed to the teeth. Each of our companies was escorted by a few wretched-looking Wehrmacht soldiers, with their rifles carelessly slung over their shoulders.

Then we passed through the suburb of Wola: to the right were great fields of little white crosses, standing close together and strewn with fresh sand. This was the burial-ground of the Germans killed in Warsaw, and there were thousands upon thousands of them. It made me think of Verdun.

We left the ruins behind, and an asphalt road led out across the fields. Here the air was fresh, there was the smell of wet rye-fields and newly-dug earth in the potato-fields. I stood aside to see how the men were standing up to the long march. I could see by the way the veins stood out in their throats and temples, and by their parched lips and shoulders bowed under the weight of their packs, that they were tired. They were no longer keeping step, some were limping, but nobody was falling behind.

'Is it much farther, sir?'

'We ought to be there in an hour. Can you hold out?'

'We've got to.'

The girls were mostly carrying heavier packs than the lads, and they looked like over-burdened camels, but they were keeping step. That was the way they wanted it.

'Sir, may we sing?'

'If you can.'

One of the girls up in front gave the signal and they all started: '*Oh the wind blows wild. . . .*'

The German escorts looked round anxiously, and glanced at each other. Obviously they'd had no instructions about singing.

Lorries full of people drove past. Someone shouted to us from one of them, and I recognised 'our' Spaniards, waving like mad.

'Long live Poland! Long live Freedom!' they shouted in Polish, unconcerned by our escort of Germans.

We passed through a little hamlet. Women came running out of their gardens, broke into our ranks and handed out apples and tomatoes and carrots to the men. Barefoot children, driven back time and again by rifle-butts, kept running up again with buckets of water.

An old man, leaning on a stick, took off his cap as we passed, and an old woman made the sign of the cross in the air.

Then to the left and below us we saw railway lines which disappeared farther away amidst the white walls of a big factory. This was Ozarow.

Here, in the big factory workshops, thousands of soldiers were lying on the cement floor which had been thinly strewn with straw. It was difficult to squeeze between them. Hundreds of new arrivals kept pushing through the single open doorway. Men with dysentery were unable to get out, and there was the stench of blood-soaked bandages, festering wounds and sweating feet.

Part of the space was marked off for the women and I made my way over to them in order to say good-bye to Barbara, my wife, as we were to be separated for the journey into Germany next morning. I found our girls crushed together in a corner.

'Do something, Lech!' Jasia begged. 'We're suffocating.'

'The stench is unbearable,' Ola said calmly.

Franciszka, smiling cheerfully, was squatting on a suit-case.

'Don't let it bother you,' she said. 'Think about something else! Try to think about the sun shining somewhere a long way away. . . .'

Friday, 6 October

I slept soundly all night thanks to a few nips of vodka which the lads of No. 5 Company gave me. The pain in my leg woke me. Pus had soaked through the dressing. Yesterday I wasn't troubled by it at all, but today every step was painful. I got out into the factory yard. We'd been shut in by high barbed-wire fences, on the far side of which many armed sentries were patrolling. Several hundred prisoners had spent the night in the open air. You could buy bread, and there was a long queue of unshaven and grubby men standing at an office doorway, where hot coffee was to be issued some hours later.

The fenced-in area included several railway sidings, where a number of goods wagons for the transport of animals were standing. Our battalion was to be loaded first. The women were to go separately. We had to wake the men so that they could pack up and move their belongings out. There was no room to hold a parade. Before we had time to get any coffee, we were ordered to get aboard. Fifty men were put into each of the manure-stained wagons. Then they slammed the heavy doors behind us and sealed them from outside.

The interior of the wagon was in half-darkness. The four narrow windows were strongly barred. It was crowded, so that there was no room to stretch one's legs. Apart from some mouldy straw, we only had our packs and cases to sit on. It grew stifling. There wasn't even a bucket, and a few of the men with dysentery tried to make a hole in the hard wooden floor with a pen-knife. It was two hours before the train moved off.

Nobody knew where they were taking us. Somebody wrote the words 'Home Army from Warsaw' in big letters on a piece of paper and tried to fasten it outside the window, while others hung their red-and-white arm-bands out.

'Our railwaymen will pass the news on to the right place.'

The irregular rhythm of the wheels cutting across points indicated whenever we were passing through a station. During short halts between stations nobody bothered about us. The long hours crept by. We realised that we were travelling south-west, in the direction of Silesia.

'They're taking us to Oswiecim.'

'Shut up! You don't know any more about it than I do.'

Towards evening the train stopped. The barking of dogs and Germans shouting could be heard.

'Have a look out, somebody!'

'Can't see anything—only fields.'

Suddenly the doors opened and there were shrill cries of:

'Raus! Raus!'

Fields stretched away on either side of the railway lines. S.S. men in black uniforms with big wolf-hounds were standing in a long file a few dozen yards away, holding machine-pistols at the ready.

'Raus! Schnell!'

More 'blackshirts' were standing at the wagon door. There were no foot-boards and we had to jump down. The wagons were standing on an embankment. I fastened my great-coat, put on my pack, and girded on my sabre, then waited until everyone had got down. I was about to jump when an S.S. man grabbed at my sabre and knocked me over. I hit the back of my head hard and fell down the embankment. Someone helped me to my feet.

'Can you walk, sir?'

'Yes.'

'Come on then, quick. They're ready to fire. Here's your cap. Put it on.'

My hair was wet with blood.

'You've got a thick skull. That S.S. man hit you like the back of an axe.'

We stood along the country road in small groups. Behind us, near the little railway station, I read the name LAMSDORF painted on a black board.

One of the Gestapo men surrounding us said in Polish:

'Any man who steps out of line will be shot. Marschiren!'

We followed a rough track through mud and puddles. Fields of beet stretched away to the left and to the right there was a six-foot-high barbed-wire fence which was divided into compounds by more barbed-wire fences. There were some low wooden barracks, and here and there long trenches roofed over with branches. This big town of barbed-wire fences and barracks looked quite dead, and it was not until presently that I caught sight of people. Wearing rags, bearded, covered with sores, they crawled up to the barbed wire and stretched out their hands like beggars.

'Tovarish! For pity's sake. . . .'

Someone threw them a few cigarettes.

Finally we reached the end of the fenced-in area and turned right, then right again. A roadway led through an open gateway into the camp. A few tall, muscular young men in sports' shirts and shorts broke off their game of ball and came over, curious.

'Russians?' they asked in English.

'No—Poles,' said Starry.

'Where are you from?'

'Warsaw.'

'Look, Poles from Warsaw! Hurrah! We're English.'

'Et nous—nous sommes français. Vive la Varsovie!'

We came into one of the compounds. There were about a thousand of us. We kept to our ranks.

'Don't break up. You can sit down.'

Dusk fell slowly. It was cold and raining a little. Colonel Pawel and some German officers walked past once or twice. Then Colonel Pawel came back alone and summoned the C.O.s of the battalions.

'I've made a very strong protest,' he said. 'I've shown them a copy of the surrender agreement, but they say that they don't know anything about it and will have to consult higher authorities about it tomorrow. As they haven't had special orders, they see no reason for treating us any differently than hitherto. We're not to get anything to eat or drink, as we arrived too late. They've ordered us to spend the night in those trenches. I had a look at them and protested that they're not suitable accommodation for men. Let's have another look at them.'

The deep trenches intended to serve us as billets were strewn with rotten straw and roofed with dry branches which gave no shelter from the rain or cold.

Saturday, 7 October

We spent the night in the open air. Some of the men tried to sleep on the wet, trampled grass, wrapped up in soaking blankets, while others dozed off seated on their packs. Very many stood up all night, silently watching the lights and flashes which illuminated the distant horizon. We could hear bombs falling in the distance. Allied aircraft were bombing the centre of the German armament industry in Lower Silesia.

Since early this morning more and more train-loads of prisoners have been arriving at the camp—all are men of the Warsaw Home Army.

CONCLUSION

Grzybowska Street—'our street'
—no longer exists. Very many of the streets of that pre-war
Warsaw of ours are now nothing more than names on old maps.
Admittedly, Warsaw rose out of the ruins and is again Poland's
capital, and the ruins and bombed sites are now covered with
new streets, buildings and blocks of flats, while new parks and
gardens blossom on what was once nothing but scorched earth.

What has become of the men and women who defended 'our
street'?

In the main, the Germans kept to the terms of the surrender.
Most men of the 'Home Army' who left Warsaw for prisoner-
of-war camps survived the war. Many went back to Poland when
they were liberated by the Allied armies.

Alexander went back to find his wife and son. Kos and Stefan
returned too, as well as Czes, old captain Zet and the two young
riflemen Staszek and Smialek. I hope that Pataszon, who went
back too, found his parents alive. Maria and Alicia went back, as
did Marta and Halina.

Some went back hopefully, others returned with fear in their
hearts. For they knew that they were going back to a country not
only destroyed by war and wretchedly impoverished, but also
enslaved, where the freedom for which they had fought on the
barricades of Warsaw was no more. And to return meant the
risk of persecution. The very fact that they had served in the
Home Army meant, for many of them, imprisonment. Nothing
has ever been heard again of several who returned.

As for the men and women who decided not to go back—they
are now scattered across the world, living ordinary, everyday
lives.